Fallen Fret

Ray Richard

Copyright © 2015 Ray Richard
All rights reserved.
ISBN:069262516X
ISBN-13:9780692625163
Dineray Press

CONTENTS

1. The Stringbender
2. Dark Knife   11
3. Johnny's Craft   24
4. Borrowed Sound   36
5. Slow Hand   50
6. Maine Blues   60
7. Stolen Sound   73
8. April   83
9. Pluck   97
10. Hard Money   103
11. Tinker Talks   118
12. Accusations   128
13. Lost Luthier   140
14. Decline   151
15. Johnny's Revenge   163
16. Fallen Fret   175

1 THE STRINGBENDER

> Pass by the barstools of Harlem's Backbeat tavern on a Friday evening and you'll overhear talk of stolen trills, unpaid gigs, and narcissistic bandmates. To hear a better tale, stay for a slow drink and listen to the bluesman sing his ballad of the O'Malley sisters; a song with thundering chords and lyrics of greed, jealousy, and murder.
> —Guide to NYC Music Haunts-2010

In 2009, Sarah, the older O'Malley sister, met the man who would compose the ballad referenced in the guide. An investigative writer by trade, she requested an interview after finding his name on a yellowed session card tucked in the jacket of a library book. He suggested they meet at Mim's, a renowned Lower Manhattan nightclub. Waiting in the walnut paneled hallway, she ignored the original artwork and focused on a row of framed newspaper and magazine articles on the wall. A 1950 *New York Times* review described saxophonist Charlie Parker's exhilarating Mim's performance despite arriving hours late with his horn in a rumpled paper bag. Another article described saxophone god John Coltrane's exhausting three hour performance on Mim's stage. Unsettled by a wayward note, he fine-tuned musical scales in the men's room during intermission. An August 1969 *Jazz Beat* article described the afternoon Miles Davis turned his back to Mim's audience and trumpeted his first jazz fusion notes outside a studio. A 1969 *Music Life* review reported on the winter night blues guitarist Jimi Hendrix singed Mim's wall varnish during his four hour set.

A barmaid carrying a folding chair told Sarah to leave because the club was closed until first show seating at six p.m. Sarah mentioned her meeting with Chaz Russell. The barmaid resentfully pointed the chair leg toward the Sanctuary, a concert room cluttered with skinny chairs and spindly tables with pizza box size tops.

Sarah sat in a maroon velvet chair in the alcove, facing a windowed wall with views of tailgating cars and hurrying pedestrians. A few minutes later, Chaz introduced himself, kissed her outstretched hand, and sat on a Victorian couch backed to the windows. Sunlight brightened the shoulders of his white silk shirt. When he smiled, tightly-trimmed, chalky, beard whiskers framed his intermittent gold teeth. His white Egyptian linen pants showed fraying at the pocket entrances and cuffs. Seconds after he sat, Sarah caught a puff of manly cologne.

He apologized when his loafer bumped her heel, then he rubbed his eyes and complained about a lack of sleep caused by playing an early morning encore. "Why would a dolled-up white girl want to interview a seventy-year-old black musician?" he asked. "You still in high school? Writing a blues book? Let me give some advice: you can't describe the blues with words, you have live it."

"I hit thirty in a few years," Sarah said. "I'm here because your name came up in my research. I'm writing a book about Miles Davis and Jimi Hendrix, two famous musicians who knew each other, but never recorded together, so they say. How'd you become a bluesman and hang with people like them?"

"I'll tell you my life story if you have a few days."

"Let's do the one minute version."

"Sugar, I do a hundred interviews a year. They've written my story many times. Born in '44 on a Mississippi cotton farm. Great-grandparents were freed slaves. Age ten, got good playing a two-string guitar made from a cigar box bolted to a canoe paddle. At seventeen, hitched a freight train to Chicago. Got a job painting a record company office. A studio musician got sick, I filled in. Led to steady work with Muddy Waters. Got tired of Mud, so I formed my own band. We've played all over America and Europe. It's a typical bluesman life of fame, fortune, misfortune, no fortune, little fortune. You've heard my story, what's yours?"

Sarah rested the tip of a plastic ball point pen on her reporter's notebook. She ran a few fingers through her long black hair. "Last two years," she said, "I've covered the city jazz and blues scene for *National Vibe*. Spare time, I'm working on my book. Trying to explain why the greatest blues guitarist and the greatest jazz musician didn't record together. Any thoughts on Miles and Jimi?"

"Loved them both. Miles, little guy, big attitude, flashy clothes. Saw him drag race his Ferrari down Broadway. Changed the whole jazz scene four or five times. Could play his trumpet loud as a firecracker or soft as a lover's whisper. Got more out of a pause than some get from a ten bar blast. Rode jazz from bebop to jazz fusion and beyond."

"What about Hendrix?"

"Sweet guy. If he didn't choke to death or get strangled in '70, he'd have recorded a hundred albums by now. His studio was across the street. Guy reinvented electric guitar. Before Jimi, blues guitarists just copied bluesman like Robert Johnson and Otis Rush. Jimi mixed blues with funk and fuzz. They call him the 'Greatest Rock Guitarist' which isn't right; Jimi had blues bones."

"The books say," Sarah said, "Hendrix and Davis booked a studio in '69, lined up a few musicians to join them in a recording session. Night before, Miles asked for fifty thousand dollars. Hendrix cancelled the session."

Chaz slid over to a shaded section of the couch, tight to his weathered guitar case. "Sugar, you only know part of the story. Jimi was like catnip to woman. More than a few times, Jimi got too friendly with Betty, Miles wife. Cooled things between Jimi and Miles. Miles was working on getting Betty back."

"So that's what happened. Did blues and jazz musicians jam together?"

"Not often. Slow nights, at the union hall, jazz and blues musicians tossed around a few trills. Blues musicians improvised, jazz musicians sampled blues, but never at a gig. Jazz clubs wanted jazz, blues clubs wanted blues. I was here the night Hendrix played Mim's. Longhairs in ripped jeans scared away the tweed and hairspray crowd. The longhairs came in with a foreign buzz, stoned on weed, didn't buy drinks. Mim counted her receipts and never brought Hendrix back. She catered to the jazz crowd who wore snappy clothes, paid stiff covers with a smile, and drank over-priced Manhattans. Over in the blues clubs, ladies in sparkly dresses snuggled in the booths with guys and carried the action to the dance floor."

"Must have been exciting with so much talent in the city."

"Sure was. I respect those long-gone musicians who created most of the blues and jazz in the bargain bin at Sharkey's Record Store. If you're hustling a musician's life, you support fellow musicians. I always drop paper money into Salvation Army kettles. I can't pass a busker's hat without chucking them a few dollars."

"Did you know any other famous musicians?"

"They all were famous in my mind. You only know about the ones who got lucky or had flash. I knew a hundred sidemen and women who'd play the pants off anybody. We passed each other on the streets. Mostly talked about how the club owners were screwing us out of money. Named crooks who'd steal an instrument to buy dope. I knew many jazz cats. I'm not sure they knew what was happening with us blues dudes."

Chaz took two bottles of iced tea from a refrigerator behind the bar and gave one to Sarah. "Why you asking about jazz and blues musicians from the past?" he asked. "Shouldn't you be listening to pop?"

"Growing up, I got hooked on jazz and blues," she said. "My hippie mom played Hendrix on her record player, dad played Miles Davis records when she wasn't around. They hated the others music. My sister and I think it caused their divorce. I became a music journalist, kept listening to Hendrix and Davis, always wondered why they didn't record together."

"Every slick music executive knows a Hendrix recording with Miles would sell ten million copies," Chaz said. "Shame it never happened. And that's how you should write it. Right from Chaz Russell's mouth, the tired old bluesman."

Sarah took the faded card from her notebook. "I found this in a Miles' biography from the library," she said.

Chaz put on his reading glasses and examined the card. "It's nothing but a Chessman Studio session ticket. I see my name next to some initials in the session box."

"You recall the session?" Sarah asked.

"I've played hundreds of Chessman sessions. My mushy brain can't recall this one."

"Take a close look at the initials. You see MD and JH? Any thoughts on the other initials I couldn't decipher?"

Chaz leaned over the couch arm and examined the card under

the light of a brass table lamp. "This is a typical session card; we used them as bookmarks or to pick our teeth. I see some session musician initials on it, could be Mark Dell and Jimmy Higgins. I did some beer commercials around that time with those guys. We pulled musicians from Harlem bars, let them play, paid them a few bucks, sent them back to their barstools."

"Are those Miles Davis and Jimi Hendrix's initials?" Sarah asked. "Did you play with those guys?"

"You're not the first snoopy writer who has asked the question. I've told everyone, I never jammed with Hendrix and Davis. Some drunk who worked at Chessman's got liquored up and told the town a crazy story about Hendrix and Miles partying and playing all night in there. Slid my name into the story. The bull began after Jimi died, heard it again after Miles died. Get it straight girl, nothing happened at Chessman's worth talking about. Don't bother asking again."

Sarah's pen slipped from her hand and slid a few feet over the oak floor. Chaz toed the pen toward her open hand. She cleaned the pen with a tissue. "Mr. Russell, sorry to upset you. I'm a reporter. I had to ask the question. I still think something happened that night at Chessman's."

Chaz stood, ready to exit the room. "Don't mention me with Hendrix or Davis. My lawyer shut down a few record companies over lies. I'll sue your ass. I'm tired of this bull."

Sarah corralled a runny tear with her index finger. "Don't get misty on me," Chaz said. "Sorry for talking cross. I loved those guys, damn shame they're gone."

"Don't worry, my skin is an inch thick," Sarah said. "I get roughed up every day in interviews. Let's go in another direction. What's in the guitar case?"

"Meet my best friend," Chaz said with the guitar case on his lap. Abraded souvenir stickers from Montreux, New Orleans, and Chicago blues festivals covered dents and rips in the black cloth covering. He released four pitted chrome clips and raised the lid. "In the 60s, I loved a gospel singer who ran off with a minister. She left her thousand dollar mink coat in my room under a note saying the minister bought her a better one. Her coat lines my case. Still smell her cheeky perfume when I open the lid." He removed a candy-apple red electric guitar and played a few notes. "Those are worried chords, they pay my bills. Some guitars have bad voodoo, this one has good.

I'm the proud daddy of Thelma, a Durrell 335 built by my man Johnny Durrell in his Arkansas shed. You ever play a Durrell?"

"Never played a guitar," Sarah said.

Chaz placed the tooled leather strap over her shoulder and steadied the guitar on her lap. "Thelma's deep tone can make a woman sob and a grown man feel guilty," he said. "You can't pull sweet sound from a store bought guitar. Don't drop her; a Durrell like this just sold for a hundred grand."

Sarah ran a finger over the inlaid headstock, wiggled the chrome lever near the fingerboard, and admired the narrow, mother-of-pearl inlay on the fretboard and body. Looking closely, she saw hundreds of scratches that began inches above a sound hole and carried across the fingerboard, smudging the etching of a crow. "You play hard," she said.

"I'm King of the String Benders. I need a sturdy guitar so my fretboard won't twist like ribbon candy. Johnny added an extra wide block of maple under the fingerboard. I'm a lefty, learned chords on a flipped over, fat-body righty. I had him build mine righty, strung righty. Johnny tried to talk me into a lefty with the fat strings on the bottom. I won the argument because I had his fee in my pocket. Now, with the fat strings on top, when I string bend, I push down, not up. It's easier on my old man fingers. It worked for the great Albert King, it's done me right."

Sarah passed the guitar to Chaz and asked him to describe string bending.

"It's a guitar style I learned from Mr. Otis Rush," he said, "when we played in the Muddy Waters Band. Us string benders marry a bunch of strings with the tip of our fingers, like this." With the fretboard a foot from Sarah's eyes, he pushed the top string down into the two strings below it, merging three strings into one. "When I amp her up, these three bent strings create a vibrato. Lets me sustain the note, vary the pitch. Can make my girl sound like a hungry hyena or a wailing baby. Handy when the song gets sad and I want the ladies to cry. Come watch me play tonight over on the stage. You'll hear some string bending. Don't get upset if you hear sniffling in the audience. Thelma usually steals the show."

"Is Thelma named after the woman who lost her mink?"

"No way. Us blues musicians name our guitars, usually after someone who got scorned or did the scorning. Thelma is the name of the woman I should have married. A simple gal from cotton country; she had ten children, two by me. This Thelma has been in plenty of cat fights and pawn shops. Got the dent on the back when a girlfriend threw her from my '62 Caddy during a tussle. An hour after the guitar skidded down Beale Street, I played her at Roscoe's. The skid improved the guitar's tone, led to a few encores. A girl I met after the show stayed with me for a few months, a world record."

Sarah strummed a few strings and asked, "How much she weigh?"

"The original Thelma; over two-hundred," Chaz said. "The guitar; just under ten pounds."

"Ten grand a pound," Sarah said." It's much bigger than my sister's Les Paul."

"She play for a living?"

"Yeah, mostly blues, She has a union card, plays with a few bands. She's a blues chick, dresses in black, big arm tattoo, beer gut. A year younger, an inch taller than me. Same Irish face. I'm better looking, but no doubt we're sisters. Few years back, her boyfriend robbed a bank. She spent a year in prison. On parole now, making a few bucks playing here and there."

"Nothing wrong with prison," Chaz said in a hushed voice. "It worked for me. I stole a car when I was a kid, slept a year at Tuskegee Correctional. Chose prison over the army. I found me a dinged up acoustic in Tusky's roomful of donated instruments. A good-hearted double-murderer taught me chords. Momma snuck me strings in her banana bread. I practiced every day. Met great pickers in there. Longer the sentence, better the picking. Day I got out, I could play pretty good blues."

"Would you meet my sister after your set?"

"Sugar, every day, ten people tell me about their niece or second cousin who's the next B.B. King. As much as I'd love to meet her, I'm too tired after work. Tell her to stay out of trouble, practice till her fingers bleed."

The barmaid nudged Chaz's buttock with an upholstery nozzle. Without softening her expression, she grabbed Thelma by the neck and held it like a pizza paddle. Chaz pried the guitar from her hands and put it in its case. The peeved barmaid dragged the vacuum to another room. Chaz apologized for her surliness, saying she was a suspect in a saxophone theft. He had watched her put the horn in a trash barrel and reported the incident to Mim, the no-nonsense woman who owned the club. Mim mentioned Chaz's name during the barmaid's interrogation. The barmaid blamed the incident on mismarked trash. Mim promoted her to head barmaid.

The barmaid returned with a squeegee and a bucket of soapy water. Chaz assumed the bubbly would land on his neck. He led Sarah to the hallway where he thanked her for the chat and requested she "be nice when you write me up." After a soft handshake, he carried his guitar into a dressing room to rest for his eight o'clock show. Sarah connected with a glass of wine at a bar several blocks away. Later that night, she fed the last twenty-five pages of her book draft into a paper shredder.

The Chaz Russell Band's two-hour set included several original songs along with sprightly standards written by harmonica god Little Walter. They covered two songs penned by the father-of-the-blues, Robert Johnson, and honored Muddy Waters with a medley of his hits. For the last song, Chaz sent his drummer and bass man to the bar. He toned Thelma down so the guitar barely covered his whispers and sang "Downtrodden and Out of Luck," a song he wrote in 1968. The crowd yelled for more, so Chaz and his band responded with a vigorous cover of Hendrix's "Hey Joe." Holding the last note, he thanked the crowd with blown kisses as the club owner, the formidable Mim, dimmed the lights.

Patrons, knowing the unpleasant consequences of lingering under Mim's closing time gaze, shuffled to the street. Chaz stayed on the stage and rubbed every inch of Thelma with a chamois cloth. He set the guitar on the mink and shut the clasps, then sat at the bar with the case pinched with his legs. The head barmaid poured him a neat whisky from a dusty, top-shelf bottle. He thanked her with a wink, closed his eyes, and downed the drink. When he opened his eyes, a smiling young woman in a blue dress was sitting on the next stool holding a blue guitar case.

"You must be Chaz," she said, fixing her bright hazel gaze on his tired eyes. "I'm Liz O'Malley. You met my sister Sarah this afternoon. The one who dresses like a banker, talks snooty, and writes about music. She's before and I'm after."

Chaz put on his glasses and said, "Sugar, your bright color scared me…Nice to meet you."

Liz leaned on Chaz's shoulder and handed him a white business card with her phone number handwritten over a blue silhouette of a young woman playing a guitar. "My sister told me all about you. She said stay away. I don't play by her rules. You got a spare minute? Can I plug in, play you some down and dirty blues?"

Chaz, pointing toward the stage, said, "See the tall, gray-haired lady on the stage? She's Mim, the meanest club owner in New York who'll get mighty pissed if you violate her rules. I've seen her punch-out a straggler who wouldn't leave at closing."

"Watch this," Liz said. "I'll give her some woman to woman jive." She strutted toward the stage holding her guitar like an infantryman carrying a rifle into battle.

Chaz shook his head, slouched on the barstool, and yawned. Exhausted from a month of steady gigs, he wanted to return to his Harlem apartment to rest for three upcoming New Orleans gigs. With the gig check in his pocket, he walked toward the exit and ignored Liz and Mim's animated discussion. Just as his shoe touched the sidewalk, he heard the opening chords of the blues classic "Born Under a Bad Sign" coming from Mim's speakers. He sucked in a lungful of dank air and went back to the stage. "What the hell are you doing?" he asked Liz.

"Mr. Chaz, sit, have a drink on me," Liz said into the microphone. "You old buzzards aren't the only ones who can play blues. Miss Mim let me play a few songs. Take a listen." Mim, seeing Chaz's shocked expression, hid her laughter in the kitchen.

Chaz sat at the bar and meekly asked the barmaid for another drink. The barmaid slammed a towel in a sink, mumbled some fowl words, and slid a half glass of speed-rack whisky his way. Liz didn't miss a note as she played way down the neck like Duane Allman, bottleneck like Bonnie Rait, and power chords like Stevie Ray Vaughn. Mim shut down the sound system after ten minutes. Chaz waved Liz to a neighboring barstool. "Dang good string work," he said. "White girls don't play blues. Who taught you?"

"Taught myself. Spent a year woodshedding, practicing chords."

"In the big house?" Chaz said with a big grin.

Liz's face reddened. "My sister told you? Twelve months in the can, I came out a guitar player. Shared a cell with Chiken Lady from Texas, she taught me chords. Please don't tell anyone I'm an ex-con. I'm trying to make an honest living playing blues."

"Don't worry about it. I've been in the can, too."

Chaz ordered another whisky. The barmaid served him a glass of soapy water. Mim tickled his shoulder with a long-handled broom, and when he stood, she patted his rear with the bristles. She broomed Chaz and Liz to the curb, locked the door, and shut off the lights. In the drizzle buffeting the sidewalk, Chaz hailed a cab and let Liz share the ride. When the cab parked near her Midtown apartment, he told her, "If I run into someone needing an axe, I'll drop your name. One more thing: stop plucking them strings, bend 'em."

2 DARK KNIFE

Bourbon Street in New Orleans welcomed the Chaz Russell Band with a nasty thunderstorm and stifling humidity. Several hours after encoring for an exhilarated Le Bluez audience, a dishwasher found Chaz near a dumpster with his white shirt and aqua slacks smeared with mud and blood. Police officers kept morning commuters from the alley. Medics sped Chaz to a hospital. Thelma rested on a bed of white towels on the ambulance floor.

Thelma fared better than Chaz. The guitar suffered a gouge on the flip side, a dinged fretboard, and a cracked fingerboard. Chaz suffered a half-inch deep stab wound in his right arm, six inches from his chord pushing hand. A surgeon used a half spool of stitching to close the wound. Ten hours after the surgery, Chaz saw his bassist Pearly White and drummer Kenny Doyle leaning over his bedrail. "Dang, you're lucky," Pearly said. "Nurse say they cut some muscle, but missed the important stuff. How'd a sly old Mississippi boy get rolled on Bourbon Street?"

"Some creep tried to clip my girl," Chaz said. "My guitar ain't for stealing." Tears flooded his eyes when Kenny placed Thelma on the bed. Chaz, holding the guitar with his good arm, said, "Sweetie, you'll get fixed up. We be playing soon."

Pearly stood Thelma's case against the bed frame. "A waiter found it behind a dumpster," he said. "Thank God it had a bunch of Chaz Russell Band picks in it."

"Dry the case over by the window," Chaz said. "Bring Thelma to

Patenaude Guitar over on Pelican Ave, the place I buy strings. Ask for Patch, the owner. Have him ship her to Durrell Guitar in Arkansas to the attention of Mr. Johnny Durrell. Johnny will know what do."

"Sure, boss," Kenny replied. "Seeing your playing arm is no good, what about the City Blues gig? Two weeks away. They pay in cash."

Chaz raised his head a few inches from the pillow. His voice changed from its normal assertiveness to a whine. "Doc says no guitar playing for two months. I'll use cousin Slim, if he's sober enough. If not, Siggy Smith from the Muddy Waters Tribute Band might work. I'll find a brother with sizzle. We'll be fine."

Three days after the stabbing, the doctor discharged Chaz with orders to return home to New York and rest. Before leaving the hospital, two New Orleans Police detectives and a police artist interviewed him in a conference room. Kenny and Pearly waited in a coffee shop. The investigation of an assault with intent to murder over a guitar fascinated the detectives, veteran observers of French Quarter criminality. For a hundred years, musicians had carried guitars in and out of Bourbon Street clubs without a problem. Chaz explained why overseas guitar collectors coveted custom guitars, especially those with Johnny Durrell's signature, and they would pay enough to inspire an assault or even murder. After the detectives ended the short interview, the artist sketched Chaz's description of the attacker: a bearded, thirtyish, white male with ponytailed hair.

Johnny Durrell replaced Thelma's fretboard with one salvaged from a Durrell singed in a nightclub fire. He figured Chaz needed a change in luck so he spent half a day fitting a replacement fingerboard: a yellow one with an etched image of a dove. He left untouched the ding on the guitar's backside, knowing that when Chaz resumed playing, he'd point to the defect and tell the audience an embellished version of his stabbing.

Johnny completed Thelma's reconstructive surgery in a week, record Johnny time. He called in a favor and had a long haul truck driver deliver the guitar to Chaz's Harlem apartment. Kenny unscrewed the wooden box and lifted Thelma from a bed of crumpled newspapers. Chaz admired the replacement fingerboard and fretboard. When he twanged the strings with his good hand, Thelma sounded showroom fresh.

He shuffled through a scuffed notebook of musician phone numbers, looking for an unemployed guitarist. He poked the telephone keys with a working finger and when someone answered, he pinched the phone receiver with his shoulder blade and jaw. Cousin Slim blended words with slobber while repeating a story from the previous month. Siggy was touring and couldn't break away. Buford Baxter, a former prison cohort, was back in Tusky, enjoying his stay. Memphis Pete wanted more than the gigs paid. Chaz even called a few white dudes, but they all had commitments. If he couldn't find a replacement, he'd be forced to cancel the City Blues gigs, leaving Pearly and Kenny unemployed for weeks, exposing him to their constant doling under fuzzy repayment terms. On a whim, he called Liz O'Malley, the plucky guitarist met at Mim's, whose flirty smirk and potent licks would bond men with drink. He left her a voicemail: "Sugar, can you help an old man out? I'm hurt, can't play guitar for two months, got gigs lined up, probably hustle a few more. Need a lead. If interested, meet me at Mim's this afternoon, bring your axe, we'll use the Sanctuary stage."

Liz strutted into Mim's on time holding her guitar case and a large latte. She wore black jeans and a pink tee shirt with an image of a bird of prey chewing carrion. Seeing Chaz sitting near the stage rubbing his bandaged arm, she asked, "What the hell happened to you?"

"Got stabbed and rolled," he said. "I'll explain later. Problem is the wound. Can't play, need a lead to front my band. You want some work? Heat-up your Les Paul. I know you can play loose with fast songs, show me you can play some slow blues."

Liz walked to a corner of the stage, wired her guitar for sound, performed a sign-of-the-cross, gazed upward toward her biological father in heaven, and played the opening chords of "Crossroads", a Robert Johnson number often covered by blues bands. Two bars into the song, Chaz flashed the chop sign. "Your Les Paul ain't the right guitar for my band. It's good for rock'n'roll, not my type of Chicago blues."

"It's the only guitar I own," Liz said. "You're the only musician in the world who doesn't like Les Pauls. I can name a hundred blues musicians who play them. Go visit the Times Square club where Les Paul himself plays. You'll hear him play jazz, rock, blues, and flamenco on a Les Paul."

The conversation stopped when the barmaid wheeled a squeaky vacuum into the Sanctuary. Chaz stormed from the room with Thelma in hand. He cornered Mim in her office and complained about the interruption. During his lengthy tirade, the barmaid asked Liz about her guitar. Liz said it was a newer Les Paul, bought from a pawn shop for five hundred dollars. The barmaid offered to buy it for eight-hundred cash. Liz declined. The barmaid said it was the right call because the guitar didn't have Made in USA stamped on the headstock, making it a 1960s model, probably worth twenty thousand dollars. Liz doubted the story, but said she'd consider selling if the audition failed.

Chaz finagled a fifteen minute vacuuming delay. He put Thelma on Liz's lap. "Thing weighs a ton," she said. "How's a chick supposed to play this sleigh?"

"Just play the dang thing," Chaz said. "Guitar won't bite."

Liz flipped the strap so she could play righty. She held Thelma to her belly and filled the Sanctuary with a few drawn out blues chords. Chaz, flashing smile gold, said, "You got it Sugar. Now play some 'Stormy Monday.' Rub molasses on the strings, slow them chords."

Liz played and sang "they call it stormy Monday, but Tuesday's just as bad." When the first stanza ended, she put her left middle finger into a chrome sparkplug socket and replayed the opening riff with the socket pressed against the strings, perpendicular to the fretboard. The pinching shortened the working string length and varied the pitch, a technique called slide or bottleneck. After she played three stanzas of slide, Chaz shook his head and grinned. In sixty years of guitar playing, he hadn't seen a white woman play slide with such flair. Before he committed to her hiring, he asked her to bend some strings. She barked into the microphone, "I'm not into bending. I've played hundreds of gigs with heavy musicians. They all say string bending is twangy. You're living old man blues; time to move on to something new."

"Baloney," Chaz said. "You're listening to the wrong people. Real blues musicians, the ones who drive old Caddies around Mississippi with their guitar riding shotgun, string bend. If you want to play in my band, stop plucking strings like you're pulling chicken feathers. Let me show you." He flipped Thelma over to lefty position, thumbed the top string into the bordering two strings and sustained a note. "Blues guitar playing isn't pick a note, think about it, pick another note. It's blending one string with the next string or two or three, like this."

On a couch near the windows, he put Thelma on her lap. Sitting close, he grasped her right wrist, planted her three finger tips on the bottom string and bent her wrist upward, forcing the bottom string into two bordering strings. The guitar made a sound like a seagull flying over chum. "So, bending makes you old buzzards sound like old buzzards," she said.

"All guitarists bend strings," Chaz said. "They just don't admit it. Get back on stage, play slow blues, try a few string bends. You're not hired yet, better play your best."

Liz played a medley of decelerated blues numbers. The barmaid returned to the Sanctuary and listened to the audition as she swabbed imaginary spider webs with a dust mop. Liz won Chaz's favor when she deftly transitioned from blues standards to jazz improvisation. "Nice work," he said. "But you're rough on the technique; we'll fix you over time." He gave Liz his business card. "Here's my apartment address, meet me there tomorrow noon, see if we can work out a deal for your services."

The next day, Liz, dressed in biker boots, denim jeans, and a gun metal blue leather vest, sat on a slippery subway car bench between a priest and a scruffy construction worker. Her wraparound sunglasses discouraged a leering rider from a pickup line. She read Chaz Russell's two page biography in the book *Blues Gods* as the car squealed and shimmied toward Harlem. The author noted Chaz played mostly electric blues except for a year when he played fusion, an electrified blend of jazz and blues. He had the same band members for over thirty years. They played over two hundred gigs a year throughout the United States and Europe.

Liz assumed a paying gig with Chaz would calm her pesky probation officer who had set her up with a whey-stirring job at a Brooklyn cheese plant. She hoped her bland social life would improve with her smooth guitar notes and sly pandering of fit males watching her moves. She needed a new romance because Steve

Maxwell, her former lover and bank robbery accomplice, had lost his appeal and would spend sixteen years in jail.

She held her pocketbook close as an escalator delivered her to the bustling Harlem street. She walked three blocks, counting sidewalk joints to avoid eye contact with men and women offering spiritual guidance. A sports car stopped at an intersection and the driver, a sullen man in a business suit, asked for a date. A tall woman in a flowery dress saw her staring at a street sign and guided her to Chaz's apartment building. Under a leafy tree, a wizened man wearing a pork pie hat sat on a concrete bench playing acoustic guitar for three old men resting on dusty dirt, sharing a bottle wrapped with a brown paper bag. Their eight somber eyes watched her trot up the granite stairs.

Chaz unlocked two deadbolts and led her to a sunny living room cluttered with song books, amplifiers, and magazines. She found comfort on a blue leather couch. Chaz settled in a black leather recliner and opened a manila envelope. "Here's my deal," he said. "I'm a one-armed dude in a two-arm business, needing temporary labor. I've got dozens of friends wanting to fill-in for me, but I like your chops. It's not wimpy, just solid blues, able to drift into jazz. When you chucked your Les Paul and played Thelma, you sealed the deal. I don't care if you're a white chick. If you're sure you'll show up sober at every gig, I'll give you an eight week contract to play lead. When my arm heals in a few months, who knows what'll happen. I've got a million friends. I'll find you another gig."

Liz asked about his bassist and drummer. "I've played with Kenny and Pearly for three decades," he said. "On the side, Pearly has played bass on hundreds of jazz sessions with you name it. His deep jazz bones spice things up. When he stays away from women and booze, he's a fine musician who lays down a tight pocket. If he doesn't, he plays like he's wearing ski mitts. Still walks with a limp, shot in the ass by a jealous husband."

"He get along with the drummer?"

"Like butter on bread. Sober, those boys play well together. They know I'll ship them out if they don't keep rhythm. They're close, claim the same mother, but don't look alike. Kenny's skin is dark. Pearly is a shade lighter. After thirty years, I still don't buy the story. Pearly is from a famous Mississippi music family, his mother was one of the best blues guitarists around. Kenny grew up in

Chicago, played with some heavies. Both have done time for stealing, not from me. My boys aren't afraid to ruffle things with a flat note. Not bad for a band of seventy year olds. We can't play from a Real Book every night; we'd have a sleepy audience, or no audience and a growly stomach."

"The other night, you guys cooked. Heard some jazz in there."

"I've played a billion blues notes and heard about five billion more. I try to lead my audience from life troubles into what the Chicago boys call 'foggin' the music; happens when listeners drift into a trance and stop concentrating on drummer's arms or guitarist's fingers. If we play tight, resolve all our dissonant notes, they'll groove on our musical conversation, enter the fog."

"Who follows your band?"

"City clubs, we play for people on the prowl, tourists, and locals. At music festivals and bigger clubs, it's white faces in the crowd and us black faces on stage. We get along, they pay us well. We rarely see our people; they listen to rap and hip-hop in clubs."

"Why you still string bending?" Liz asked. "It's not heard much these days. The sustain sounds corny, like country."

"You're about two seconds from getting kicked out of here," he said. "Don't bad mouth my style. I've made a lot of money playing my way. When my guitar cries like a scorned woman, eyes wet. If you play for me, you'll need to play like me. This ain't a rock band."

"I'll give it a try if you lighten Thelma's strings. I got a blister from the crane cables on there."

Chaz took two contracts from the envelope. He promised to install lighter strings and keep Thelma at his apartment between gigs and practice. Liz signed the contracts after he promised to stop calling her Sugar. Chaz clipped a five hundred dollar signing bonus to her copy. She left the apartment with a song list and directions to a rehearsal at Chessman Studio, ten blocks away. Chaz told Pearly and Kenny the Guitar Lounge gigs would go on as scheduled and they'd meet the new guitarist at a band rehearsal in two days. He'd play one hand piano while his hand healed.

Liz entered Chessman Studio wearing a white blouse, black slacks, and red plaid heels. She breezed past pitted metal chairs, over scuffed pink linoleum, to the production studio. Corky Chessman, a sixty-year-old, lean black man with short cornrows, welcomed her with a cool handshake and passive smile. Chaz beamed when she entered the room. She sat on a tall stool next to the primary microphone and dipped her shoulder as Chaz guided Thelma's strap over her nape. Corky plugged a wire into the guitar's belly and then sat behind a clear glass partition, tweaking sound settings. When the essence of heated amplifier tubes pervaded the studio, he said, "Mike one, you're live. Fire-up the Durrell."

Liz sent dozens of no-nonsense blues chords to the amplifiers. The lighter strings made playing Thelma tolerable. Wanting to hear the guitar's limits, she plucked and pushed the strings during a frenzy of blues trills borrowed from Sister Rosetta Tharpe, Blind Lemon Jefferson, and Robert Johnson. Chaz kept a steady smile. Corky shut his eyes and tapped the beat on the console. When Liz played the first notes of Hendrix's "Purple Haze," Pearly and Kenny entered the studio, looked at their new bandmate, and left in a cab without saying a word. Chaz covered his face with his hands.

"What the hell happens now?" Liz asked. "A Salvation Army gig outside Macy's? Chaz Russell's three-hand band?"

"It'll take a few hours," Chaz said. "I'll find the bastards. This music business is full of head cases like them. I know where they went. You stay here, get friendly with Thelma. If you pop a string, Corky has plenty."

Chaz kept a change of clothes in a Chessman's closet. He changed into a blue, pin-striped suit, tucked a heavily starched baby-blue handkerchief in his lapel pocket, combed his hair, clipped his nails, and rubbed a few drops of manly French cologne on his face. He hailed a taxi and sat in the back seat. The cabbie asked, "Sir, what street you go?"

"Take me up Malcolm X Boulevard to 142nd Street, to the Cotton Palace," Chaz said.

After the cab driver swore in Kurdish at a driver who cut him off, he told Chaz, "Sir, I no go those streets. I stop at 129th. I'm Iraqi. Those streets worse than home."

"Listen my friend. How long you been in the United States?"

"Sixteen weeks."

"Let me tell you how this country works, my friend. In the U.S. there is the king president, Barack, and a bunch of little presidents like me. I'm president of the Harlem Musicians Guild. Drop me off at the front door of the Cotton Palace. I'll make sure no one bothers you."

"You the President? I take you there," the cabbie said. He parked on the Cotton Palace VIP lane behind a white limousine and a red Ferrari and showed Chaz ten fingers. Chaz handed him a twenty-dollar bill and waved change. The cabbie chanted an Arabic blessing. Chaz tipped five singles to the velvet-gloved woman who opened the cab door and strode like a president to a mirrored façade where he combed his hair in the reflection. A security officer let him enter the marble-floored restroom. Several minutes later, he winked at the velvet-gloved lady and walked a block to the Backbeat, a friendly bar favored by musicians, ladies-of-the night, and thieves. He opened the windowless, dented metal door with bullet holes near the lowest hinge and waded past three dandies fogged by cigarette smoke. A couple immersed in vodka-drenched love talk waved a hello. A few regulars patted his back and asked about his recovery from the stabbing. One asked to borrow sixty-dollars. On the stage, Big Jock Parker smoked a Churchill cigar while playing a rollicking blues number with the Frisky Mamas, his all-women rhythm section. Walking toward his rhythm boys, he passed hunched drinkers pontificating about bad marriages, slimy agents, and life in general. At the far end of the longest bar in Harlem, Pearly and Kenny shadowed empty gimlet glasses with fresh ones in hand. A blond-wigged woman sitting next to Pearly moved over one stool. Chaz ordered a whisky and "something for the lovely to my right."

Pearly leaned toward Chaz and said, "We feel bad you're getting senile. Of all the blues guitarists in the world looking for work, you pick a white babe to play your fat guitar. I see ten slingers in this gin mill better than a white chick. You trying to jump her? We're afraid you'll end up on life support over at Harlem Central."

Kenny added, "You feeling frisky, like in your twenties? Don't you get it? You're an old bluesman with one good wing. She's a floozy, not a musician."

Chaz stirred the thin striped straw piercing his drink. He pursed his lips and drew the straw between his teeth. "First of all," he said, "I'm old enough to be her grandfather, you idiots. Second, she's a hell of a blues player, copped some jazz along the way. I damn near fell over when she snuck in a few Coltrane licks with "Born Under a Bad Sign." Third of all, I agree, blues musicians are a dime a dozen, especially drummers and bass players. Looking around this gin mill, I see plenty of each. Here's my deal: Get your black asses down to Chessman's or you're both fired. I'll borrow Jock's backup ladies; they're better looking than you guys and they play tighter. Probably work for half the money."

Pearly and Kenny gulped their drinks and left. Chaz conversed with the woman who had yielded her seat: Ruby Ralston, a well-traveled thief and prostitute whose salacious gait and sultry voice enamored most of the New York City blues scene. Her alluring perfume, spray of blond hair, and sultry smile masked a savvy grifter who delivered local fences a steady flow of sweet-toned guitars. One blues musician claimed she stole his denture studded with gold teeth and he couldn't sing until a dentist made a new set. The police knew she sold stolen guitars and musical memorabilia to a broker who shipped them to collectors in Japan. Last year, she sold Chaz a vintage acoustic owned by Reverend Whitley, a legendary Harlem gospel choir leader. Chaz paid Ruby two hundred dollars for the guitar. In the middle of a night, he put it in the Reverend's church and tiptoed away without leaving a written note. When Chaz wasn't touring, he hosted Sunday afternoon acoustic guitar gatherings in his Harlem apartment so friends could strum and gossip. The previous winter, Ruby talked her way into one of the gatherings and when she walked in, bluesman coddled their guitars like mothers huddling infants on a cold day. When nature called, they took their guitars. Chaz set a trap. He put a recording tape and reel in a box in his closet and wrote Jimi, Miles, and Me on the cover. During the gathering, someone stole the tape. Ruby was the only suspect.

Chaz finished his drink and gave Ruby a quick hug. A whiff of her perfume gave him a hot flash. "Know anyone looking for a nice Flying V, for short money?" she asked.

"No thanks," he said. "You're selling the guitar stolen last week from Eddie Kiefer's apartment."

On the way out, Chaz gained three lipstick smears on his cheek, loaned fifty-five dollars, collected two hundred dollars owed, bet ten dollars in the numbers pool, and rain-checked six drink offers. When he got back to Chessman's, Liz was practicing chords on Thelma. "You've been gone for two hours," she said. "I thought they murdered you. Where's the rest of the band?"

"Give them ten minutes," he said. "I go through this foolishness a few times a year. Last time it was Kenny shaking me down for a new kit."

Right on time, his giggly bandmates swaggered into the studio. Kenny carried a brown cardboard box holding a dozen plain donuts. Pearly asked for an introduction to "this lovely young lady, our new leader."

"Here's Lightning Liz, the best available blues guitarist," Chaz said.

Pearly stepped forward wearing brown and white saddle shoes fit for a country club. He eased his hand from his white linen sport coat. His long, leathery fingers held Liz's hand with the same tension one would have when carrying a parakeet to its cage. Kenny nudged into the conversation. Years of kick drumming had worn thin the toes of his butter-colored loafers. His sinewy fingers squeezed Liz's hand with the same tension a Major League Baseball player would apply to a bat when hitting a home run.

Musicians spend more time with their instruments than with their lovers. When they find an instrument with the right fit and sound, they marry it. If the tone flattens, they are quick to divorce. Pearly showed Liz his Durrell JD-2 four string bass named Lucas. The bass looked like a thinner Thelma with two *f*-holes on the body and two rounded protuberances facing the fret board. Inward facing banjo tuners made on-the-fly adjustments dependant on limber fingers. The bass begin its working life in 1972 with a flawless sunburst finish. The business side varnish now had a foggy patina caused by rubbed-in barroom smoke. Decades of palm pressure had worn the varnish from the outer radius. Years of friction from showy belt buckles dug a silver dollar-sized abrasion on the back. Scratches running below the fingerboard indicated he occasionally strummed the bass like a guitar. Deep, throbbing notes sounding like an elephant's heartbeat tumbled from the speakers when he pinched the strings.

Liz watched Kenny unpack the rounded black cases holding his kit and set up his twenty-six, fifteen, sixteen, and eighteen inch drums. He removed his prized Turkish cymbals from a brown leather bag. "Love when shine comes out of the bag," he said. "I've lost my clangers a dozen times, they always comes back. One time Pearly filled my bag with tin pie plates. Chaz told me to drill holes in the plates, play them that night. I got an electric drill and did my duty. Pearly told me it was a prank. Chaz told the audience the story, they laughed like hell. Some still call me Pie Plates."

Kenny and Pearly gained partial sobriety by emptying the donut box. Chaz waved his bandmates to the center of the sound room. "Listen up," he said. "I rented this studio for twelve hours. Spent half my time chasing two idiots. We're playing until 4 a.m. Do your talking with your instruments." He rested his five good fingers on the piano keys. "Let's start with 'Born Under a Bad Sign' played fast. Liz, D-chord heavy; Kenny, warm them pots and pans; Pearly, work a tight line." Chaz snapped his fingers. Although these musicians had played this song hundreds of times, the first few bars sounded like a high school band after summer break.

"Liz, you're out of tune," Chaz said. "Get it right. Tuning is like airplane maintenance, well worth the effort." After the tuning break, he shouted a speedier "ah-one, ah-two, ah-three." The band picked up the pace. Chaz yelled, "Sounds tighter. Now, improvise, anything you want."

Liz snagged a riff from Miles Davis' *Bitches Brew* album then she sent Pearly the primary chords of "Born Under a Bad Sign." Pearly repeated the D, A, G chords four times, then held his bass like a guitar and finger picked a thirty second improvisation pinched from John Coltrane's acclaimed album *Blue Train*. Kenny took the hook and played a drum solo so fast his sticks blurred. Chaz, wincing when he touched a key with the thumb of his bandaged hand, ended the improvisation with a simple piano solo. He had disregarded his doctor's directive to refrain from instrument play during his recovery.

"Damn impressed," he said. "Kenny, Pearly, not bad for three-sheets-to-the-wind. Liz, those jazzy licks sounded sweet. I knew Miles, he's smiling down on us."

The band practiced dozens of blues standards and the music tightened as the night darkened. Chaz pushed them until the final minute. Knowing he had the makings of a credible blues band, he shut off the lights and led his band across the street to Suki's Mandarin.

Suki owned the only all-night restaurant in this neighborhood of night clubs, instrument shops, and recording studios. Tipsy drifters, hungry from a night of carousing, couldn't resist his tasty food and edgy scene. Most nights, Suki stood in the foyer in a three-piece suit schmoozing with customers. On a few occasions, his black belt karate skills subdued drunken toughs skipping a check. Suki greeted

Chaz with a bow. He grabbed four menus and led the party past booths of beery, wide-eyed musicians who kept a steady eye on the guitar and horn cases leaned against the wall. In the last booth, a vintage platinum blond wearing glittery stockings leaned over a man in a wrinkled tuxedo.

The band sat at an oblong table under a cloudy light. Suki said he'd bring the usual. Chaz sat on a throne-like chair with CR carved on the back. Liz sat between Kenny and Pearly on a soft, vinyl covered bench. Chaz asked Kenny about a musician sitting a few booths away who had recovered from health issues. Pearly answered the question, just like a husband and wife. Liz said she'd have a used Les Paul for sale soon. Pearly recommended a close friend who paid fair prices for used instruments. Suki delivered four Korean beers. They clanged bottles and promised to play their best over the next few months.

3 JOHNNY'S CRAFT

In 1988, the City Blues owner converted an electronics store near Times Square into a nightclub that attracted discerning music listeners who didn't mind paying a stiff cover charge and fifteen dollars for a drink. The newly renovated façade and lobby flashed more chrome than a car bumper factory. The enhanced Chaz Russell Band arrived at the club several hours before their eight o'clock show. After a testy exchange over gig payment, they set up on stage. The sound tech fiddled with the mix. Liz practiced riffs on Thelma. Pearly and Kenny bickered over a bass line. Chaz, loaded with pain medication, practiced a piano ditty. He approved the sound mix after lengthy fussing. In a dressing room, they shared a soul food spread sent by the Backbeat owner.

Five minutes before the first note, Chaz followed his band to the stage. The front row seats held respected New York City blues musicians Jimmy Shine, Clark Monroe, and Big Mama Washington, along with three fawning newspaper reporters. In the second row, a carload of well-lubricated Backbeat regulars howled over a dirty joke. Japanese tourists and dozens of familiar faces filled the other fifty seats.

Liz caught a glance of her sister's face in the third row behind a woman wearing a big hat. The hat blocked the view of an individual sitting next to Sarah. Liz assumed it was a date because this gig was too small for her to review. Sarah lifted a tan notebook from her pocketbook. If the book folded sideways it was a phone book and if it folded up, it would be a reporter's pad, indicating Sarah was on assignment reviewing the concert. When she flicked the notebook upward and began writing, Liz told Chaz, "I'm outta here. I'm not playing if my sister is reviewing my work."

Chaz made Pearly walk ten steps to a Hammond B3 organ and play "Green Onions," a catchy blues instrumental often played during hockey intermissions. Kenny added a limp drum line. Chaz shuffled Liz into the dressing room and asked, "What the hell is going on?"

Liz's complexion had the color of boiled lobster. "My asshole sister is in the audience reviewing my playing for *New York Vibe*."

"Why do you care?" asked Chaz with a look of despair. "Maybe she'll like the sound. I'd take the free publicity."

"She's a bitch. Ever since she went to the high-brow Ivy League school on the Upper West Side she's been talking down to me. Telling everyone about her sister the perp. I can see the next *Vibe* headline: 'Parolee Bungles Chords in City Blues Debut.'"

"Go get your sister. I'll flip a coin. Heads, she stays, you play. Tails, I fire your ass and pull Jimmy Shine from the front row to play lead."

A minute later, the club manager led Sarah into the dressing room. The two sisters stood face-to-face. "Why you here without my permission?" Liz asked.

"Lay off," Sarah said, pushing her sister away. "I got this assignment a month ago. You should thank me for setting you up with this fine gentleman."

Liz drove the nail of her index finger into Sarah's belly. "You didn't set me up. I talked my way into this gig. Why'd you tell him I did time?"

Sarah, noticing a fresh run in her silk blouse, said, "You owe me two-hundred bucks for the top. And stop pretending you're an angel. Your trial was all over the news. Everyone knows you're a thug."

The club manager interrupted the verbal combat by shouting into the dressing room, "My audience is sick of 'Green Onions.' Stop the foolishness, get on stage, or I'll send you home, have Big Mama sing with Clark and Jimmy."

Chaz herded the sisters to a corner of the room where he told them in a fatherly voice, "You're damn lucky to have a breathing sister; mine ain't. Many years ago, a gator got my baby sister. Little thing, playing by a crick, chasing a froggie. Buried her the day after

Easter in her pretty pink dress and hat. They put her favorite dolly where her arm was two days before. I cried more tears than was in the crick. I talk to her up in heaven every morning. Be thankful to dear God you've got a breathing sister. Give your sister a squeeze."

Liz gulped water and fired the crumpled bottle at a wall. After a few deep breaths, she sobbed, "You're my only sister. Bailed me out of trouble many times. I've been a bad girl, sorry for dragging you into my screwy life."

The sisters hugged. Sarah returned to her seat and readied her notebook for ink. Liz held Thelma, ready to play. Chaz winked at the club manager, an old friend from Chicago who knew Chaz never had a sister. The manager announced to the audience, "Please welcome the Chaz Russell Band and the debut of Lightnin' Liz O'Malley."

Kenny tapped his snare twice. Liz's guitar lagged a half beat behind the bass line. Pearly waved his hand upward and by the third bar of "Crossroads" she played tight to the beat. A minute into the song, Chaz felt like hiding behind the piano when Liz tried a string bend, broke a fingernail, spilled blood, and stopped playing. A band-aid applied by the manager allowed her to resume playing. The next song, with its tight chords, timely beats, and fluid improvisations, put the audience in the fog. They played ten more songs over two hours, ending the set with blown kisses and bows. The club manager ignored calls for an encore because another band had to set up for their midnight set.

Chaz, exhausted after the successful debut of his reconfigured band, made a few phone calls from his apartment with his throbbing arm on a pillow. He told his bandmates, a booking agent in last night's audience liked what he heard and offered him a thousand dollar gig at the Guitar Lounge on 41st street, two blocks from City Blues. The house band had the flu and couldn't play a happy-hour gig scheduled for that afternoon. Chaz accepted the light fee with short notice knowing it was only an hour of work and music industry big shots frequented the club.

The Guitar Lounge filled half of the ground floor of the ten-story Landing Hotel, a tired edifice with a gray facade and cloudy windows. The last three New York City mayors wanted the building demolished. Despite its sordid appearance, sentimental preservationists prevailed. Pedestrians hoped for the best as they speed-walked under the sagged marquee. The Landing rented rooms to musicians, lower-tier Broadway actors, and transient dreamers looking to make a splash. Cigar smoke, Chanel #5, and a faded mauve rug emulated a 1970s Las Vegas casino. An unemployed musician who booked a room and hung out in the art deco lobby could hook a gig if they dressed smartly, knew music lingo, and acted somewhat sober. The lobby wall held twenty paintings of blues legends including one of young Chaz playing Thelma with the top two strings bent into the third string.

Chaz introduced Liz to a group of well-dressed men and women sitting on clubby leather chairs. "She's a pup with nice technique," he said. "She's playing Thelma while my claw heals. As long as her fingers hold up, we'll be fine." Sherry Greenberg, the owner of Temptation Records, asked if Liz preferred electric or acoustic blues.

"Mostly electric with some jazz." Liz said. "I'm not afraid to sneak in a Hendrix lick, a little Miles." Sherry handed her a business card and suggested they talk about an upcoming project. Chaz interrupted the conversation by telling Liz to find the boys and set up.

Over the next half hour, black cabs discharged passengers to the sidewalk across from the marquee. The lobby filled with Italian suits, sculpted pantsuits, and shiny shoes. When the gossip and small talk ran dry, they drifted into the Guitar Lounge and sat at a long table covered with a white tablecloth. They avoided eye contact with sullen souls parked on barstools quaffing wakeup cocktails. At a corner table, a twentyish man wearing his father's sport jacket stared at his soft drink and fidgeted with an envelope holding his resume. His girlfriend, a sturdy figure in a frilly dress made by her mother, circled help wanted ads in a music trade newspaper.

Depression-era craftsman had built the oaken stage with Maine timber. Only cracker-thin musicians enjoyed playing on the cramped platform. Chaz sat at an electric piano, a foot from Kenny's biggest drum. He began the session with good-natured needling of the bartender who had recently celebrated his fortieth anniversary working the bar. The headstock of Pearly's bass brushed Liz's hip when he played. Chaz ribbed the music executives between songs and they responded with hearty laughs.

After the gig, the mischievous audience went to a tony uptown restaurant to talk deals and more deals. The bartender toweled ten feet of prime real estate and served drinks to Chaz and his band. Halfway through his second whisky, Chaz told Liz, "Your playing fills my backbone with ginger ale. You'll fit as my second lead after my hand heals. We got to fix our guitar shortage, but keep your Les Paul in its case. If you promise to play in my band for a year, I'll order you a lighter Durrell. You'll have to visit Johnny's shop for a fitting."

Stunned Liz focused her eyes on her drink. Having her own Durrell would led to a long productive career as a guitarist. Memphis producers would beg her to play session work. The best blues singers would want Liz and her sweet-sounding instrument in their bands. If she needed money, the guitar would pawn for ten thousand dollars. She shared a high-five with Chaz and promised to fulfill her side of the deal.

Sarah lauded Liz's City Blues performance in her review. This led to a teary, reconciliatory phone call with her sister. After a few glasses of Chablis during a long lunch, they hugged like sisters should. Liz, needing an accomplice for the guitar fitting trip, talked Sarah into the role of copilot.

A week after their reconciliation, the sisters sped across the George Washington Bridge in a rental car toward Johnny Durrell's Arkansas shop. After fifty tranquil miles on the New Jersey Turnpike, Liz asked Sarah about her book.

"Agent's pissed over my slow production," Sarah replied, "sources slinging fluff. I'm stalled until I figure out why Hendrix and Davis scheduled the ultimate session then bailed out. The music would've sold twenty million copies. Never happened, so they say."

"Sounds like you think it did,"

"Yeah, there's more to the story. The Hendrix bios say Jimi set up the session. Tony Williams, the jazz drummer, was in on it. Miles called Hendrix the night before, demanded fifty grand before he'd blow a note. Williams asked for the same. Jimi said no way. I added the story to my first draft. Things changed after I borrowed a book from the library. Tucked in the jacket, was a session card from Chessman Studio with Chaz Russell written on top. I'd heard Chaz's name in my travels, but I knew little about him. I didn't tell you what happened when we met at Mim's. I showed him the session card, he growled so hard he damn near popped one of his gold crowns. His smooth talk turned to stutters."

"You think he knows more than he's saying?"

"I've been around enough men to know when they're slinging shit. When I asked about a couple initials on the card, Chaz squirmed like a whore in church. Looked at the floor when he spoke. Claimed he couldn't recall anything about the session. He really got testy when I told him the card had JH and MD penciled under his name. I'll pry the real story out of him someday; may mix truth serum with his drink."

The sisters spent the first night in a Knoxville, Tennessee motel. The following afternoon, they took a right turn after Little Rock and drove an hour down a two-lane highway to the Ozark community of Lincolnville where they got directions from a general store clerk and then drove two miles to a rusty, guitar-shaped sign nailed to a tree. They followed the long, dusty driveway to a white farmhouse and parked next to a rusted Harley leaning on the fat trunk of a shade tree.

Not quite five-foot tall Johnny Durrell greeted each sister with a sturdy handshake. His white tee shirt luffed in the breeze. Fine yellow sawdust on his dark cheeks and forehead made him look younger than his seventy-one years. His tooth count of twelve equaled the amount of new guitars hanging on his shop wall.

Johnny's late father, JD, was the preferred guitar builder for the best Memphis session players. He dropped dead after leaning his Harley against the tree and Johnny hadn't touched the motorcycle since the death. During JD's prime years, 1952 to 1969, he built guitars for paroled bluesman and if they made some money they paid him back. If they returned to prison, he bribed guards so the convicts could take their guitars with them.

Johnny built his first guitar at age twelve with his father guiding every move. JD was a finicky craftsman who made Johnny work seven days a week. Johnny, wanting a lighter schedule, left for New York City on his twenty-second birthday. The country boy found excitement and a living wage when he met Chaz in a bar. They toured in the early 60s with Gabby Walters. Chaz played lead and Johnny served as Gabby's guitar wizard and woman getter. Johnny returned to his native Arkansas in 1974 to care for his newly widowed mother. In 1979, *Guitar Build* magazine named him the Best Luthier in America and he unplugged his shop phone soon afterward.

Ordering a new guitar from Johnny involved persistence, luck, and intrigue. The morning after the Guitar Lounge gig, Chaz had his Mississippi-based cousin drive six hours to Johnny's shop. The cousin sat on the rusted Harley for an hour while Johnny fussed with a varnish application. Harried Johnny eventually let him into the shop. The nervous cousin ordered a new guitar without mentioning his Chaz connection. Johnny muttered his standard response to walk-ins: "Two years wait, two-hundred down, cash only, you'll get a postcard when I'm ready to deal with you. Don't wait at the post office for the postcard, could take three years. If you can't wait, go buy a pawn shop guitar." The distraught cousin called Chaz and gave Johnny the phone. Their twenty minute brabble ended when Johnny agreed to a speedy build that would begin with Liz's guitar fitting.

Liz and Sarah followed Johnny a hundred feet down a path to the shop, a low-slung hodge-podge of repurposed chicken coops crowned with a crumbly roof. Wood chunks and serpentine shavings hidden by sawdust made for dangerous walking across the shop floor. Guitar carcasses littered a corner of the shop. Autographed pictures of guitar gods and goddesses covered the back of the door. On a wall, a long maple rack held a dozen Durrells fit for a museum. A closet door had the words STAY OUT painted in runny red. A workbench served as a guitar triage with three dinged Durrells awaiting repair. In the far corner, near a pot-belly stove, three deerskin covered chairs and a table made from a wooden crate served as a sales office and at night, a place to sip moonshine.

Liz and Sarah sat on the deerskin and rested their feet on the crate. Johnny tossed a handful of cedar cutoffs into a storage bin behind the cold stove. He sat on an inverted five-gallon drywall bucket and held a piece of wood with a rope nailed to opposite ends. "Chaz wants Thelma's baby sister made," he said. "Let's start with this here prop of pine and pig iron. Try it out, see how it feels. Soft wood lets me change the shape. Chucking a little iron will lighten it. Plan is to try, tweak, try again, build her right the first time. Don't want to shave a few ounces after I build the real one. Happened a few times."

Liz put the strap over her shoulder and strummed a few air chords on the wooden form. "The body's too fat. Can you shave the face a quarter inch or so? Lighten her up, too."

Johnny said he'd make the adjustments. He stood on the bucket and measured the distance from Liz's picking hand to her shoulder, her arm length, finger width, waist, and the distance from the floor to her belt buckle."You ladies head over to Miss Simpson's, near the general store, for a tea and biscuit. I'll shave the prop."

An hour later, Johnny placed the thinner, lighter prop over Liz's shoulder. "This is perfect," she said.

"Let's talk finish and wood," he said, "I get guitar stock from Jose` Pez, my wood broker in Brazil. Seeing you can't chop down a guitar wood tree down there, Jose` waits for a good storm, buys the windfall from the government, ships me mahogany. I send back shine and greenbacks."

Johnny and the two sisters followed a weedy path to a brick and concrete kiln built by a crematorium contractor. "I cook the wood in here," he said, "and store the dry stuff in the next building." Liz asked why the kiln looked unused. Johnny claimed he scrubbed it after every batch because an undertaker used it to cremate big bodies.

They walked a few steps to a wobbly hencoop stuffed with mahogany planks. Johnny horsed three planks onto a picnic table and splashed water on the boards. "Take your pick young lady. Water tells the story. Get a lookie at the tight grain. Don't want knots or rot. Tight grain makes sweet sound."

Liz chose a tightly swirled plank with a reddish hue. Sarah nodded despite her inability to distinguish balsa from ebony. Johnny brought the board into his shop. "I'll get working on your guitar two seconds after you leave," he said. Liz put five, hundred dollar bills in his pocket.

"No money," he said. "Chaz paid for it." She yelled her approval and offered to buy dinner.

The sisters booked a room in a motel behind the general store. They returned to Johnny's farm at dusk and met his spry 85 year-old mother Mae. She graciously declined Liz's dinner offer because she had to babysit her great granddaughter. Before they left, she thanked the sisters for taking Johnny on his first date in thirty years.

Johnny sat on the front seat, tightened his seat belt to a child's setting, and navigated Liz over three miles of gravely side roads to Molly's Roadside Grill. The restaurant sprouted from a gas station in 1952 when the owner, angered by a two cent a gallon gasoline tax increase, shut off the pumps, married two abandoned mobile homes to the rear, and opened a barbecue joint. Since opening night, anyone driving with their windows down on State Road Four near the Lincolnville town line breathed barbecued smoke from Molly's.

The first years in business, Molly, the owner's wife, cooked and served barbecue while her husband toured Arkansas and surrounding states, buying tender pork and beef directly from farmers. In 1958, they opened a tennis court sized addition with a two-story tall stone and cast iron grilling pit on the middle. The wait lines doubled, so they doubled the seating in 1962. Customers walk by the original gas pumps on their way to the dining room.

Molly's daughter Moline inherited the restaurant in 1989. She bellowed a greeting to Johnny while tossing meat on smoky iron. Johnny and the sisters sat at a table covered with a shiny checkerboard tablecloth. Johnny smirked at a pretty waitress and ordered a pitcher of Ark Ale, a local brew known for a quick kick. When the waitress returned with the ale, Liz asked her for a menu. The waitress said they didn't have menus because Molly's served only ribs, white bread, and pralines, and they didn't want to embarrass customers who couldn't read, or had bad eyes.

Johnny's steady hand filled three frosted mugs. He offered a toast to Liz's new guitar. They tapped mugs, but before his first swallow, he swished ale in his mouth for a few seconds then gargled; the procedure done every afternoon to rinse sawdust from his throat. Three sips into his visit, he caught the waitress's attention and flashed three fingers with one hand and one finger with the other. She delivered three floppy paper plates stacked with baby back ribs, a loaf of bread, and three rolls of paper towels. Johnny ten-fingered a saucy rib a half second after his plate touched the table. Liz and Sarah cut their dinner into pieces and ate with a fork.

Moline's husband Ralph sat at their table with his black guitar resting on his boot toe. The sisters admired his polished cowboy boots, black dress pants, black long-sleeved shirt with white embroidery, and string tie. Ralph served as Molly's house musician, playing blues every week night on a one-man stage tucked in a corner. Locals considered him a newcomer. When an injury ended his professional football career in 1982, he spent several years traveling the Bible Belt, playing guitar in churches and juke joints. In 1984, heading to Tuscaloosa in an open convertible, a whiff of barbecue outside Lincolnville led him to Molly's. Teen-aged Moline noticed his caring eyes and sincere smile as she served him lunch. Ralph has stayed close to Lincolnville since their wedding three months after they met.

Johnny pointed at the gold Durrell script on the headstock of Ralph's guitar. "She's a Double Trouble named Blackbird, looks like a boomerang, built it for King Miller. King loved the sound, but got signed by a paying guitar company. I swapped the guitar for a month of barbecue and ale. Best deal I ever made."

Ralph, watching lazy bubbles rise from the bottom of Johnny's mug, played a few notes. "She's one bad-ass fiddle," he said, "goes with me to church, powers them spirituals. Had some big money offers for her. I'll only sell if they outlaw barbecue."

Johnny showed the waitress one finger and pointed at Ralph. Moline saw Johnny's finger action and howled louder than a coyote stuck in a crevice. She followed the scream with a full shoulder and arm gesture first pointed at Ralph and then at the stage. Ralph stood and told Johnny, "Woman feeds and houses me. I best go to my corner and play music so I'm not eating Miss Simpson's stale biscuits all week."

Ralph went to his corner and dawdled with his guitar, playing off-key standards mostly ignored by customers. Johnny and the sisters chased their ribs with a plateful of pralines then they faced their chairs toward Ralph and ordered another pitcher of Ark Ale.

"Chaz is good people," Liz said. "Only known him a month. He set me up with a new guitar by the legend, Mr. Johnny Durrell."

Johnny's eyes leaked tears. "I've known him since my early twenties. Sometimes he sends me a few dollars after a good week. I tell you, he's played with everyone, even a few local pickers who could play the boots off anyone. Shame that woman stabbed him in New Orleans, damn near cut off his picking hand."

"You sure it was a woman?" Liz asked. "He told the cops a man knifed him."

Johnny's boney fingers brushed his hair. Sawdust plopped into his mug and floated on the foam. He chugged a few swallows, lowered his head, and whispered, "Chaz told me a woman stabbed him. He couldn't see no skin, but it was a woman's hand wearing a glove. Got a good whiff of a French perfume. He knows the brand."

"It wasn't a woman," Sarah said. "He's feeding you garbage. I read the police reports and newspaper articles. They all point to a white guy with greasy hair. A woman wouldn't have the nerve to stab a man, snatch a guitar."

"Chaz is an honest boy," Johnny said, "Men perps don't wear perfume. He wants to find out who did it before telling the cops. Mama told me to stay out of others business. Let's talk about the weather."

Liz didn't want to discuss the unbearable Arkansas humidity so she mentioned Mae's niceness. This initiated a lengthy Johnny sniffle and sob session with detailed, dramatic descriptions of his mother's arthritis and her doctor visits over the past two years. When Johnny's handkerchief couldn't hold another tear, he asked Sarah what she did to pay the bills.

"I write for a music weekly," she said, "review concerts, write columns. On the side, I'm writing a book on the 60s music scene; it's about Hendrix and Miles Davis."

"I built Jimi a guitar," Johnny said, "boy broke it, by mistake, not part of the show. Those two were from different planets. Miles wouldn't play with Jimi so he hired Johnny Mac who tried to play like Jimi."

"What happened to Jimi's guitar?" Sarah asked.

Johnny, looking like he witnessed a murder, excused himself for a restroom visit. He returned and said, "Jimi's guitar got burnt after he died. He played it one time, didn't like the sound. Turns out, worms got into it. It fell off a counter, broke into a thousand pieces, not worth fixing."

Sarah, feeling like she hooked a fish, asked Johnny if Chaz jammed with Hendrix and Miles. Johnny swallowed a half mug of ale and slammed the empty glass on the table. Everyone in the restaurant stopped talking. Ralph put down his guitar. Moline walked toward Johnny holding a skewer with a white-hot tip and put the warm end inches from Johnny's ear. Johnny stood and apologized for misjudging the distance between the bottom of his mug and the top of the table. Moline returned to the pit, Ralph resumed a sappy ballad, and diners savored their barbecued meat.

"Jeezus Miss Sarah," Johnny said. "You trying to end our friendship? Here on in, I ain't talking about any secret session. Chaz gave his word to those boys."

"You think they played together?" Sarah asked.

Johnny's posture straightened. "Stop city-talking me," he said with henchman's eyes. "I ain't talking about nothing."

Johnny's false toughness didn't last long. Several more glasses of ale turned him into a chirpy supplicant. He danced three bouncy songs with Liz, gave Moline a friendly pat on the rear, and accompanied Ralph on a song. Sarah, sensing a scoop, wrote three pages in her notebook while in the ladies room. Around midnight, per Moline's directive, the sisters shambled hiccupping Johnny into the back seat of their car. He sounded like an out-of-tune calliope as he wheezed and whinnied on the ride home. He awakened when Liz drove into a deep pothole in the driveway. Now feeling like the Don Juan of Arkansas, he sat on the rusted Harley and invited the sisters into his shop to sip moonshine. They declined his overtures and went to their motel room.

The next morning, Johnny, in crisp dungaree overalls, red suspenders, and no shirt, led the sisters to the chairs near the shop stove. Sitting on his bucket, he asked Liz to name her guitar. Most luthiers carve a serial number in each new guitar, but Johnny didn't like numbers. He wouldn't let a new guitar leave his shop without writing the guitar's name on a rib visible from the sound hole. Liz named her guitar Jasper, after her high school music teacher. Johnny promised to start building her instrument after a chocolate milkshake and nap. He told the sisters to return in a month for a final fitting and sound check.

"You can't build a custom guitar in a month," Liz said. "You'd have to work twenty hours a day."

"I'll do it," Johnny said. "Chaz wants it quick."

Around noon, Johnny hugged the sisters and watched their sedan disappear into a cloud of driveway dust. When they passed the Arkansas state border, Sarah thought about Johnny's evasiveness about the 1960s Manhattan music scene. She hoped to squeeze more information from him on their return visit.

4 BORROWED SOUND

The day after the sisters returned from Arkansas, the Chaz Russell Band played a well-received gig in a Queens nightclub. After the show, the band went to Suki's for an early breakfast. "The last month, we've had quite a run," Chaz said. "Liz added fire to the band. Kenny and Pearly kicked it up a notch. Overall, we've done fine. My only problem is my aching hand hurts when I play piano. I'm taking two weeks off to rest and line up more work. You are free to play with anyone. I want you all back after the Fourth of July. Liz will have her new guitar by then."

A few days a week during the break, Liz practiced on Thelma at Chaz's apartment. One afternoon, she entered the spare bedroom while Chaz napped. The dark, musty room was a hoarders dream with dozens of memento filled boxes stacked on the floor. Guitar straps and a two-string, cigar box fiddle hung from hooks. She moved a few amps blocking the walk-in closet and parted a rack of gaudy clothes on hangers. On the closet floor, she found a metal box holding a dozen recording tapes in aluminum canisters. One canister had Chessman Studio Oct. 24th 1969 painted on it. She put the canister in her backpack, wrote Chaz a puffy note, and left the apartment.

On the way home, she bought two reels of previously recorded tape from a used record shop. Tad Morgan, a semi-retired sound technician and close family friend from her Brooklyn neighborhood, agreed to play the recently acquired tapes for the sisters. During his forty years in the music business, he had recorded and mixed music for many prominent record companies. After his wife Ginny died, he sold their brownstone and moved to a lower-Manhattan neighborhood where he could meet friends for a drink or record select jazz musicians. Tad's fourth floor windows faced elevated railroad trestles converted into a densely landscaped park. Industrial shelving lining his apartment hallway held hundreds of tape canisters redolent of aged celluloid.

Tad welcomed the sisters with fatherly hugs. Walking the dark hallway, he said, "Don't bump the shelf. Fifty years of music will crash to the floor. Mostly outtakes mixed into better sounding albums. Sometimes I get calls to remix old tapes, so I don't throw anything out."

He led them to a bedroom converted into a robust recording and mixing studio. To shield neighbors from noise, thick foam covered the walls and ceiling. Three inches of squishy padding made walking on the carpet perilous. Six inch soundproofing insulated the door. Liz put a lumpy plastic bag on a table. "I've got three reels," she said. "I don't know if I have garbage or a lost masterpiece."

Tad unrolled a few feet of tape and repeated the process on the other two tapes. "They're all four track," he said, "I see 7 ½ i.p.s. painted on the reel. I'd guess an hour and a half of music on each one. Let's hear what's on them." He removed a canvas cover from his tape machine. The sisters watched from folding chairs. "I bought this AG 440 B back in '70," he said. "Replaced the AG 440 that drove me crazy. You had to slow the tape down before you stopped it. If you didn't, you'd have a room of loose tape."

He cleaned the recording head with a small, feathered brush. When the analog tubes smelled right, he took a reel, threaded the tape over the head, and toggled a switch. A few pops and scratches spilled from the speakers followed by a maladroit accordionist playing a Hungarian polka. Tad muted the tape after a few seconds. "I was mixing delicate jazz guitar before you arrived. This stuff hurts my ears."

"My gypsy friend loves polka," Liz said. "I'd like to hear all of the reels before I call her."

"No problem," Tad said. He gave headphones to each sister. "Listen to the recordings through these. I'll paint my bathroom ceiling without hearing a note." He showed the sisters how to thread the reels and left with paint roller in hand.

Sarah asked Liz, "Have you lost your mind? A beautiful summer day, you've stuffed me into this overheated studio listening to off-key accordion."

Liz, ignoring her sister, switched reels and hit the right buttons. A raspy voice said "test, test, test" into their headphones, and, after a crackly pause, "Chessman's. Take one, and a one, and a two and a…" The sisters winced as guitar feedback pounded their ear drums. Liz lowered the volume. Four deep, sustained blues chords followed the feedback. A guitarist repeated the chords four times then a trumpeter played the same chords four times. The song gained heat when the guitarist and trumpeter sped the beat and tossed the vamp back and forth. They gave way to a deft guitarist who blended the vamp with samplings of jazz-rock. All hell broke loose when more guitars, a saxophone, bass, piano, and a big drum kit joined the jam. For ten minutes, this mystery band pounded out a thrilling meld of jazz and blues.

When Liz paused the tape, Sarah asked, "What the hell was that?"

"Bargain bin, ten bucks apiece." Liz said.

"The raspy dude sounded like Miles Davis." Sarah said. "The guitar riffs sounded like Hendrix. You think Miles was on trumpet? And the bass line? Not sure who drove the beat. It was someone who could really cook. Drummer played like he had four arms."

"I found the tape in Chaz's apartment. It's a borrow, not a steal. On the way back from Arkansas, I decided to check out his apartment for old music. The other day, when he slept, I found this reel."

Liz let the tape spin. On track two, the sisters first heard musicians tuning their instruments then the raspy voice said, "You mothers are something. Jimi been talking about us getting together. I'm damn happy we did. Macca nailed the bass; Chaz, nice second lead; Joe, far out piano; King's sax made me shiver; Tony, you're the best drummer in the world."

A slow talker with a barely audible voice said, "Miles and I been talking about this for years. Glad you all are here. Tonight, let's rattle the jazz and blues gods, see what happens."

A woman asked why Chessy was recording the session, intended as an informal jam between friends. The slow talker said he wanted to record it and play it later so he could learn a few tricks. He promised copies to every musician in the room.

"Hendrix talked that way," Sarah said. "You've got gold here."

They next heard the unique opening notes of Hendrix's "Crosstown Traffic" played at a slow, jazzy tempo by a guitarist not afraid to let each chord do its work. A piercing trumpet joined the conversation, followed by snarling, twisting, feedback driven guitar. The saxophonist added steam, then sent the vamp to another guitarist who played a bluesy solo in a higher key. The trumpeter concluded the song with twelve unhurried, jubilant notes.

"You've found the mother of all recordings." Sarah said between songs. "We'll get millions for this."

"Or a million years in prison," Liz replied.

The next track began with the raspy voice saying, "Let's play Jimi's 'Red House,' then I'll walk you through my latest, 'In a Silent Way.' " And do us a favor Chaz, quit bending strings, sounds like backwoods country. We're in New York City man, not at the Grand Ole Opry. Nobody plays your way anymore. You gotta evolve, man. Play something new."

"Cut the bull," Chaz said. "Chicago boys still bend; Jimi does on occasion. Just let it be, man. You're mad because you can't play guitar like me, you're stuck playing a silver kazoo."

"Sit this next one out," said the raspy voice. "I can't stand string bending. We've got a half hour of time left. Let's move on without country boy's guitar."

Over the next minute, the sisters heard yelling, breaking glass, and a door slam. When the ruckus ended, Hendrix played the first chords of "Red House" like he did with the Jimi Hendrix Experience. Halfway through the third bar, he drifted into a meandering improvisation; twisting the "Red House" vamp into a passionate jazz statement lasting five minutes. Having said all he wanted with his strings, he offered the vamp to any takers. The trumpeter took the bait and married the vamp with the bones of "In a Silent Way." One-by-one, the other musicians assimilated the riffs and beat of this newborn song and joined the improvisation, ending with a collective return to "Red House."

"This will knock the blues and jazz world on its ass." Liz said as the tape rewound.

"I've got serious writing to do," Sarah said.

Tad entered the studio and offered assistance. "The last tape had some catchy rhythms," Liz said. "The gypsy will like it. Can you copy it to CD?"

"Sure can," Tad said. He wiped a paint dab from his finger and detached the tape from the deck. "Figuring ninety minutes of music, an mp3 burn will take two CD's. It'll clip the highs and lows, sounds you can't hear. Lossless transcription will copy every nuance from the tape. I prefer lossless; you can dilute the music later to mp3. Best to keep the source music intact and play with the mix on other media. It doesn't matter to me. I've got cases of blank CDs."

Liz requested lossless. Tad clipped the tape to the deck, plugged a CD burner into a port, and pushed the recording button. Listening through headphones, he heard a few pops, confirming a connection between the burner and the deck. Happy with the setup, he removed the headphones and watched thin arrows on tiny screens bounce to the output. When the arrows spent too much time in the red zone, he said, "This isn't polka. Is it heavy metal? Let's hear what you got."

When he reached for the headphones, Sarah cawed like a crow. She collapsed to the floor with her hand pressed to her stomach, moaning about a sashimi dinner. Seconds after landing, she closed her eyes and stopped moving. Tad, suspecting a ruptured appendix or food poisoning, prepared to administer mouth-to-mouth resuscitation. When his lips got inches from Sarah's face, she regained consciousness, apologized for fainting, and requested a drink. Tad took a few deep breaths to lower his heart rate. The incident reminded him of the night his wife died in his arms. Amazed by Sarah's speedy recovery, he gave her a bottle of water. He offered Liz a glass of wine to settle her nerves. She said it was a fine idea. Holding their wine in red plastic cups, they talked about wayward family members, but avoided mention of Liz's past legal troubles. Tad checked the recording gauges every few minutes while Liz held the unplugged headphones. When she reached for a refill, Tad noticed Robert Johnson's image inked on her arm. "You're a real blues musician," he said.

"I'm all in playing blues," she replied.

Sarah asked Tad about the musicians he recorded in the 60s. "I worked mostly jazz," he said. "Coltrane, Monk, Mingus, nice people. Not with Miles; he was into fusion and funk. His snappy attitude was too much for me."

"You ever hear about Hendrix and Davis playing together?"

"The rumor is older than dirt. They say Jimi got tired of playing the Experience songs, wanted to play jazz. Miles dug the Hendrix sound. He wanted to top Jimi, so he put together a fusion band with guitarist John McLaughlin. Jimi figured a jam with Miles would open some windows. Jimi scheduled a session, Miles backed out night before. Everyone knew it was about Jimi bedding Miles wife; a sweet girl named Betty."

Tad stopped the recording after the last few feet of tape unrolled. He gave Liz the reels and two recorded CDs. The sisters promised to take him to lunch when the weather cooled. In the lobby, Liz professed guilt about holding stolen music. Sarah kicked the wall and said, "Earth to Liz. Don't you get it? I'm broke, close to living on a Central Park bench, and you're not sure what to do? I'm sure your 'wink-wink' money will disappear soon. Sell the damn music, screw Chaz, screw everyone, take the money, get your ass tucked, your teeth capped, buy a Porsche, marry a band leader with a back catalog."

The spat continued on the sidewalk. Liz threatened to take a cab without her sister. Sarah, standing on the curb, unloaded a batch of angry tears. "I'm fed up with your cushy lifestyle," she said. "I'm broke as a newborn. My clothes are threadbare. I see you fresh out of prison, working here and there, living in a nice apartment, without a care, spending bank robbery money."

"Cops stole the money," Liz said. "I'm living on Aunt Ruthie's Savings Bonds, playing guitar, gigs pay good. You spend too much time on your stupid book. The Hendrix story has been told, same with Miles. People don't care. Let it go, get a real job before someone punches you out. You're smoking around gunpowder asking questions people don't want to answer."

Liz pushed her sister into the back seat of a cab and followed her in. They didn't speak until Sarah found comfort on the convertible sofa in the sunny alcove of Liz's apartment. Liz made sandwiches on the granite countertop in the long kitchen next to a brushed steel refrigerator and ten gallon sink. In the living room, two cat-clawed Victorian chairs faced a stereo system purchased by their uncle on the way home from the Vietnam War. Few New York City apartment sound systems sounded better than the coppery amplifier powering two beefy speakers.

Liz connected her laptop to the amplifier, inserted the first *Chessman* CD into a drive, and aimed both speakers at her sister. The first Hendrix guitar notes nearly cracked the picture windows. Liz lowered the volume. "If my neighbors hear this, they'll come knocking on my door. You don't play guitar, you wouldn't know, he's inventing while he plays. It doesn't sound like the white Strat he played at Woodstock."

Sarah shut off the sound halfway through the first song. "I'm curious to find out how much the music is worth, "she said. "My friend Lenny knows the record business, he markets old music, published the Coltrane tape found in an old suitcase last year, made a big score."

"Chaz owns the music," Liz said. "He probably doesn't want it played because Miles yelled at him. Even if he approved, you'll need the Hendrix and Davis heirs to sign off. It will be like settling an Irishman's estate; after the lawyers pick it clean, all the heirs stop talking. Record companies will take their chunk. We'll end up with nothing but a pissed-off Chaz, who pays my way and knows every blues musician in North America. If he presses charges, I'll be back in the can with Chiken Lady. I'm in no rush to sell. The reel is going back to Chaz's apartment tomorrow."

The next morning, Liz found Chaz, sitting in his favorite chair, picking Thelma's strings with the index finger of his wounded arm. Hundreds of envelopes and receipts cluttered the floor near his slippered feet. A cable connected Thelma to a vintage amplifier that emitted soft, neighbor-friendly notes. Liz put her backpack on the floor. "Nice to see all those gig checks," she said. "How'll you spend all your money?"

"Not a cent in the pile," Chaz said. "I ain't seen a gig check in two weeks and my mattress money is getting thin, bedsprings are pinching my ass."

"I'm hankering to work," Liz said. "Any gigs coming up?"

Chaz rubbed the gauze pad covering his wound. "I've got gigs lined up, starting in three weeks. I hope the arm feels better by then. I visit Doc. Jones next week."

Liz strapped an electric massager on Chaz's arm and took her usual seat at the end of the couch. "I'm with yah," she said. "I need a dark nightclub smelling of stale beer and cheap perfume, with us playing blues. Money wouldn't hurt either."

Chaz downed a few pain pills. Fighting to stay awake, he cut a story short, dropped his chin, and slept. Liz tiptoed into the spare bedroom and put the Chessman tape back where she had found it. She browsed old magazines in the kitchen until the massager's beep awakened Chaz. She put Thelma near his leg and said goodbye.

Mornings during the band hiatus, Liz sat on her stoop with a coffee, reading the *Daily News*, waiting for the mailman. One day she got a postcard of the Lincolnville Arkansas General Store with "Jasper near done. Come by, Johnny" written on the back. She immediately called Sarah and said they'd leave for Arkansas in the morning.

Sarah wouldn't cancel an important interview. Liz wouldn't drive alone to Arkansas, so the next afternoon she boarded a southbound train in Penn Station. She preferred older trains that stopped at small towns and attracted simple folk willing to chat. The velour seats felt like her grandmother's sofa. She had traveled on shiny express trains, but found the seats too firm and the passengers more interested in pushing laptop keys than conversing with an edgy guitar chick. A few hours into the trip, she spread a newspaper over her lap and ate a pastrami sandwich from a Fifth Avenue deli. She later unpacked a skeletal practice guitar made of bent chrome tubing. Earphones connected to the device fed string work to her ears. Passengers within earshot only heard wheels riding steel. A half hour of string bending practice blistered the tip of her thumb, so she repacked the device and spent the night snoozing or watching the lights of sleeping towns streak by her window. On a muggy Sunday morning, the train hissed into Little Rock's Union Station. She gained a heavy dose of God's advice while walking from the station with hundreds of gussied men and women going to a Baptist service.

She arrived at Johnny's shop around noon in a rental car. Johnny hummed a country tune while smoothing a new guitar with fine sandpaper. He jumped three feet when she tapped his shoulder. "Jeeeeez," he said. "Glad to see you back in guitar heaven."

"What are you sanding there?" Liz asked.

"Just another axe," he said, "made just right so their momma or daddy can make them cry and whine."

Johnny unlocked the door with the drippy lettering and led Liz into a wood-paneled room with a shiny floor made of mahogany, cedar, oak, and maple scraps. She sidestepped a glass-top table made from a failed upright bass project and sat on a wingback chair that wouldn't look out of place in a Victorian parlor. Johnny tuned a gospel music program on a bureau-size radio. "Close your eyes, be right back with your baby," he said.

Johnny took Jasper from a closet hidden by wall photos and draped its strap over Liz's shoulder. She snuggled the guitar and opened her eyes. "I love it! I love it! I love it! Thelma's little brother! Look at the dove etched into the pick guard! Thin strings! Ice blue, my favorite color!"

"You're holding a sum cunnin' guitar," Johnny said. "Chaz and I talked for some time on how to beef it up like Thelma, but make it fit a girl. Spent days on the shell. Got the pickups from a '72 Durrell smashed up in a car crash. Used a spare headstock. Paint came from Ollie, my neighbor who sprays cars, same color he used on an old Buick. I sanded it smooth as a baby's bum, sprayed on six coats of paint and two clear. If a nuclear bomb heads your way, hide under this guitar. You'll be fine."

Johnny adjusted the guitar strap so her hand met the strings just the way she liked it. She stroked a few strings and said, "Let's hear this baby howl. Got an amp around here?"

"Momma won't let amped music on her farm." Johnny said. "She's OK with acoustics, thinks electrics are tools of the devil; may have a point. We'll try it out at a church down the way. The minister is my cousin. Come, let's go."

Johnny settled in the back seat of Liz's car holding a coffee mug nearly filled with a clear fluid that could fuel a dragster. She put Jasper on his lap. "If you see me heading for a crash," she said," toss the guitar out the window before we hit." Johnny giggled after a sip.

Liz refused to take Johnny's bumpy shortcut, so they rode five miles on smooth asphalt to the only steeple in downtown Lincolnville. In 1950, townsfolk built the largest church in the county on the foundation of a defunct Packard dealership. Every Sunday service since opening had full pews, stirring sermons, and loud blues music mixed with gospel singing. Johnny put his empty mug on the seat and asked Liz to carry Jasper to the church strapped to her shoulder ready to play. The previous summer he had taken a swaddled mandolin into the church and a passing rumormonger told townsfolk it was a real baby of Johnny's making. Johnny used every muscle on his string bean frame to open the hefty church door. He latched the door open to ease his departure. "This place cooks when Ralph strums Blackie and the choir ladies belt out 'John the Revelator' from the balcony" he said as they walked down the center aisle past rows of empty pews to the pulpit.

Minister Martin Lancaster, a portly black man wearing a black pinstriped suit, crisp white shirt, and pink tie, bellowed a welcome and shook their hands. Per Johnny's suggestion, Liz handed the minister a twenty dollar donation. The minister, showing a pious smile, performed a sign-of-the-cross with his fingers pinching the currency. He stuffed the bill in his pants pocket and said, "May God bless, young lady."

The minister laid Jasper on a baptismal table on the far side of the pulpit. He read from a ring-bound notebook: "Oh holy God, please bless this fine guitar built by Mr. Johnny Durrell for Miss Liz from up north. Let this union of wood and wire play sweet music. Please dear God guide Miss Liz through the trials and tribulations of her music life especially around scummy agents." The minister sprinkled a few drops of holy water on the guitar body. Liz held it steady to keep beaded water from a sound hole. The minister followed his drawn breath with the first words of a two-page prayer.

"Hey cuz," Johnny interrupted, "the prayer takes ten minutes. Cuts into our guitar time."

The minister said the opening sentence would do the trick. He went into a back room filled with beefy amplification equipment donated by a parishioner who had made millions selling plastic food containers. He connected a long black cord into Jasper. "There's enough juice in the room to crack our roof timbers. Don't touch a string until I say OK."

Johnny and the minister walked down the center aisle and climbed twenty narrow, squeaky stairs to the balcony. Johnny leaned on the balcony rail and savored the summer breeze sweetened by freshly-cut hay. The minister adjusted several dials on a console. When the settings seemed right, he spoke into a microphone, "Ma'am, give the thin strings a tickle or two, just a few chords, don't want feedback." After hearing smooth notes, the minister told Liz to "let her rip."

A hundred feet from the balcony, on the walls behind the pulpit, plaster torsos of John the Baptist, Paul the Apostle, the Blessed Virgin Mary, and the good Lord himself watched Liz pull a gilded pick from her pocket, a borrow from Chaz for the first notes on her new guitar. It was the same pick he used on Thelma's first chords. She pushed the pick onto the thickest string. A deep, worried note bounced from the pulpit speakers to the church timbers and out the eve windows. The first note led to a tender play of "Amazing Grace," the haunting spiritual written by a repentant slave ship captain. Liz slowed the tempo to funereal pace, letting each chord resonate through the church. The statues held their placid smiles. Johnny wept like a young widower as he sang along. The minister watched the sound meter and the parking lot.

Liz yelled toward the balcony, "How's it sound boys?" Johnny and the minister hollered their approval. She shouted back, "Seeing this is a church, can I play blues, or should I stick with spirituals?" The minister told her to play anything but salsa. He'd pull the plug when the choir ladies arrived in about twenty minutes. The potent opening licks of Robert Johnson's "Dust My Broom" spilled down the aisle, out the vestry, across the parking lot, and dispersed in the shorn field. She spiced the livelier Elmore James version with a few bars of slide. After a dozen bars, she snagged a five-note vamp from the song and fingered a five-minute improvisation that included licks from Sonny Boy Williamson II's "Eyesight to the Blind." To show respect to Chaz, she string-bent a few bars. Jasper didn't flinch, but her thumb blister felt ready to burst. She began a throbbing Hendrix number while the choir ladies parked their cars. The minister, seeing two dozen angry women headed his way, cut the speaker power, hurried down the stairs to the lot, and told the women he was testing the sound system. Liz and Johnny ran out a service exit and drove away.

Liz offered to buy Johnny dinner. He replied, "Anyplace but Molly's. Let's have biscuits and coffee."

"I'm not eating Miss what's-her-name's shoe leather rolls," Liz said. "My belly ached for a week after drinking her grainy coffee. I'm in barbecue country, we're going to Molly's."

"I'm not going there," Johnny said. "People say they serve horsemeat. Moline tells people where I live. Ralph can't play a lick. They got slow waitresses, serve flat beer."

Liz didn't want to eat alone so she let Johnny show the way to Destiny's B-B-Q, ten miles from Lincolnville. A quarter mile from the diner, manure scented air wafted into their car. Liz nearly drove by the low-slung restaurant hidden by an unruly hedge. She parked between two rusty pickups with farm plates.

Destiny's would fit into Molly's dining room. None of the fifty customers looked up from their plates when Liz and Johnny sat at the bar. A fiftyish woman with a puffy afro came from the kitchen and told Johnny, "Hun, you get better looking every day. How come you age backwards?" She landed a kiss on Johnny's cheek and tendered a country handshake to Liz. "I'm Destiny. I serve the best ribs in the county, better than the old gas station with the off-key music."

Liz ordered an Ark Ale. Johnny asked for a glass of milk with an ice cube. "What the hell is going on here?" Destiny asked. "I've known you for thirty years. You worship Arky. What's up with the milk?"

"Me and Arky parted ways," Johnny said. "Felt like a train ran me over last time this here girl drank it with me. I'm done forever."

Destiny's face soured. "I don't serve milk at my bar. If you want milk, get out of here, go to the general store, drink it on the porch, with the pigeons. I'll find Miss Liz a more exciting dinner companion."

Sulking Johnny slid off his stool and headed toward the exit. On the way, he caught a whiff of Arky from a passing tray. Like a hound dog, he followed the tray to the bar. "You win." he said from his counter seat. "Just a splash of double A. Don't fill it to the top."

Every customer and waitress watched Destiny fill a one-ounce shot glass with Arky and take great care centering it on a cork coaster under Johnny's frown. On a return trip, she brought Liz a tall Arky with a razor-thin head. The bar crowd barely held laughter when Johnny took the tiniest sip ever drawn in Arkansas. He drank like a hummingbird while Liz and Destiny discussed the local man scene. After his tenth sip, he asked Liz about the weather forecast. "I'm taking a train," she said. "I don't care about the crummy Arkansas weather. And, by the way, you look foolish drinking beer from a shot glass."

"Them little-bitty sips are downright painful," Johnny murmured.

Liz ordered another round. "I'll take the same. Give Johnny a big-boy glass of Arky and a shooter of top shelf whisky. Let him catch up to where he would have been if he drank a big boy glass on the first round."

Destiny walked toward Johnny with a smile wider than a dollar bill. She placed a tall Arky next to a glass of fine whisky. He chased the boilermaker with a wave of revered brew. His frown turned to a grin. Over the next hour, Liz and Johnny split a pulled pork sandwich and emptied two pitchers of Arky. Johnny told a few hilarious stories about his local guitar playing buddies, using wild gestures to emphasize story elements. He said one doesn't own, only rents Arky, as he left for his third visit to the men's room. The brew raised his voice an octave, to that of an adolescent elf. He dragged his consonants and hiccupped through every sentence. Liz, tired of corny stories without punch lines, asked him about the guitars he had built for famous musicians.

"Everyone famous died," he said. "And stop interviewing me. My man Chaz warned me about you and your sister asking too many questions about Hendrix. Chaz is mighty pissed over the way Miles treated him that night. I sure as hell won't talk about it."

Liz, facing away from Johnny's boozy breath, ordered a sandwich to go. She paid the check and pointed to the exit. Johnny went behind the counter and gave Destiny a besotted hug. He waddled back to his bar and ordered an Arky in a doggie-cup. Liz twirled him off the barstool and whisked him to the back seat of her car where he gabbed, hiccupped, and eventually slept. She made it back to the farm despite dense fog and a malfunctioning copilot. Parked next to the Harley, she tapped his shoulder to wake him. Startled Johnny threw a haymaker, missing her head by five feet, landing his fist on a headrest. He apologized all the way to his shop, blaming it on a bad dream.

Johnny got comfortable on his pail seat with Jasper on his lap. He said it was the finest sounding guitar he had ever built. He settled Jasper on the red velour lining of an old guitar case and latched the cover. Liz put a hundred dollar tip in Johnny's tee shirt pocket. After getting a clingy hug, she drove to Little Rock and boarded the New York City bound train. As the train eased from the station, she took Jasper from its case and put it on her lap. A few miles into the trip, the bold city skyline softened into gentle foothills and low sun bathed the guitar's flawless finish. When the train sped through a forest, sunlight flickered over the guitar like a strobe light. When the train passed over an undulated plain, Liz tilted the guitar to let a sliver of sunlight enter the sound hole and illuminate the innards. As Johnny promised, Jasper had a fat block of wood running down the middle of the body. She could bend strings and never worry about breaking its backbone. On the side of the block, Johnny had written "Jasper for Miss Liz . Johnny Durrell, Ark. 2009."

5 SLOW HAND

Six hours after departing the train in Manhattan, groggy Liz strutted into Mim's wearing a spray of Sarah's best perfume, a light blue dress, and four-inch heels. Per Chaz's invitation, she carried Jasper into the Davis Room, so named after young Mim spied Miles Davis roiling on the carpet with a European princess. Chaz, Kenny, Pearly, Ruby, and several dozen friends of Chaz applauded her entry. Hugs and high-fives made way for requests to see and hear the new guitar. Liz thanked Chaz, Johnny Durrell, and Mim. Everyone in the room, including the nasty barmaid, got a close look at Jasper's build.

Mim wheeled in a cart of nibbles after Liz played a slick blues number. Chaz thanked everyone for attending and said his doctor would allow him to resume two-handed guitar playing provided he didn't play two days in a row. Many attendees had gigs that night so the gathering abated after they devoured a guitar-shaped chocolate cake.

Chaz, needing to reestablish his guitar verve in front of a friendly audience, booked the Backbeat for the following Monday, Wednesday, and Saturday afternoons. The morning of the first session, a ticket line ran from the Backbeat to the next door flower shop. Grizzled musicians, dolled-up divas, and twitchy ticket scalpers stood in line with plaid suited agents and predatory music producers. All three sessions sold out in an hour.

An hour before the first session, the Backbeat neighborhood

emptied. Dusty's Dating Bar posted a sign saying Closed Mon Wed Sat. Thick steel mesh shielded a bodega's facade. A cabbie parked his vacant taxi in front of a shuttered liquor store. In the Backbeat, four bartenders hustled drinks. Record company big shots sat on the best seats. The crowd kept carousing as Chaz tested the monitors and microphones.

For these sessions, the Chaz Russell Band adopted a format conceived for tired, old band leaders: Let the backing band stir the crowd with a few dazzling songs, then have the rested band leader make a kingly entrance. When the crowd settles, have the geezer play a few songs from a chair. Hold him steady when he takes a bow then send him back to the dressing room with a stirring tribute. Call it a night after a few more songs from the backing band. If the crowd demands an encore, call the bandleader back to the stage for a quick number. If no encore, let the bandleader nap.

Famed blues radio host Black Peter started things off with a sugary Chaz tribute and pandering introductions of Liz, Kenny, and Pearly. Liz drowned the chatter with dozens of staccato chords. Kenny and Pearly drove a brash beat. During a pause, a lady in a slinky gown escorted tuxedoed Chaz to a chair next to the center microphone. She swept back her washy hair and told the room, "From our Harlem streets, our very own King of the String Benders, world famous Chaz Russell and his band."

Chaz fluttered both hands at the audience, let out a hoot, and nailed the tricky riffs of "Fabled Ways", a song he wrote in the late 1970s. He summoned enough strength to play three songs loaded with string bending. With his tender hand aching, his band serenaded him with a bluesy "Hail to the Chief" as he floated through the crowd to kisses, romantic propositions, and drink offers. Liz led the band for several songs, but the crowd wanted Chaz back on stage. Invigorated by adulation, an ice pack, and a whisky, he ascended to a chair wrapped with silver foil and gave the audience a full dose of power-chord blues lasting long enough for him to realize his band had one extra guitarist.

Many of the same individuals attended all the Backbeat sessions despite missed work and the same song list. Saturday, after his mid-set breather, Chaz joined the band for several blues standards. A leather-lunged man demanded an encore, so the band returned to the microphones and delivered the goods. Liz stood five steps behind

Chaz to let him savor the good karma. After the encore, the lady in the gown escorted Chaz through the parted sea of revelers to a horseshoe-shaped booth decorated with foil and welcome back signs. He swapped one-liners with a waitress while his bandmates ate complimentary entrees and liquids. When the owner stopped the flow of free food and cocktails, Kenny and Pearly fled to their favorite bar stools.

Liz, seeing Ruby slink toward the bar, told Chaz, "She sure likes to show her assets. First session she had on a tight red-sequined dress. Second session, a black mini something missing a few threads. Today's outfit didn't hide a bump or roll."

Chaz whispered to Liz, "Don't tell a soul. Ruby is no good. I know she's snooped through my spare bedroom looking for booty. Room is filled with sparkly junk. Got some *Superfly* suits from the 70s. I'm sentimental about those days. Want to keep my stuff around."

"She steal anything?" Liz asked.

"Nothing of value," Chaz said with a sneer. "I'll check my closet when things settle down. All my stuff has little pencil marks that line up. If someone messes with something, I'll know. You watch your back around her. She's a nasty gal. I'm sure she stabbed me in New Orleans. She palled with Pearly that night. Figure he polished-off too many gimlets, she put him to bed, grabbed a steak knife, sliced me up, tried to steal my guit. I'm not a hundred percent sure. Never saw her face. Long gloves hid her arms and hands. Did get a whiff of her perfume, the expensive stuff worn by all the Harlem street walkers, sold by truck jackers."

"Why'd she stab her buddy Chaz?"

"Grab Thelma, make fifty or sixty large, that's why. Don't listen to Johnny. He thinks all his guitars are worth five hundred bucks, same as what his father charged in the 60s. He doesn't believe they'll pay a hundred grand for a Durrell. Thelma's ripe for picking. You keep Jasper close."

"You tell the cops about Ruby?"

"Naw, if she's back in jail, I'll have Kenny, Pearly, and the Backbeat scene mad at me. My boys drink less and play better when they spend time with her. I told her to stay away from my apartment. I hid everything worth stealing. She won't bother me if I've got nothing to take."

The Monday after the last Backbeat session, Sarah and Liz met for lunch at a hotel restaurant facing Central Park South. They sat outside at a round, copper table next to a marble angel spewing forest-scented mist. A waiter brought them tall menus with tiny type. Liz couldn't find anything she liked on the page, so she ordered a beer and a cheeseburger. Sarah chose Parisian escargot in Bordeaux sauce and a bottle of French water.

Liz stopped the small talk after a few sentences. She had listened to the *Chessman's* a dozen times and identified the musicians on the recording. She read from a handwritten list: "Jimi Hendrix on guitar; Miles Davis, trumpet; Billy Cox, bass; Mitch Mitchell, drums. The organ player had to be Miles' buddy Joe Zawinul. Chaz and Roy Buchanan played the other guitars. King Curtis played the funky sax on the first and third song."

"That's quite a crew," Sarah said. "I agree on Hendrix, Davis, Chaz, and Roy Buchanan. I'm not so sure on the bass and drums."

"Billy Cox played bass in Hendrix's band after Noel Redding got the boot," Liz said. "Mitch Mitchell remained true to Hendrix even after Buddy Miles stole his job."

"I've got a different take. We know Miles wanted fifty grand to play with Hendrix, Hendrix laughed him off. Tony Williams kept the session alive. He was a world class jazz drummer who worshipped Hendrix. Miles mentioned him on the recording. Williams led his group Lifeline into some mean fusion in the late 60s. He's the one who got Hendrix to jam with Davis."

The effusive waiter told Liz the chef refused to make a common cheeseburger. He suggested a Maine lobster tail on a crushed ice bed for fifty dollars. Liz decided to skip food and drink another twenty dollar beer.

"I've never heard of Tony Williams or Lifeline." Liz said.

"Check out their album *Emergency!*" Sarah said. "What a band. They invented fusion. Jack Bruce on bass, organist Larry Young, John McLaughlin on guitar. I know their sound. It has to be Young and Williams on the *Chessman's*."

"Sounds possible, so whose playing bass? It's someone with a Rock and Roll vibe."

"Paul McCartney."

Liz coughed on her beer. "No, No, No. You're whacked out.

The Beatles were together then. He never played jazz."

"A month before the session," Sarah said, "Hendrix and Williams sent McCartney a cable inviting him to play with Hendrix, Davis, and Young in New York City. McCartney's rep cabled back, claimed McCartney was on holiday and unavailable. Some restaurant owns the original cables. I think Paul changed his mind, snuck into the city in the fall of '69."

Liz pledged to listen closely to the bass line that night. "You squeeze Lenny to buy the *Chessman's*?" she asked.

"He's interested, wants me to bring them to his office, listen to it in his sound room. Will you go with me, make sure he behaves?"

"He's your squeeze," Liz said, feeling a shiver. "Guy makes me uneasy. I don't want to watch him feel you up. I'm also leaving for a gig in Massachusetts"

"He only does the feely thing when he's drunk. I've known him for five years. He's as honest as they come."

"Yah, right. Honesty in the record business?"

"Call me in the morning with an answer. I'm in a financial hole, with one way out. I've got to score something big."

Sarah's eyes turned to the curb across the street where groomers shined their horses and black carriages. They didn't discuss the *Chessman's* until their taxi ride when Liz told Sarah, "You want a split of the action? Get pretty. Do some dirty work. Tease your boy with the music, use your big bag of tricks. I'll copy the source CDs to mp3. I don't want Lenny to listen to the music in lossless, files he can secretly record and publish."

Sarah, dressed in a pastel sundress, took the watered-down *Chessman's* to a high-rise tower near Rockefeller Plaza. She found Lenny in the lobby reading a yoga guide. Despite thirty years in the record business, he maintained youthful vigor by running marathons and spending leisurely weekends at his Southampton, Long Island home. A burnished Art Deco elevator lifted them to the twentieth floor offices of his Goldenvibe Records. Sarah glanced at the red leather couch in the lobby where months before, she and Lenny had engaged in horizontal frivolity after a corporate Christmas party. Lenny hung his blue yachtsman blazer on a hanger and sat behind a glass-topped desk next to floor-to-ceiling windows with views of the Hudson River and New Jersey skyline. With his lizard-skin loafers resting on a foot rest, he said, "So, sweets, you holding mystery music played by the famous?"

Sarah leaned over the desk and put her face inches from his. "Sure do. Let's play it,"

She followed Lenny past a row of interns pecking keyboards, down a hallway to a cozy sound room. "My moneymakers listen to their final takes in here," he said. "You wouldn't believe who sat in here last week." They walked down the gently-sloped aisle to three long couches. Sponge panels plated the ceiling and walls. Four hefty speakers faced the couches. Sarah sat on the middle cushion of the couch closest to the speakers. Lenny slid the *Chessman's* into a player in a sound room then he sat next to Sarah and controlled the system by remote control. She told him to fasten his seatbelt.

Miles said his raspy words then the hundred thousand dollar speakers shook with guitar feedback. Lenny's software eliminated the source recording hiss, making the tracks sound better than live. They listened to both discs, slow dancing during the last song. They hugged for a few minutes after the music stopped. Lenny gave Sarah an adoring look. "Outstanding, I want it. I'll talk to my partners, we'll make an offer. Let's consummate the deal right here, right now." His hand slid her dress zipper down an inch.

"This isn't the time," she said. "Maybe after you pay for the tracks. One problem, before you offer anything, we don't own the music."

"Don't worry about who owns what," Lenny said. "My lawyers will bust any rights. Here's my deal: The mp3 is useless to me. I'll give you a hundred thousand for the source tracks. My forensic guys will figure out who's playing on it. We'll negotiate royalties with their estates or lawyers. You'll get thirteen percent of any download or CD sale."

Sarah put the discs in her pocketbook and said, "Let me run this by my sister, she's away for a few days. By the way, what will you do with the argument at the beginning of the last track?"

"We'll erase it along with the guitar work of the guy who got pissed and left. It's only background music. The overall product won't suffer."

Sarah promised to push her sister for a sale. On the way home, she tossed the mp3 discs in a trash bin.

Liz got a one sentence update on the meeting while driving to gig at The Mooring in Fall River, Massachusetts. In the early 1990s, an enterprising non-profit group converted the second floor of an abandoned mill into a comfortable space for three hundred patrons. The venue attracted listeners from nearby universities and Providence, Rhode Island. The Chaz Russell Band sold out ten years in a row and had a handshake agreement to return every summer.

A brigade of timeworn hippies met the van and conveyed guitars and gear up the elevator to the stage. The planked floor chirped as patrons filled rows of patinated church pews that hadn't heard prayers in decades. Stage-side tables held seniors tasting wine, students eating Chinese from cartons, and a tweedy academic lusting at three Durrells within grabbing distance.

The show began with a mellow introduction of Chaz and his band. Chaz sat at a table and watched his cohorts open with a run of stirring numbers. After a drum roll, spotlighted Chaz strode to the stage. He pinched, wiggled, and splayed Thelma's strings for four songs, then called it a night and went to the dressing room. The crowd thanked him with hoots, hollers, and whistles. Liz tried hard to outshine her boss on the next two songs, but the crowd responded with soft applause and cat calls. Chaz returned for a two song encore. The crowd left, thirsty and spent. After the show, the band lingered near the stage, holding their guitars while signing autographs for sleepy boomers and bright-eyed, young musicians looking for an edge.

Around eleven, the manager gave Chaz the gig payment. "I tell you every year," he said, you've got a sweet Durrell. Thelma's got the best tone. The blue one the girl plays has a nice kick, too."

"Johnny is a good axe man," Chaz said. "Only bad thing is you got to keep his guitars close by, or they'll end up stolen by someone like the dude in the tweed sitting down front."

"You're getting paranoid," said the manager. "He's a history professor over at the state university. Wife says he hoards and hides guitars, harmless guy, buys them legit. Speaking of paranoid, Johnny's nieces played the Golden Sisters here last winter. A goon with a gun guarded the guitars every second."

"Be easier to play my old acoustic and keep Thelma in a vault," Chaz said.

The wizened hippies, showing signs of missed bedtimes, loaded the band's gear into the van. The Chaz Russell Band arrived in New

York City as a logy all-night radio talk show host passed the microphone to the chirpy morning crew.

The morning after the gig, Liz drifted around her apartment wearing a towel turban, hotel bathrobe, and gaudy sunglasses. Sarah dropped by around noon with details of Lenny's offer.

"A hundred grand?" Liz shouted. "I'm scratching and clawing for bucks. You're talking a hundred grand?"

"It's a real deal," Sarah said. "Done by me, not you.

"Yah right. You know whose deal it is? Chaz Russell's. I stole his recording, the one he doesn't want anyone to hear. You want to sell it so half the world can hear him get insulted by Miles?"

"Don't worry about Chaz. Lenny's engineers will remix the music, remove the argument, erase his guitar, make him disappear."

"If he gets wind of this, he'll bash my head with a crowbar." Liz said, pacing the room.

"Chaz is an old coot. He won't live forever."

"I wouldn't bank on his health failing," Liz said. "Bluesmen live long lives. Some of them have ten farewell tours. I don't like your arm-twisting. If you didn't have such uptown tastes you wouldn't be in this jam."

"At least I'm upfront about my money or lack of it," Sarah said. "You flash hundred dollar bills all over town and think nothing of it. Nice apartment, new computer. Where's your money coming from?"

"I told you, from my college fund. Might as well spend it."

"What happens after you spend all the funny money? You'll be broke like me. Let Lenny publish this lost masterpiece. Let the next generation of musicians hear legends jam."

"I'll sleep on it," Liz said through a yawn.

Sarah borrowed twenty dollars from her sister and went to the library. Liz sat on her bed, listening to the *Chessman's* with her best headphones. The direct sound exposed the subtle give-and-take between the blues and jazz musicians. On the first track, Hendrix snuck a few jazzy licks into a blues bar. Miles' sharp ear heard the tweak. He mimicked the Hendrix licks with his trumpet. Their conversation lasted a half-minute with the drummer and bassist keeping pace as they switched from blues to jazz.

On the second disc, Liz heard a sampling of a solo Hendrix played at his August 1969 Woodstock appearance. She loaded the

DVD *Jimi Hendrix: Live at Woodstock* into her laptop. Hendrix played Woodstock on the last morning with his new band, when most of the sodden crowd had left. He had moved on from the Jimi Hendrix Experience to the hastily configured Gypsy Sun and Rainbows with guitarist Larry Lee, longtime Experience drummer Mitch Mitchell, percussionist Juma Sultan, and Jerry Valez on congas. He had replaced long time Experience bassist Noel Redding with close friend Billy Cox.

In the mire facing the stage, thousands of bloodshot eyes saw Hendrix prance to the microphone in a white dashiki, holding a white Stratocaster. When he let loose a few hefty chords, the crows on the speaker towers fled to farmland across the street. The crowd felt rushes of adrenalin when hearing "Message to Love" and tapped their feet in the mud during "Spanish Castle Magic." This was the first time the band had played for an audience, so it took a few songs to get comfortable.

Midway through the two-hour set, Hendrix played his stellar take of "The Star-Spangled Banner." After gaining his breath, he led a solid rendition of "Purple Haze." Hendrix seemed to leave the earth when he paused after the song and gazed at the dewy hills and mass of young people smudged with blue smoke. Perhaps it was the effects of the joint he had smoked earlier in the set, the tightened groove of his new band, or energy from the muddied skin on the hill, but something provoked Hendrix' guitar meanderings on the next song, "Woodstock Improvisation," a dreamy blend of blues, jazz, gypsy, rock, and country riffs.

Liz watched "Woodstock Improvisation" three times then she replayed the portion of the last *Chessman's* track, where Hendrix drifted from "Red House" to "Woodstock Improvisation." The two versions had different conclusions. On the Woodstock recording, Hendrix returned to his typical muscular chords after the improvisation. On the *Chessman's*, he must have felt comfortable in the private setting because he followed "Woodstock Improvisation" with seven bars of mellow jazz.

Liz jotted the "Woodstock Improvisation" chords from the *Chessman's* on a notation pad. When she couldn't identify a sound, she wrote a question mark. She propped the pad on a pillow and put Jasper on her lap. Hendrix was a lefty who played righty guitar upside-down, strung like a conventional left-handed guitar. For this exercise, she played Jasper upside down with her left hand pushing chords. She tried to work the strings like Hendrix, but her fingers couldn't play "Twinkle, Twinkle, Little Star" that way. She moved Jasper to righty position and spent hours practicing the chords. By midnight, she could imitate a few bars of the "Woodstock Improvisation" heard on the *Chessman's*.

Unable to sleep, she thought about the "Red House/In a Silent Way" track, the last song on the *Chessman's*. In ten years of blues listening, she had heard hundreds of blues pickers and slingers who played close to the blues book but were afraid to venture into other genres. They preferred to stay true to their blues brethren by filling their compositions with traditional blues chords. Hendrix disrupted this conformity when he replaced night-after-night repetition of Experience hits with exploratory compositions and weighty covers of Bob Dylan compositions. Around the same time, Miles Davis, abandoned his stable quartet, bible salesman suit, and skinny tie, and recorded the Hendrix influenced *In a Silent Way* with John McLaughlin, Joe Zawinul, Tony Williams, and Larry Young. These four seasoned musicians, tired of playing by the rules and willing to create something new, drifted from their money-making sound into controversial, cross-genre exploration.

Sarah's high pitched phone call interrupted Liz's morning solitude. Sarah's mortgage company wanted her condominium vacated in two weeks so they could ready the unit for auction. Between sniffles, she asked to move into Liz's apartment. Liz promised a decision when she returned from a Maine blues festival in a few days.

6 MAINE BLUES

On the last Friday morning of July 2009, Liz drove a loaded van northward toward the coastal community of Leeward Maine, the site of the biggest blues festival in the Northeast. Kenny and Pearly, dressed in identical florid shirts, relaxed on plastic lawn furniture wedged between baggage, gear, instrument cases, and a cooler. Chaz, buckled tight to the passenger seat, wore baggy Bermuda shorts, a white tee shirt, and a Greek fisherman's hat. The Leeward trip continued a ten year tradition for the Chaz Russell Band. Some years they performed on stage under the sun and other years they sat in the shade watching the performances and renewing friendships. This year they'd play the festival on Saturday afternoon. At the Connecticut border, Chaz turned to his rhythm section and barked, "Same rules this year. Don't be biffed when we get to Leeward. And don't try the half-fill the soda bottle with rum trick, either."

"I know they have beer in the cooler," he told Liz. "If I hear a can open, I'll dump them boys on the side of the road. Back on the '04 trip, we got to Maine about midnight with my band curled up like pretzels, passed out drunk. I parked in a dark corner, left softly, checked in the hotel, and soaked in the biggest hot tub in Maine. Slept like a breathing corpse. Next day, they walked like spiny crabs to the stage. Played like crap. I fired them, hired them back an hour later. They promised to stay sober for a year. Promise lasted until dinner."

Liz drove by the Welcome to Leeward sign around ten p.m.

Police cruisers with flashing lights blocked traffic from a half-mile section of Main Street crowded with revelers. Every few hundred feet, a blues band played on the sidewalk, powered by electricity donated by store owners. She parked in the Anchor Inn parking lot, a block from the Main Street festivities. Blues beats and laughter spilled from the four story hotel. The Wilde Island foghorn serenaded them with a spare, bluesy vamp as they leaned on a harbor front handrail and breathed salty mist, a scent much different than the stale hops and cheap perfume respired during club gigs. The rail led to the dark festival grounds where hundreds of dew-soaked camping chairs set up for the next day's music faced the stage.

In the Anchor Inn lobby, Chaz, with drink in hand, greeted guitarists Kid Baxter, Lonnie Lynn, and one-armed drummer Cull Smith. He sidestepped a club owner who had bounced his gig check in '78. Kenny and Pearly chatted with the Walling Brothers, the rhythm section of the festival's headlining band. Liz introduced herself to Fiona Foley, a petite Canadian guitarist with strawberry tinted hair who would open the festival the following morning.

When live music drowned the lobby conversation, the swarm of conviviality moved a few dozen steps to the lounge. Chaz gave his empty glass to a waitress and walked toward the parking lot to get his suitcase. A festival volunteer intercepted him on the veranda, returned him to the lounge, and bought him a drink. She later handed him three room keys and claim checks for the band's gear and luggage.

Around ten o'clock, after the house band played a last call boogie, the lobby filled with celebrants ready to shift into second gear. Chaz found Kenny and Pearly on a bench next to Ruby. Her lobster red dress looked shrink-wrapped to her body. Chaz tossed them a room key. "If you don't show tomorrow," he said. "I'll rent a percussion machine. Liz will play lead. I'll play keyboard bass, we'll split the gig money fifty-fifty. You guys can thumb home."

The party-primed horde walked a block to the Timely Pub, a two-story nightclub on Main Street considered the unofficial festival headquarters. On the back corner of the club, on a plywood stage, wannabe musicians jammed with respected performers who had arrived early for their festival gigs. Liz found comfort on a corner stool at the street-level bar. Tina, a seasoned barmaid with cheeks dotted with silvery sparkles, served her a margarita. On nearby stools, a bearded biker wearing a Stevie Ray Vaughn tee shirt argued with his brawny girlfriend. When Liz took her first sip, the girlfriend landed a rabbit punch on the biker's jaw. Liz thought he was dead before he hit the floor. Tina flipped a wet bar towel to a waitress. A few minutes later the biker ran to the street pressing the bloody towel to his leaky jaw. The girlfriend moved to a table of rival bikers. Kenny and Ruby sat on the vacant bar stools and ordered a round.

"You Chaz's new guitar chick?" Ruby asked.

"Honey," Liz said. "I'm no chick. I'm a guitar player who makes a living standing, not on my back, like you."

"Didn't mean it that way, sis," Ruby said. "Us ladies from the 'hood call white girls chicks. I'm a long time friend of Chaz, looking out for his well being."

"Well, I'm a short time friend of Chaz, looking out for his well being." Liz said. She downed her drink, shook Kenny's hand, gave Ruby a curt smile, and returned to her hotel room.

Chaz had a longstanding friendship with festival promoter Ben Block, a balding, energetic man in his late-fifties who had turned bar napkin doodles into a thriving festival that drew twenty thousand blues fans to this seaside city an hour and a half north of Portland. Ben began his working life managing an edgy bar in a working class Leeward neighborhood. Over a decade, he made it the liveliest music club in Maine. Thursday nights, after the local fish processing plants passed out paychecks, the club hosted a check cashing party featuring a Maine-based rock band. Savvy customers first downed a two-ounce tequila shot to offset patron fishiness. The plants threatened to shut down Friday work because half the workforce showed up with debilitating hangovers.

In 1990, Ben and a lawyer friend, looking to capitalize on the success of the Thursday night concerts, created the first Leewardfest, a one-day rock music festival held on the last Saturday in July on the Anchor Inn parking lot. Ben rented the lot for a dollar. The Jewell brothers donated flatbed trailer served as the stage. The Leeward movie theater loaned him speakers.

Ben hired three local rock bands to play the first festival. Each band got two hundred dollars and souvenir tee shirts for their one hour performance. Needing a somewhat famous group to headline, he called Fats Snelling, a Boston booking agent who represented

Chondrite, a Las Vegas-based hair band. Ben agreed to pay a thousand dollars and two dozen steamed lobsters for Chondrite's two hour show.

The morning of the first festival, three Massachusetts State Police cruisers stopped the Chondrite tour bus a mile short of the New Hampshire border and arrested the lead singer for attempted rape of a fifty-nine year old groupie. He claimed she was at fault because she had grabbed his privates. The cops assumed the singer was an innocent victim, but the earliest they could release him was after his Monday arraignment. Fats didn't hear about the arrest until noon, five hours before Chondrite's first scheduled note. Ben didn't respond to numerous frantic phone messages. Panicked Fats called in a favor from the governor's brother who had the Maine State Police reroute a substitute band from the Maine Turnpike to Leeward.

In a 2002 *Blues Scene* magazine interview, Ben recalled:

> An hour before show time at the first festival, I had a parking lot packed with stoned bikers, spiked-hair groupies, and tipsy locals, all primed for loud rock. I sold five hundred tickets, three thousand showed up. The first two bands blasted off-key, hard rock. Crowd loved it. Hundreds danced on the street. When I saw my police detail move cones, I looked for the Chondrite tour bus with the flaming meteor painted on the side. Damn near freaked-out when a yellow school bus with Mississippi plates parked next to the stage.
>
> Back in 1990, nobody in Leeward Maine, including me, had ever seen a blues band, let alone a Mississippi blues band. When the school bus parked, the only noise in this part of Leeward came from the Timely Pub air conditioner. The quiet continued as a dozen musicians from the Eddie Williams Band came off the bus. You could have seen Eddie Sr.'s yellow pants from the Wilde Island lighthouse. Eddie Jr., the lead guitarist, had long cornrows hanging over his yellow blazer. When three gorgeous lady singers in skimpy yellow dresses stepped from the bus, a biker yelled, "Look at them yellow jackets ready to sting."
>
> Eddie shouted in my ear, "Fats couldn't reach you. Chondrite had a problem. We're your headline band. Sonny boy, don't worry, steam be coming off the stage in a few minutes." I heard a threat from the audience to burn

down the town, so I had a buddy climb a church cupola, watch the crowd, and call the National Guard if a riot broke out. When I told the crowd Chondrite wouldn't appear, Tiny Pinkham's wife threw a lobster salad sandwich at me. Seagulls took care of the mess.

Eddie and his band played smoking blues for three straight hours. His women singers sang so loud they didn't need microphones. Bikers danced with their dollies. Fishermen sold their catch and boogied with the fish plant girls. The crowd demanded and got four encores. After the show, Eddie set a table near his bus and signed CDs and tee shirts until he ran out. I had to pay him, but we hadn't talked money. He asked for a thousand dollar bank check. I laid two thousand cash on his hand and told him to keep the change. Leeward Police had one arrest, for jay walking. Turned out he was a deaf guy who'd lost his glasses. Next day, I quit rock music and formed the Leeward Blues Festival.

Late Saturday morning, on the festival grounds, muggy sun gradually replaced briny fog. Sound technicians tugged on cords and tested microphone output. Several thousand patrons waited on their chairs for the first note. A few thousand more watched the action from a shady hillock. Fried seafood aromas wafting from food trailers tempted the mostly white crowd. A blond woman, defying stern cholesterol warnings from her doctor, nibbled on a breakfast of fried scallops and onion rings. Miles out in Leeward Harbor, lobster boats chugged toward their soaking pots.

Ben scheduled five bands for the first day, limiting each to a one hour set. Fiona Foley opened the festival with a set of endearing acoustic numbers. Beanpole Woodley's band had everyone standing for an hour. Chaz, Kenny, Pearly, and Liz stood under a tent next to the stage before their set and watched a Zydeco band leader dance his fingers across accordion keys. His lead singer, a sinewy man with a sweet voice, tapped his spoons on a frottoir, or washboard, strapped to his belly. After their set, roadies quickly replaced their drum kit and xylophone with Chaz Russell Band gear and instruments.

Despite the humidity and scorching sun, Kenny and Pearly wore black pants, black tee shirts, and black sport coats with white CRB script on the lapel. Chaz looked dapper in a black sport coat with bold red swirls, black slacks, and red leather alligator boots with Texas toes. Liz stepped to the stage with several hundred eyes locked on her black halter top, black skirt, and tall heels. As the sound crew shuffled monitors and connected cords, Liz replaced a Jasper string, Pearly limbered his fingers, and Kenny complained about his microphone volume, telling the sound tech to "gas it." A guitar tech set Thelma in an opened suitcase with a built-in stand, the same one Chaz used at all his festival shows. Under the stage-side tent, Chaz bantered with the Zydeco band leader. Kenny got the microphone volume to his liking. Liz gave Ben a thumbs-up. He shouted into the microphone, "Show some love for the Chaz Russell Band."

Chaz sipped lemonade as his band opened with a ten minute cover of Little Walter's "Key to the Highway." They kept playing while Miss Leeward, a recent high school graduate, escorted Chaz to the seat at the center of the stage. He rested Thelma on his leg and played a mean take of "Downtrodden and Out of Luck." When he slid into the opening chords of "Born Under a Bad Sign", a wave of cheers whooshed from the shade, over the stage-front chairs, to the stage. Liz drew a few lusty whistles when she played Jasper behind her back with sweaty belly skin exposed. A willowy woman leaned on the stage and flashed Pearly a cardboard sign bearing her kinky nickname and a phone number. Kenny shed a pound of sweat during his three minute drum solo. Chaz heard cheers when he added the lyrics: "I haven't felt well for a while… now feeling fine, back here, bending for you Maine folk."

Chaz hushed the crowd by saying. "Let's take it around the block. Meet Kenny on tubs, Pearly on bass, and our newest member, Miss Liz playing Jasper, her brand new Durrell, baby brother of my Thelma."

Liz introduced Chaz as King of the String Benders. He responded with a few bent notes. "Seeing my band's been so good to me," he added, "I'm letting them add their own touches to our next song. See if we can kick it up a bit." Liz led off with a dark instrumental she wrote in her prison cell. She passed the vamp to Chaz who responded with twenty seconds of string quivers and warbles. He added adrenaline to the song with a few bars of surf music. Kenny's drum sticks blurred during his minute-long solo. When everyone thought he was spent, he tossed his sticks to the crowd and pounded the snare with bare hands. Pearly held his bass like a lead guitar and finger picked a few bars. Halfway through his run, he sampled a few bars of Rogers and Hammerstein's "My Favorite Things." With his message said, he nodded toward Liz. She flashed an upward thumb to the sound man next to the stage. He turned a dial, doubling Jasper's volume. When she unloaded a sustained C chord, the husky tone bounced off the Timely Pub clapboards. Her thrilling string work, played by instinct, not forethought, muffled every audience conversation and silenced every boat engine. A few seconds after the solo reached its highest intensity, her fingers loosened a fret, causing it to extend a quarter inch from the fretboard, making the guitar unplayable. Sweat-soaked dancers stood at rest on the parquet. Ben begged the crowd for a fret press. A luthier from Skowhegan ran to the stage, took a pliers-like device from his backpack and pressed the wayward fret into its groove.

The repair took less than three minutes, enough time for Liz to rest for her grand finale. With Jasper running on all cylinders, she played a dead on cover of the "Woodstock Improvisation" from the *Chessman's*. A police officer on Main Street closed his cruiser window to hear a radio call. Chaz, hearing Hendrix's ghost, dropped his pick and reached into his pocket for a replacement. When the song ended, a woman in the front row yelled, "Hey old timer, anything left in the tank?"

Chaz mumbled to himself about retiring to the Bahamas without a guitar. He drew a deep breath, scowled at the woman, and hammered a stray vamp into a five minute medley of riffs borrowed from the Hendrix catalog. The staccato chords disrupted a church service ten blocks from the stage. Timely Pub barmaids took drink orders by hand signal. The woman who questioned his stamina hid under a broad straw hat.

Ben, leaning on the side of the stage, used his fingers to signal a two minute warning. Chaz, Liz and Pearly delivered a final string barrage. Kenny's drums shook like they were in a bad earthquake. The bouncer guarding the stage kissed his caring wife who had insisted he wear ear plugs. Ben cut the song short by announcing from the stage, "Let's hear more love for Chaz Russell and his band."

The crowd begged for more. Chaz, too sweaty and spent to play another note, told them, "I'd throw my pick to yah, but it may burn somebody." On the way down the stairs, Chaz told Liz, "Nice

Hendrix action."

Roadies put Thelma, Jasper and Lucas in their cases and carried the guitars to a walk-in storage box near the stage, guarded by Ben's cousin, a drossy oyster shucker from a Maine island with a hard-to-pronounce name. Liz poured chilled water on towels and gave them to her bandmates. When their bodies cooled, Kenny and Pearly followed Ruby to Pierpoint, a bar perched on pilings a few hundred feet from the stage. Ben led Chaz and Liz to a nearby dock where the wooden lobster boat *Sea Princess* awaited hungry performers. On the aft deck, a blue plastic barrel filled with seawater held lobsters plucked from Leeward Harbor that morning. A few feet away, their cousins boiled in a ten gallon pot. On the dock, a barbecue pit made from a locomotive boiler simmered ribs and ears of corn.

A mate with few teeth guided Chaz and Liz to soft landings on the *Sea Princess* deck. Chaz found comfort sitting next to his friend Bucky White, the plump Zydeco accordionist whose band had played the set before the Chaz Russell Band. Liz introduced herself to Bucky's washboard player, Spoons Walker, a sixtyish Zydeco veteran with more gold teeth than fingers. She squinted when his washboard reflected sunlight into her eyes.

"You have a Hendrix flashback up there?" he asked. "You left the earth for a bit, came back playing like Jimi. Slammed a Hendrix riff, fired us up. Never seen a white girl play Jimi."

"Just playing some chords," Liz said with an air of indifference. "Never know what my new axe will deliver."

Spoons positioned his hands in air guitar mode. "I once played guitar, couldn't get no work, ended up swatting tin," he sang.

"How long you known Chaz?" Liz asked.

"We go back to the mid-seventies. I'm a New Orleans boy. Down there, you play Zydeco, cook Cajun, or drive piles. I don't like work, so I chose Zydeco. These days, I tap metal, sing up a storm, pay the bills."

"Where'd you get the swampy groove?"

"Sheet, I was born into Zydeco music. Aunts, cousins, brothers, sisters all played a type of Zydeco that's half swamp and half New Orleans blues. We play it, sing it, or say it, but don't give the audience a second of silence. You watch: Bucky tells little stories and tickles soft accordion notes between songs. When I'm not playing, I'm dancing and swinging my arms to the beat."

"Got to keep the crowd from thinking about overdue bills or bad love." Liz said.

"You know what I'm talking about. You guys got the right guitars. Johnny is the best guitar builder I know. I've been down his Arkansas shop with my cousin who plays with Sonny Boy Maxwell. Man, Johnny has a hollow leg; saw him down a gallon of local brew in about an hour. I drank a glass, the room spun."

"Locals call it lighter fluid. I swear they cut it with moonshine. I've emptied a few glasses with Johnny, stuff packs a punch."

"Can I take a peek at your Durrell?" Spoons asked.

Liz pointed toward downtown. "We're jamming tonight at the Timely. Stop by before ten. I'll let you play a few notes. Chaz will be there. Take Bucky, we'll jam."

"Will do. I'll bring my belly metal."

The mate served the guests tin plates overloaded with seafood and local produce. A half-hour hour later, the plates held only shells, cobs, and bones. During the ice cream course, the old bluesmen swapped stories about characters met while touring. Liz returned to the tent next to the stage. Ben's cousin unlocked the storage box after checking Liz's driver's license photo. She took Jasper to her hotel room.

Around 9 p.m., a Timely doorman escorted Liz and Jasper to open stools. Three guitarists, a saxophonist, and a keyboardist played a timely song on the stage. Tina ambled behind the bar in a pink tank-top with two-inch wide leather bands on each bicep. Liz told her, "I've got a Zydeco singer coming in. An accordion and another guitar might show up."

Tina read from a clipboard, "You're set for ten. Wait near the stage five minutes early. I'm not your babysitter, so be ready to plug in and play."

Spoons washboard shimmered as he crossed the dance floor. He ordered two beers for himself and a margarita refill for Liz. Every woman, single or married, old or young, drunk or sober, rubbed the washboard when passing his stool. Spoons humored the women with stale one-liners like: "Take me home, I'll launder your sheets in the morning." A few lady hands tugged on his gold belt buckle. One woman said lightning was forecast so he should stay the night at her place.

A few minutes before ten, next to the stage, Liz handed Jasper to Spoons. He looked into the sound hole at the Johnny Durrell signature. Satisfied it was a real Durrell, he tickled a few strings and flashed a ten-caret smile. Tina escorted Bucky and Chaz to the stage. Bucky plugged-in Beulah, his prized pink accordion. Chaz offered to cover rhythm with Thelma. Bucky suggested a key and song then introduced the Muddy Swamp Band. His speedy accordion riffs drove a dozen couples to the dance floor. The woman who had bloodied her biker boyfriend the previous night danced tight with her new paramour. A tall man under a ten gallon hat boogied with a woman in a pink tee shirt and white shorts.

Bucky screeched like a buzzard during "Jambalaya", a song he had performed thousands of times over forty years. Chaz loosened Thelma's two thickest strings and covered the bass line. Liz added a few backing licks. Spoons spanked his washboard and sang. When Bucky sipped a beer, the woman brawler shouted, "Hey Bud, play something slow."

"Sweetie, we don't play slow," Bucky replied. "You want slow, go to church in the morning."

Bucky's accordion drove a forty minute Louisiana swamp medley. Body heat from the dance floor overworked the air conditioning. Tina waved the musicians off the stage a few minutes before eleven. Spoons introduced Liz to the tall man under the big hat, a record company owner named Stevens who had produced one of Spoons' recordings. Stevens invited the Muddy Swamp Band to his nearby yacht for a nightcap. Chaz and Bucky, claiming old man fatigue, declined the invitation. Liz and Spoons accepted the offer. Tina stored Jasper and Spoon's washboard and spoons in an upstairs storage room.

Liz and Spoons walked over the festival grounds to the Leeward town dock. Fog dimmed the lights of yachts tied to slips and fuzzed the view of moored lobster boats pointed at the gentle southwest breeze. They passed the *Sea Princess* on the way to the wobbly slip hugging the *Blues Groove,* a sixty-foot motor yacht named after Stevens' record company. Stevens stood on the boat's deck steadying a brass ladder, insuring a safe landing on the dark blue carpet. Liz sat next to Spoons on a cushioned bench built into the sweeping curve of the stern. Stevens sat on a white leather fighting chair used the previous week for shark fishing off Nantucket. His dance partner, now a pert mate in a dress uniform, brought them drinks.

"Old friend, where's your great voice taking you these days?" Stevens asked.

"Still singing Zydeco and God's music for food and shelter," Spoons replied. "Just guested on a gospel album in Nashville. Take a listen." Spoons walked across the deck, climbed a ladder to the cabin roof, and another ladder to an aluminum tuna tower where he stood with outstretched arms thirty feet above the water. In perfect pitch, he serenaded the harbor with the slave spiritual "Going to the Promised Land." When he finished, applause spilled from vessels hidden in the murk.

Spoons returned to the stern and sat closer to Liz. "Your voice gets better with age," Stevens said. "We should do a spiritual album. I'll get some New Orleans heavies to play along. Your voice will make us big money."

"Cool thought," Spoons said. "I make nice cash as a chrome belly, but singing is my love. I grew up on a church balcony watching mama sang. And boy could she sing. Church had no money for amps. Big girls like mama carried the sound."

"How'd you get connected with Chaz Russell?" Stevens asked.

"Liz plays in his band. I met him in the 70s. He and Bucky been friends since '60s Chicago. Them boys seen it all."

"Chaz's arm got stabbed, so he hired me," Liz added, "Now he's somewhat healed, I'm second lead. When his hand bothers him, I play lead."

"I heard about the stabbing," Stevens said. He caught the mate's attention for refills. "Glad he's back, he's the last of a breed. Otis Rush doesn't play much these days. Albert King is long gone. You the Queen String Bender?"

"No way. It's too twangy. I fell into this gig. See what happens. I'm learning plenty playing with these boys."

"Chaz was there on blues best days," Stevens said. "Ask him about the late 60s, with white kids digging blues, blues clubs everywhere."

"He won't talk about the past. My sister found out the hard way. She's writing a book about the blues. His name came up. She asked him if he had played with Hendrix. Got yelled at."

Stevens leaned forward, stirring his fresh cocktail with a long silver spoon. "Funny you mentioned Hendrix. Late 60s, I worked in

Manhattan for Player Records, a long-dead label. A drinking buddy, Tinker Martin, worked as a sound tech for Chessman Studio over in Harlem. One night he told me a lush tale. Claimed a few days before, he showed for work, old man Chessman—we called him Chessie—had him set up for an all-night jam. He figured Chessie would leave at supper time. Tinker wired microphones, put fresh recording tape on the console, and loaded the coffee pot for a long night babysitting the studio. Turns out, Chessie stayed the night, sent Tinker home early. Tinker figured something was up so he hid in the bushes. Saw a couple limousines drive in. Swears Hendrix and Miles went into Chessman's service entrance with a couple flashy women. Other dudes carried guitar cases and horns. Some white guy had a Hofner bass.

"The next afternoon, Tinker found the studio clean as a whistle except for a String Bender guitar pick near a microphone stand. Chessie had removed the recording tape. Tinker can't hold a secret, especially with a beer buzz. Within days, all the Brothers Pub regulars heard all about the Hendrix and Davis session. Hendrix left for London the week after the rumor broke, died a year later, never spoke about it. Miles yelled insults when reporters asked about the session. Chessie died without saying a word about it. His kid ain't talking either. The rumor has haunted me for forty years." Stevens handed Liz his business card. "Call me next week. I'll give you Tinker's contact info. Have your sister talk to him. I'll tell him to get his story in print before he checks out."

"You think the story is true?" Liz asked.

"Could be," Stevens said. "Tinker still swears it happened."

An hour after midnight, a stiff ocean breeze plowed the fog from Leeward Harbor. The mate draped a blanket over Liz's shoulder. Stevens talked about his music business accomplishments for a half hour. Liz and Spoons, tired of one-sided discourse, returned to the Timely where they found Tina mopping the dance floor. Liz thanked her for watching their instruments and gave her a ten dollar tip. They followed her up the stairs to the storage room. When Tina stepped on the top stair she screamed. The storage room door was open. Toppled metal shelving, curtains, and broken bottles littered the floor. Liz saw a guitar neck under a heap of movie posters, but it was only a cheap acoustic. They pored through toppled cardboard boxes and beer signage without finding Jasper or Spoon's washboard and spoons. Liz yelled dozens of guttural curses. Spoons cried over the detritus, "Had my frot for thirty years. I'm nothin' without it. My soul's in the steel. Them spoons pounded a million beats. Thank goodness I had a voodoo bless them. I'll get them back."

Tina called the police from the bar phone. Within minutes, officers and a detective interviewed the nervous Timely staff. The cleaning man, doormen, and barmaids swore they saw dozens of musicians walk in and out of the bar with guitar cases that night and none looked suspicious. They didn't see anyone other than Spoons wearing a washboard.

The police left about four a.m. without a lead. Before Liz and Spoons departed, Tina topped three shot glasses with bar whisky. "I'm pissed," she said. "Maine blues scene is tight. They'll smoke out the crook, hang 'em with guitar string." They each downed a shot. Dazed Liz and Spoons walked to the street. Tina called her boyfriend, a motorcycle tough who knew every thug in Maine. Liz retired to her hotel room, madder than a thrown cat. Spoons wept most of the night on his bunk in the tour bus.

7 STOLEN SOUND

Sunday morning on the festival stage, Ben told the crowd, "Hard to believe someone stole a guitar, a frottoir, and a couple silver spoons last night. If you see a blue Durrell mini-335, or a washboard with a golden S on the middle, call the Leeward Police. I'll pay a nice reward." He showed a stack of dollar bills thick as a paving brick. "Cash money, nothing asked. Let's get these instruments back so their owners can make a living."

Ben introduced Liz who described Jasper as "made by the guitar god, the great Johnny Durrell." A roadie handed her a semi-hollow guitar made by a local luthier. "You find a stray baby-blue Durrell, turn it on its side like this and peek in the sound hole. If you see Jasper written near Johnny's signature, call the Leeward cops. I'll be your friend for life. May even write a song about you."

Spoons wobbled to the microphone with drenched eyes and puffy cheeks. He sniffled into a handkerchief, hacked some cigarette revenge, mumbled a few sloggy words, and left the stage. Ben told the crowd, "See what those instruments mean to these hard-working people?"

A waitress serving breakfast mentioned the theft to Kenny, Pearly, and Ruby. "Liz got no damn guitar," Kenny said, glaring at Ruby. "You know anything about this?"

"Not me," she said. "I told you all, never take a Durrell on tour. Fences love them. They sell quick, for big bucks."

A cleaning lady told Chaz about the stolen instruments. He

walked to the stage and saw Thelma and Lucas secure in the guarded box. He met Liz and Spoons at the festival gate passing out flyers with images of the stolen goods and spouting revengeful jive and vindictive curses to anyone who'd listen. Feeling faint in the relentless heat, he offered condolences and then retreated to the hotel shade with a suspect in mind.

Standing four hours under high sun yielded Liz and Spoons sympathetic squeezes, bizarre theories, acute dehydration, and few leads. Sage Winslow, a doyenne in a tie-dyed dress, said a man ran by her bedroom window around midnight holding something wrapped in a curtain. Liz jotted Sage's phone number on a flyer. Tilly Barker, a windburned lobsterwoman back from a haul, mentioned getting cut off by a car with New York plates a few hours before the bars closed. The guy "from away" drove a white sedan with a woman crouched in the passenger seat. Tilly's boyfriend was saving her a coveted lunchtime bar stool, so she invited Liz to stop by her fish boat in the morning to talk.

The sun slid behind the Timely as the festival ended with a five-guitar encore. Ben had begged the audience for information about the thefts after each act. Wilted, angry Liz sat near the exit, passing flyers to departing attendees. Few had the will to chat after twenty hours of steamy music over two days.

Bucky's bus driver summoned his passengers with three air horn blasts. Liz and Spoons exchanged phone numbers outside the idling bus. She promised to text him with any news about the stolen instruments. Standing on the bus stairs, Bucky played a parting tune on his accordion and sang lyrics with a promise to pay some Cajun alligator hunters to find the thieves. The loaded bus departed to a Boston Massachusetts gig where Spoons would get a replacement washboard and two duplicate spoons.

After the dark bus fumes dispersed into the cottony sky, Liz walked thirty paces to the Timely for a draft beer with ice cubes. At the same time, on the Anchor Inn veranda, Chaz listened to his rhythm section pitch conspiracy theories. Pearly offered a heated denunciation of Timely security, blaming them for letting a pickpocket follow him into the two-stall restroom. Kenny blamed Tina, saying he knew first hand she had slept with bad men.

"Stop blaming imaginary pickpockets," Chaz said. "You

probably spent the missing money on drinks. Tina wouldn't steal a toothpick. My suspect has long legs, sometimes blond hair, body splashed with stolen perfume. I figure when you guys got glued, she snagged the booty. We're not leaving Leeward until she brings me the stuff."

Kenny and Pearly bolted from their chairs faster than greyhounds chasing a bunny. They returned ten minutes later with Ruby who slid onto the rocker next to Chaz and with cuddly voice said, "Baby, I don't steal no more. No hooking or crooking for this girl. I'm a soldier of the Lord Jesus Christ."

"Like hell you are," Chaz said, pointing a finger at her head. "You're suspect number one, you'd steal my shoelaces."

Ruby pushed Chaz's hand away. "Don't point at me. I'm on God's side now."

"How'd this happen so fast?"

"A few weeks ago, Reverend Whitley found me weeping on a Saturday night at the Backbeat. I told him hay fever was causing the tears, but he figured I was sad. Talked me into staying with him that night. Next day, he took me to Sunday service. In front of a full house, he forgave me for stealing his guitar, the one I sold you cheap and you gave him back."

"They let you into a church?" Chaz asked. "In a stretchy dress?"

"Usher made me wear a men's raincoat from the lost and found. Nine in the morning, fifteen balcony birds started things off with "My Savior." Reverend Whitley blasted a ten minute sermon then some Broadway star walked the middle aisle belting out "We Are All God's Children." Three cats in red jumpsuits played guitar up front. One had a Fender worth twenty large. You musicians talk about the fog, when the music is so tight you leave the earth. When the big gal sang and them cats played, I left earth. Lord himself asked me to join his team. I came back near the Reverend and yelled to the congregation, 'I'm a soldier of God.' Reverend kissed me all over my face and neck."

Chaz, looking like a prison guard hearing an inmate complaint, asked, "All your stealing and one church service cleaned your slate?"

Ruby took a white leather covered bible from her pocketbook. "Sure has. This book runs my life. They found it in the hands of my murdered mom. You can see a spot of her blood on the cover. Every day, I read these pages, think of her, try to keep the devil from stealing my soul." She read aloud a passage from Genesis. When she got to the part about Adam and Eve's inability to play by God's rules, Kenny and Pearly, feeling uncomfortable, scurried to the hotel lounge.

Chaz asked Ruby, "Pretend you know nothing about last night's theft. In your past life, how'd you sell stolen instruments?"

Ruby closed the bible with her index finger serving as a bookmark. "Clip it and ship it," she said. "Get it out of town fast. Don't let the cops find you with the booty."

"Who'd steal a one-of-a kind guitar?" Chaz asked. "What do they look like? Who'd want an old washboard? Would they melt the spoons?"

"All the thieves I know look like normal criminals. Stolen axes sell quick, especially Durrells. Back when the devil had my soul, fences offered to pay me fifty grand for one. A few asked for Thelma. I only stole from suckers or bloodsuckers. My fence sold to collectors, gave me a percentage in cash. Sometimes I skipped the fence, went direct and met some kooks. Guy in Philly had a hundred stolen guitars on his wall: Fenders, classic Les Pauls, Bo Diddley's homemade. He'd dress up like a bluesman, play them in his mansion."

"You steal stuff from me?"

"Baby, back when I was the devil's dolly, I took a tape from your bedroom. A friend said you recorded with Miles and Hendrix, thought I found the tape to prove it. Shipped it to a collector in California. Guy sent it back, madder than mad. Tape was of some lounge singer. I put the tape back in your bedroom."

"Right back in the closet," Chaz said. "Kenny and Pearly know you stole my stuff?"

"Those guys know nothing about nothing. They'd brain me if they found out I stole from you. They think you're the best guy in the world except when you yell at them."

Chaz sighed. He had met hundreds of grifters and drifters over the years who had offered him stolen goods. Most ended up dead or in jail, but a few had abandoned thieving for honest work. Ruby sounded like a survivor, tired of face slaps from drunken Johns and price beat-downs from greedy fences. When Ruby talked about God, her expression changed from woman on the prowl to woman at peace. He went to his room for a nap. She spent the afternoon on the veranda, rocking back-and-forth, reading the Bible, feeling uneasy about staying in Leeward.

The next morning, Chaz asked an Anchor Inn receptionist for directions to a business able to pack and mail a parcel. She recommended Freeman's Stationary, four blocks away, on Main Street. When he pulled the handle on Freeman's screened door, a cowbell signaled his arrival. A clerk with ponytailed hair adjusted his drugstore glasses and greeted him with a warm welcome and tight handshake.

"I played the festival," Chaz said. "Had someone ship a busted guitar. I want to be sure it went out."

The clerk took the weekend shipping log from a hook and asked for the shipper's full name.

"Not sure who did the shipping," Chaz said. "I gave a roady cash and a guitar. His buddy packed and shipped the package."

The clerk had shipped eleven packages over the weekend. Ten were overnight envelopes addressed to mortgage companies or lawyers. A twenty-two pound box shipped Sunday noon to Port Townsend, Washington. The clerk stroked his chin while thinking aloud. "Right after I opened on Sunday morning, some city slicker brought in a box. Pleasant guy, in his forties, hadn't shaved...hundred dollar haircut, didn't say much...box wrapped like a mummy, must have used ten rolls of tape, paid cash for express overnight. Got a truck from Augusta to pick it up. Sounded like scrap metal in it."

"You've got the one," Chaz said.

The clerk gave him a copy of the shipping slip. Chaz left the store and walked a few blocks where he found Liz at a crosswalk. She promised to meet him on the veranda after visiting the Leeward Police station.

Liz began her meeting with a police officer by calling Ruby Ralston the prime suspect. "Ten people told me she did it," the officer said. "We had her in this morning, she denied any involvement. She's got a rap sheet thick as a Sunday newspaper. I'd call her a religious woman. After questioning, I drove her to church, other side of town, she prayed all the way. Might have prayed she wouldn't get charged."

Liz mentioned Sage Winslow's recollection of a man running

past her window carrying something wrapped with a curtain.

"I'll check it out. Sage's son is a buddy, a fireman in town. Her clutch is slipping. Wouldn't take her word as gospel."

Liz told the detective about Tilly Barker who got cut off by a man driving a fancy sedan with New York plates. The officer fumed, "You know how many New Yorkers pass through Leeward on a summer day? Hundreds? They park them rentals in fire lanes. It's like Coney Island around here in July. My ex-wife is a New Yorker. I wish they'd all stay home…" The officer heard a call for assistance and ran to his cruiser.

On the festival grounds, Liz asked a town employee pushing a lawnmower where to find Tilly Barker. He pointed to a green-hulled fish boat tied to the commercial dock. She found Tilly stacking lobster traps on the *Harp's Luck*, a creaky vessel on the hunt for lobsters four days a week. Tilly waved her aboard. "You're the girl who lost her guitar." she said. "Let's talk. I'm good until high tide, about an hour."

Liz found a place to lean, near the doghouse, far as possible from a barrel of fetid chum. "You recall the car that cut you off?" she asked.

Tilly pulled a toothpick from her lips. "Sure can," she said. "I was headed to my boat about two in the morning, needed to pull a hundred bugs before nine to buy fuel and pay my way into the festival. Turned my truck into the town lot, guy in a Lexus, wearing shades, cut me off. Around here, only people who wear sunglasses at night are crooks or blind. Locals drive rusty pickups, not fancy sedans. Car damn near sideswiped my truck. Got a good look at a guy with black shiny hair wearing a pink shirt. Woman in the passenger seat bent over. I only saw her white hands and a baseball cap on her head."

Tilly smiled as she stirred the chum with a canoe paddle. Houseflies from far and near hovered over the barrel, savoring its bouquet. Liz felt a wave of nausea after a wind shift sent a whiff her way. She asked where to find a cold beer and good sandwich, far away from the dock. Tilly pointed to a building perched on the southern shore, a quarter mile away. Liz declined a parting handshake in favor of a wave. She followed the splintery boardwalk to the restaurant built on the granite block foundation of a failed fish processing plant. At the outdoor bar, under an awning, she savored a beer and light sandwich. On her northern view, cloud shade darkened the purple and tan face of the Camden Hills. The southern view showed puffy white clouds in no rush to slide away. The serene setting cleared her mind, allowing her to recall the events of the previous two days. She couldn't fathom how the thief had walked into the Timely and descended the stairs carrying the stolen goods. It had to be an inside job, done by a waitress or bouncer who created a diversion to help others perform the heist. On the back of a placemat, she wrote a list of the individuals seen Saturday night in the Timely: The sixtyish couple wearing tee shirts and shorts, the dude with the bad Elvis haircut, the fisherman with yellow teeth who drank shots and tried to pick her up, the loud, rummy woman called Day Pass by her friends. They all seemed like typical blues music fans having a good time.

Sage's story about the pink-shirted man running with the curtain seemed credible. The ransacked Timely storage room had curtains strewn on the floor. The guy running with the curtain was probably the only man in town wearing pink that night. Blues festival attendees don't wear pink golf shirts. The Timely staff denied seeing anyone fitting this description.

After her lunch, the restaurant manager gave her a golf cart ride down the boardwalk to the hotel. She found Chaz on the veranda reading a newspaper. "Yesterday morning," he said, "someone shipped a guitar size box from Leeward. Clerk thought the box held tin cans."

"Who sent it?" Liz asked.

"A snazzy white guy. Short, in his forties. Initialed the packing slip PSM."

"Who got the package?"

"Some woman in Washington State. This has a Ruby ring to it. She's been to Seattle, tried to take Kenny and Pearly. I canned it, we had gigs. She's using God in a new scam."

Chaz wanted to distribute festival paychecks and extract more information from Ruby so he invited his entourage to dinner at The Rockery on the northern shore of Leeward Bay. Liz drove the crowded van five miles to the winding entrance road lined with breezy maples. A valet, seeing Harlem Rentals on the van door, shooed her to a service lot behind a garage. The unlit, crushed shell path leading to the restaurant made for unsteady footing. Ruby and Liz, wearing dresses and heels, nearly fell onto a prickly hedge. Kenny stubbed his toe on a landscape timber. Pearly ripped his pants pocket on a fence post. Sweaty, winded Chaz tipped the valet ten cents.

A hostess seated the Chaz Russell party at a round table overlooking the long jetty protecting Leeward Harbor from ocean swells. They dined on seafood bisque and lobster without a mentioning the stolen instruments. After dessert, Kenny and Pearly had a smoke on the patio. Liz tempered her anger with an aperitif at the bar. Chaz stayed at the table with wary Ruby, drinking coffee. He interrupted the chilly scene by asking, "You know April Peters from Washington State?"

"Don't connect me with the bitch." Ruby snarled. "April is part of my former life. I ain't going back to bad living."

"Remember when I bailed you out of Riker's last year? The five hundred you forgot to pay me back?"

"Yah, I remember." Ruby touched the coffee cup rim to her red lipstick and took a slow sip. In a calm voice, she replied, "Scripture says be upfront with all God's children. I know April Peters, been to her house. She's a hippie chick, pushing sixty, house full of Woodstock stuff. Living room has a painting of the stupid seagull sitting on a guitar. Place stinks of patchouli. Must have a hundred lava lamps. Fluffy parachute nailed to her living room ceiling. Blue lights in every room. Smokes weed constantly. Loaded with money. Collects guitars and weird musical stuff. Buys vintage axes, fiddles, mandolins. Never sold her nothing because of her scumbag boyfriend. We tried doing a deal, April went to the bathroom, dude threatened my life unless I slid him a vig. I told April I felt sick, took my swag, ran out the door."

"Where does she live?" Chaz asked.

"Way out west, Port Townsend, Washington, near mountains, in a big house, looks over water. Her husband was a big shot banker, died in a plane crash, left her fat with cash. She told me a gallon of maple syrup got mixed with his jet fuel. Bet she got some on her fingers. Her boyfriend knows every fence and crooked pawn in the world. He gets whatever she wants, by hook or crook."

"We're heading back to New York in the morning. We'll talk some more after we get home."

"No prob," Ruby said. "I'm bussing it. I'll see you there."

Chaz passed out paychecks in the lobby "I took out travel expenses and split meals. Ben paid for the rooms. You each get $255.65." Kenny claimed his check had the wrong date. "It's dated the day we get back to Harlem," Chaz said. "The last time you guys cashed paychecks in Leeward didn't go well."

Late Tuesday morning, with downtown Leeward approaching Ecuadorian temperature, Liz visited Sage's apartment. Sage pointed out her window at the alley used by the man carrying the curtain. Liz walked the alley and found no footprints on the path, but under a trash can lid on the ground, she found a silver spoon with the bottom of the bowl and back of the handle showing heavy wear. She put the spoon in a stray plastic bag, put the bag in her pocket, and thanked Sage without mentioning the find.

Around noon, Liz drove south with her three bandmates fighting sleep. When she passed the Thomaston town line, she had the only open eyes. Two hours into the ride, at a coffee shop inside the Kennebunk rest stop on the Maine Turnpike, Chaz asked Liz about a replacement guitar.

"I'm screwed. I'll have to play my Les Paul," she said.

"No way on the Les Paul," Chaz said. "Here's what's up: My cousin is driving to Johnny's shop, leaving this morning from Mississippi. He'll borrow a guitar, drive it to Harlem. Johnny will keep an eye out for Jasper. If he has to build you another guitar, so be it."

"He's not building another Jasper," Liz said with fury. "I'll find the original and bash heads when I do."

"Four days till our next gig," Chaz said. "Probably ten axes looking for homes, in Johnny's shop. One will do until we find Jasper."

Kenny and Pearly nearly suffered cardiac arrest when Chaz pounded the side of the van with his fist. He gave them a five minute restroom visit. Liz powered her cell phone and scrolled text messages from Sarah with headings: Need a decision!!!!!; What are you going to do????; I need $$$$$!!!

Entering New York City, Chaz decided to unload the equipment in the morning. Around ten p.m., Liz dropped Kenny and Pearly at their apartment. Liz volunteered to sleep in the van in front of Chaz's apartment. He gave her a shiny 9mm hand gun and said, "This baby is loaded, It's a good argument settler. Be careful."

"I carried heat for a couple years," she said. "I'm so pissed about Jasper, I'll make chum out of anyone who messes with me."

Chaz retired to his apartment hoping the gun would remain unfired. Liz pushed aside a guitar case, tossed a few cushions on the floor, and slept within minutes despite frequent taxi horns and ambulance wails. Early morning, an intruder jimmied the locked driver's side door. Liz leaped from the cushions, snarling like a mountain lion. She flashed the pistol. The bad guy dropped his pinch bar and fled to a park. Liz fired three shots into the trees over his head.

Over the next few hours, streetlights, sirens, anger, and adrenalin kept her awake. A cold beer from Kenny's cooler tasted good so she had a second. Her thoughts focused on the man in the pink shirt and his accomplice who could be the woman who stabbed Chaz. Someone had to stop these Durrell obsessed psychopaths before they attacked another musician. And, she thought: how did the thief know where to find custom guitars? This information didn't come from the tight circle of Durrell collectors who kept a low profile, meeting once a year in a secret location. She wondered why Kenny and Pearly acted nonchalant about the missing instruments. Could they behind the theft? No way, she concluded, they couldn't steal cookies from a jar without acting guilty. Stage roadies couldn't have done it because their livelihood depended upon reputations as trusted instrument babysitters. Could a co-conspirator be the Great White Shark, the big dude in brown overalls who leaned on the Leeward stage and kept order with a cold stare and pointed finger? The night of the theft, she saw him carry a guitar case to the Timely upstairs. It couldn't be him for he was an earthy native who crabbed for a living. Ruby Ralston remained her prime suspect. Liz doubted she had straightened out after years of crime. She decided to visit Reverend Whitley to get the truth about Ruby's religious enlightenment. When dawn light nixed the streetlights, she finished her beer. She slept until late morning when Chaz tapped on the van window. She lugged Chaz's gear to his apartment, dropped-off Kenny and Pearly's equipment, and drove to the van rental office.

8 APRIL

Dropping off the van turned unpleasant when a bullying agent charged Liz a thousand dollars for a scuff mark that turned out to be shoe polish. Liz reached over the counter, grabbed the agent's neck, and squeezed tight until he apologized for his rudeness and deleted the charge. She eased her grip and warned the agent to play nice with musicians experiencing stolen guitar syndrome. Disgusted with life in general, she went home, pulled her window shades tight, and slipped under her bedcovers with the air conditioning on full-blast.

Across town, Sarah spent several hours in a coffee shop interviewing a young Brazilian guitarist named Stephan` who claimed responsibility for the rebirth of bossa nova, a smooth South American jazz genre popular in the 1950s and 60s. Mid-afternoon, she entered Liz's bedroom holding Lenny's offer sheet for the *Chessman's* stapled to a photocopy of a hundred thousand dollar check with Liz O'Malley the payee. Liz, awakened from a disturbing dream, rubbed her eyes, hacked, wheezed, and cleared her throat before acknowledging her sister's presence. Sarah, accustomed to sluggish post-gig greetings from her sister, leaned on a wall, reading the fine print of the offer sheet.

Liz gained full facial function after a second coffee. Sarah, seeing her sister running on all cylinders, asked, "Why'd you blow me off? Lenny doubled his offer. Sign this. You'll get the real check later today."

"Shut up," Liz said. "Big horror show in Leeward. Jasper's gone, clipped from a bar. Met a nice tin gut up there, they stole his washboard. I'm not dealing with Lenny until I get Jasper back. I'm chasing a strong lead that a West Coast collector has it."

"Go rent a guitar from Ed at Fret Rent," Sarah said. "He's got hundreds, one will sound right. Or, have Johnny build a new one."

"Why are you so damn guitar stupid?" Liz asked. "Guitars don't all sound the same. I want the real Jasper back. Forget about Johnny building a new one. Getting a new one built would take more trips to Arkansas, more hangovers, more dusty rides."

Sarah stormed into the living room and sat on the recliner with her black pumps resting on the footrest. "Every time you sit in that chair you ask for money," Liz said.

"I'm short this week," Sarah pleaded. "My only work is a two hundred dollar article about the cockiest guitar player in the world, a punk named Stephan`. My mortgage is six months behind. I'm sinking fast. If you're tired of loaning me money, sign Lenny's contract, save my ass."

Liz slammed her mug on the table, splashing hot coffee on her wrist. She cooled the burn with a wet sponge. "I'm not signing anything until I get Jasper back," she said. "I could care less about your problems. You spend money on flirty clothes on Fifth Avenue and I buy used jeans from street people. Why don't you find a husband? Stop chasing uptown suits who dump you after a few bangs for the next cupcake."

"Speaking of lifestyles," Sarah replied, "your numbers don't add up. You must pay three grand a month rent, working a few measly gigs. Still able to cuff me a couple hundred here and there. You living on robbery money?"

"Don't meddle in my life. I've saved my money. When you get kicked to the streets, move into my place, split rent. Just find another place to stay when I snag a hot date, which isn't often."

Sarah, seeing her sister's burn bubbled and crimson, bought bandages and salve from a local pharmacy. Using rubber gloves and a tender touch, she salved Liz's burn and covered it with a bandage. Calmed by care and a glass of milk, Liz described the Leeward trip and how Chaz's street sense led to a strong lead on who had Jasper. She showed Sarah the baggie containing the spoon found outside Sage's window. "This was stolen with the guitar and frot. It holds the DNA of the thief."

"You're crazy," Sarah said, "You can't connect this spoon to anything. It's a yard sale special, all tarnished. The scene on the handle looks like the *Last Supper*. Some church probably threw it out. I'd toss it. Thing may be spooked."

Liz put the bagged spoon in her pocketbook, without comment. She claimed Jasper was in a private collection on the West Coast and in a few days, she'd fly west to steal the guitar from the Port Townsend, Washington address on the shipping log. She showed her sister a satellite image of the property, currently valued at two million dollars. "I'm headed west to get my baby. Prison girls gave me a PhD in breaking and entering, busting doors, stealing stuff."

"You're not going alone," Sarah said. "I'll go with you."

"Not this trip. I've got someone in mind. You're too prissy for a B&E."

"I'm tougher than you are. I have to deal with snarly musicians and mean editors. All you do is play guitar and flirt."

"Lay off."

"What'll I tell Lenny?"

"Tell him you have a family emergency. You'll get back to him in a week."

"His offer is good for five days."

"Hold him off. Use the O'Malley jive mom taught us."

A couple hours later, Liz went to Harlem's Divine Intervention church to meet blind Reverend Whitley. The church was built in 1950 in the shell of an abandoned five-story brownstone. Workers made the cavernous interior by removing the floors from the first three stories. Steel beams kept the building upright during the Reverend's fervent sermons. A brass railing ran from the front doorway, along the left wall, past a few dozen pews, to the pulpit. Another railing ran from the pulpit, twenty feet to an office door.

Liz, standing on the aisle between the first pews, shouted, "Anyone home?"

A tall, bearded, black man wearing a red cloak and clerical collar appeared outside the office. "Who you?" he asked in a deep, cultured voice. "Who cometh to the Lord's house?"

"I'm Liz from Chaz Russell's band."

Reverend Whitley held the railing with both hands. "So you're the girl bank robber helping my dear friend Chaz," he said. "You're working for a wonderful man, full of the Lord's grace. What brings you my way? Seeking the Lord's advice?"

Liz walked down the aisle and grasped the Reverend's arm. "I've got a few questions about one of your congregation," she said.

The Reverend offered to provide personal references on anyone who attended his church and kept up with weekly donations. "Ma'am," he added, "before I get to talking, could you help me figure out who you are? When I meet new woman friends, seeing I can't see them, I like to Braille them." Before Liz could respond, he ran his clammy palms over her hips, shoulders, and legs. "You a white chick?" he said. "You got a nice ass." When his hand drifted into uncomfortable territory, Liz pushed it aside.

"Reverend, if I needed a feel down there, I'd call an old boyfriend. Let's get back to why I'm here. Can you answer a few questions about Ruby Rallston?"

"Sorry for getting carried away," he said. "I like women of all shapes and sizes. I need to know if you're a hard belly or a senior citizen so I can talk the right talk. Now I know you're a hard belly, I'll help you out."

The Reverend waddled to his desk chair. Liz, sitting a safe distance from his wayward paws, asked, "Now you know my physicality, can you tell me about Ruby becoming born again?"

The Reverend, fidgeting with an empty tin cup, replied, "Seems every week a cop or crook knocks on my door asking about one of my congregation. I can't see, but I damn sure listen to what happens in this part of Harlem. I know who's sleeping with who, who's stealing from who, who shot who. I can't be known as a snitch, so I can't comment on Ruby other than saying she's a well-built woman."

"Here's my situation," Liz said. "I need her help getting back something I own. I want to be sure she straightened out her act."

"I'll tell you her story if you perform a favor for our church. We use a few drops of spirits in our services, mix it with fruit juice, make a holy wine. Stuff eases my eye aches. Right now, we're running light. If you perform a small tithe by going across the street to Shill's and buying me a jug, I'll answer all your questions. I like the Russian stuff. Tell Shilly it's for the Reverend."

Liz returned ten minutes later with a two-liter bottle of Rabinakov vodka. The Reverend ran his fingers over the bottle and chirped when he felt the distinctive nub on the neck. Liz poured the vodka into his cup. The Reverend downed hearty swallows and exhaled hundred proof sighs. When the cup emptied, he shouted, "Hallelujah to the Lord…Ask me anything about anybody."

"I need Ruby's help recovering my stolen guitar," she said. "Most of Harlem knows she sold her body and stole instruments. Now she's gone straight, found the Lord, changed her life. Is she telling the truth?"

"She sure as hell is born again. She's the real deal. Began when I found her crying in the Backbeat. I was preaching, drinking shooters. A woman friend told me Ruby wanted to talk about maybe killing someone. We went to this office, stayed awake all night, talking, getting to know each other. When the sun came up, she showered up, put on her shiny dress, went to service in a man's raincoat. Halfway through the sermon, she yelled her love of God almighty. She gets dunked in New Jersey in a week, making her a dues paying soldier of our church."

The Reverend tapped his cup with the gold ring on his finger. Liz poured halfway to the rim. "Can you switch a hooker to God in a day?" she asked.

"Sure can. I'll set you straight for two-hundred cash. If you want to change your ways, stop banging for bucks and robbing banks, spend an hour with me in the sophistry. You'll feel the Lord's presence take over every inch of your body. It starts with a tingle. When you get it, you'll know it."

"Maybe some other day," Liz said. "I must go. Thanks for your time."

The Reverend raised his mug and said, "C'est la vie."

That night, in a coffee shop, Liz asked Ruby to accompany her to April's house to steal back the stolen instruments. Liz promised to pay all expenses plus a five hundred dollar bonus if they recovered Jasper and the washboard. If Ruby agreed to go, they'd depart from JFK the next evening.

"I wouldn't call it easy money," Ruby said. "Couple problems: April's boyfriend is a wacko who'll shoot our asses. And your offer fits into a category of sins that'll get me a long spell in purgatory, with no parole."

"We're not stealing anything," Liz said. "We're returning stolen stuff. If the trip drifts into sinning, makes you uncomfortable, I'll pay to fly you home. I need your help. You've been to April's house. You know her."

Ruby checked her calendar book. "I suppose if I steal something stolen and give it back to its owner, it's not really stealing, it's returning. God wouldn't mind. I'll do it, but I must be back in four days. I get my sins washed next week. No quick splash for this girl. I'll need a good soak to clean my slate."

Thirty hours after the coffee shop meeting, Liz and Ruby boarded a Seattle-bound flight at JFK. When the jet reached cruising altitude above Pennsylvania, Ruby parked her head on a pillow and slept. Liz studied Ruby's face. She felt compassion for this woman-of-the-street who had stolen and slept her way to survive. Although Ruby claimed forty-nine years of age, her lined complexion could pass for sixty. Liz had met many women like Ruby in prison, good people ruined by drug dependency, abusive relationships, alcohol abuse, mental illness, or lack of common sense. She recalled one of her cellmates, Cynthia, who spent countless hours on her bunk with a pen and legal pad writing a memoir about chasing a trick or copping a fix on Newark streets. Liz couldn't forget her opening sentence: "Thawk, twack. I opened the door at three a.m. My pimp smacked me three times. As blood trickled down my white nightgown, he yelled, 'you open my door after one knock, not two.'"

Turbulent air over the Great Divide awakened Ruby. "You had a rough spell," Liz said. "Sounded like a bad dream."

"I live bad dreams," said Ruby as she stretched her arms. "Raised in a cold-water flat with druggies cooking a fix next to mama cooking dinner. Those memories make for bad sleep."

"How bad?"

"Bad-ass people 24/7. One dude ripped off mama, shot a hole in our refrigerator. Made our last gallon of milk leak all over the floor. Baby sister drank Kool-Aid until we made a score. Another time a junkie kidnapped my older sister. My uncle got her back by swapping her for a stolen Mercedes."

"How long you been working the streets?"

"From age fifteen, did my first trick, made ten dollars. Done so many, I've lost count. Only got beat up once, by a pimp. I fixed his ass. Friends hid dope in his car. I dimed him. He got fifteen in Attica."

"How long you known Kenny and Pearly?"

"I've known them boys about twenty years. One night, I walked into the Backbeat. Back then Kenny was a stud. I sat next to him at the bar. Pearly got mad because I stole Kenny's attention. He sat at the far end of the bar and sulked. Kenny and I had drinks and played footsie. We wanted to continue the conversation at his apartment. He hailed a cab and just before the cab door shut, Pearly jumped in smelling like a menthol factory from all the gin he drank. Two blocks from the club, he passed out on Kenny's shoulder.

"Cab got stuck in midtown traffic. I tried to make time with Kenny. Pearly snored loud as a truck without a muffler. We dragged Pearly to their apartment floor where he passed out. Next morning, we all had tequila sunrises for breakfast. We forgave Pearly for the previous night horror show because his memory stopped working after his fifth gin. After our third tequila, Pearly's crying jag got old. I took a commuter bus home with my runny makeup, wrinkled dress, bare feet. Looked like I got run over by the bus. You should have seen the looks from yuppie chicks going home from work. Those boys are like my brothers. They talk to me, entertain me, love me, loan me money, and give me a free room that's really a closet. Good people, if you keep them somewhat sober."

"What drew you into the music scene?"

"Despite my bad childhood, I was close to an uncle who played bass. I met some famous musicians back then. Mr. Coltrane bought me an ice cream, Thelonious Monk let me sit on his lap when he played piano."

"You ever meet Hendrix?"

"Saw him play couple times in the city. I was just a little girl with pigtails. When Hendrix moved to London he asked my uncle to join him. Uncle couldn't go. He had a steady gig and an unsteady wife."

"Chaz know Hendrix?"Liz asked.

"So they say. Once, when Chaz was away, Pearly and I watered his house plants. We got to messing with Chaz's stuff. I put on his white lacy boots and a funky white overcoat covered with sparkles. We laughed like hell. Another time, I clipped a tape from his closet. It wasn't worth anything, so I put it back. Happened when I was stealing. I don't steal anymore."

"Why'd you turn to God?"

"I punched out a white babe outside Central Park. Never hurt a woman before that night. I was leaning on a rail outside the Cherry Blossom Hotel, looking for a date. Some bitch, all dressed up, told her friend I was a ten cent trick. If she called me a five-hundred dollar trick, nothing would have happened. She found out I knew boxing when I landed three rabbit punches on her jawbone. Got some of her makeup on my knuckles. Heard her jaw bones crack. Down she went, flat on the sidewalk. Out cold, thought I killed her. Lifted twelve hundred from her purse, paid the rent. Got a hundred for her credit cards. That night I had the worst nightmare. Over and over, heard her moaning for her mama, pretty girl with a busted face, dropping tears and blood on concrete. A movie of her laying there played all night in my head. Bothers me to this day."

"She die?"

"Not sure. I don't read newspapers or watch TV, guess she's OK. Next day, I saw a big red stain on the sidewalk next to some flower pots and candles. Oh God, forgive me. If you wouldn't mind, got to stop talking about my bad days, catch up on some scripture."

Steel gray moonlight washed Mount Rainier's snowy slopes as the jet approached Sea/Tac Airport. By the time they got their luggage, the tall concourse windows gleamed with morning sun. Liz and Ruby, suffering from cramped seat fatigue, had a stormy confrontation with a rental car agent who wrote Liz's credit card information on a scratch pad. Ruby, seeing a scam in motion, grabbed the credit card and pad from the agent and made a loud request to see her supervisor. The manager apologized for the error and upgraded them to a bright red convertible.

Ruby guided Liz to the Bainbridge Island Ferry on the Seattle shore. From the ferry dock, mid-morning sun made the Space Needle shine. After the ferry landed in Winslow, Liz drove an hour to the Northeast corner of the Olympic Peninsula. "When we smell the paper mill, we're close to Port Townsend," Ruby said.

Nineteenth century Port Townsend was an important port and railway terminus for the vibrant Olympic peninsula logging industry. Calls to designate it the Washington state capitol never materialized because railroad barons and politicians preferred Seattle's mainland location. Ornate administrative buildings and expansive Victorian homes remain from the prosperous years. Renovated buildings with shops and restaurants now line both sides of Water Street, close to the harbor. A renowned boatbuilding school sits on the east end, near a port of refuge protecting classic wooden boats from nature's anger. A long wave of glacial till shaped like a Himalayan serac hovers over cars entering downtown.

Four blocks up the hill from downtown, Liz and Ruby checked into the Dungeness Guest House, named after the tasty crabs thriving in the nearby sea. The proprietor, a salty extrovert, put their cash payment in his pocket and led them up a stairway to an end unit with a slider facing the sea. When he spread the drapes, they awed at the magenta Olympic mountain range. Looking east, they saw a cruise ship bound for Alaska.

The proprietor, a retired school teacher, began a well-rehearsed Port Townsend history lesson. Ruby's exaggerated yawn ended the proprietor's narrative after the second sentence. After unpacking their luggage, they drove a quarter-mile to April's house and parked across the street. Ruby pointed out the iron cannabis leaves on the wrought iron perimeter fence. The top of each fence post had a bronze casting of the splayed fingers of the 1960s antiwar peace movement.

"The guitars are in the dull building out back," Ruby said, "locked up good. Place has wide, narrow windows and a couple sky lights."

Someone in the house spread a curtain. Liz, driving away, said they'd get a closer look at the property later that night.

Around 2 a.m., Liz tried to awaken Ruby with a shoulder push. Ruby uttered a few bad words, pulled a blanket over her head, and resumed wheezy sleep. Liz, dressed in black jeans, dark blue hooded sweatshirt, and black sneakers, walked to April's. Many houses had a barking dog announcing her passage. When she walked down April's street, the barking stopped.

Foggy floodlights made April's house and grounds look like a coastal prison. When Liz opened April's wrought iron gate, the hinges squealed like a braking train. She froze for a few seconds, waiting for a bark or shout, but only heard the dull sound of a faraway boat engine. She tiptoed toward the house, pushed aside the limbs of a dense rhododendron, and peered into an unoccupied room with avocado leather furniture. A sky blue rug with woven cumulous clouds made the floor look like a summer sky on the Kansas prairie.

A saggy parachute covered the ceiling. A wall held a six-foot tall Woodstock poster of a seagull loitering on a guitar. The mantel of the fieldstone fireplace held several blown glass water pipes.

She followed a row of bushes to an attached stucco building the size of a small ranch house. The bland structure looked like a munitions depot, the style unfit for this neighborhood of pretentious homes. Iron cages covered a row of long, narrow transom windows. She climbed a fir tree next to the building, crawled across the roof to a skylight and shined her flashlight on an interior wall. She counted twenty guitars, a saxophone, and a mandolin, but no Jasper and no frottoir. A small stage held big speakers and a large bag of potato chips. After ten minutes on the roof, she shimmied down and returned to the Dungeness.

The next morning, Liz scrubbed black pitch from her hands. She promised to tell Ruby about the late-night romp during lunch. They walked to the Uppity Deck, a pub on the second story of a former Water Street bank. Those who ascend the eighty steps to the pub are rewarded with a fine view of the harbor and mountains. Those who park too long at the bar jeopardize their lives descending to the street on the steep treads.

Liz and Ruby sat on tall stools on the outdoor balcony. A few cagy seagulls perched on a wire envied the bowl of taco chips brought to their table by a young woman with a lip ring and streak of pink hair. Far across the harbor, a crane at the munitions port loaded armaments onto an aircraft carrier.

"I got the lay of April's place last night," Liz said. "I tried to shake you awake. You were chasing bunnies in your sleep. Is April all there? Her living room floor looks like a thunderstorm."

"I'm sorry," Ruby said, "I got wiped out by jet lag. April's got a loose screw. Happens when you smoke a trainload of pot."

The waitress brought them coffee. Liz opened her notebook to a page cluttered with doodles and arrows. "Here's how we'll get my guitar back," she said.

"Better be Lord approved," Ruby said, glancing upward.

Liz pointed to the primitive sketch. "I'm sure the man in the clouds will OK this. Let's call my plan a drop, snag, and run. We'll use a cable and winch. I'll set a pulley on the big tree limb overhanging her roof. I'll open the skylight, you lower me in, winch me out with the goods."

Ruby gave her a look that would scare a bear. "Sister, you crazy? How'll I raise your white ass up and down? Where you getting the circus stuff?"

"Don't worry about it. I grew up around pile drivers. Daddy was in the rigging business. I know all about shackles, sheaves, turnbuckles, cable. Phone book shows ten rigging shops in Port Townsend, some rent rigging."

Ruby begged Liz to replace the winch plan with lipstick, flashy clothes, perfume, and sexy talk. She restated her fear that April's boyfriend would shoot if he heard any suspicious noise. It took a Rueben sandwich, four colas, and a hundred dollar bill for Ruby to go along with the winch plan.

They descended the stairs after lunch without incident. Ruby spied a church spire a few blocks down Water Street. "I'm going to visit God," she said, "say a few prayers, make sure the cables don't break. See you later at the Dungeness."

Liz drove a few minutes to Kanga Rigging, a boxcar-like building sheathed in shingles last painted during the Eisenhower administration. She strode over the crushed shell path to a screened porch where a caged mynah bird cawed a lewd greeting. A lean man about fifty, in dungaree overalls and greasy leather vest, introduced himself as Jerry the owner and offered his grimy hand. "I need to raise a big birdhouse up about fifty feet," Liz said, shaking his hand and looking into his eyes. "You rent rigging?"

Jerry rubbed his eyes, put on his glasses, and panned Liz from her eye shadow, across the bumps on her black blouse, over the V in her jeans, to her pink sneakers. "Not used to slick woman with bright eyes in my shop. Usually grubby riggers in here. You play the Blues Festival? You a blues queen?"

"Yah, I'm kind of a blues queen. I'm not playing. I'm here to help a friend."

"Which boat you with?"

"I came by car. A friend wants to do something nice for her sick mother by hanging a birdhouse way up a tree. The mother loves watching birds from her bed. I want to shackle a few chokers under a headache ball and pick and place the birdhouse. Thing weighs a hundred and fifty pounds."

Jerry removed his glasses and rubbed his beard. "Thirty years in this shop, never heard a woman talk rigging like you. What type of birds you attracting with a hundred and fifty pound birdhouse?"

"Seagulls."

"You two-blocking me? Seagulls don't live in birdhouses."

"Maybe it's crows or pigeons. I'm a city girl, not into birds. I need to rent enough rigging to raise a big load."

"Where's the house? I've got a buddy in the tree business with a bucket truck, looking for work. He'd pick and place the birdhouse for short money. You'll get squished like a pancake if the rigging slips."

"Don't worry about me and rigging. I could probably out-rig your ass. My daddy was a union pile driver. We had spools of two and a quarter cable in our back yard. I stacked shackles and turnbuckles when I was a kid. The pick has to happen when the mother is asleep. It's a surprise, a loud bucket truck won't work. I need a one day winch and cable rental. Don't give me junk. I'll pay in cash so you can buy paint for your shingles."

Jerry nodded like a seasoned waiter. He walked a few feet to a wash station, squirted orange soap on his hands, and said, "The more you talk about this, the wackier it sounds. Come back in an hour, I'll see if I can rustle up what you need."

Jerry shuffled through his back room thinking the boat school crew was retaliating for a prank. Liz walked a few hundred feet to a stone jetty and watched the long schooner *Adventuress* sail from the harbor basin. Several dozen passengers wearing puffy lifejackets waved from the deck. She watched the vessel round a corner, headed toward the strait. When it vanished behind a knoll, she walked back to the rigging shop. Jerry wheeled out a suitcase-size metal box. "This'll do the trick," he said. "One day rental, ninety-five bucks plus tax, call it a hundred. If you get minced by the cable, have your next-of-kin return the rigging as is. I'll pressure-wash your gizzards off it."

Liz gave Jerry a hundred dollar bill. He waived her behind the counter to the back room and opened a gear box. "Pay attention," he said. "Here's a hundred feet of cable that'll handle a three hundred pound load. Use these leather gloves, those tiny broken cable wires called meat hooks will turn your girl fingers bloody."

"I know all about meat hooks," Liz said.

"I'm sure you do," Jerry said. "Wrap the pulley and chain around a high part of the tree on a limb wider than your neck. Dance the cable over the sheave to the ground then clip the headache ball to the end. It weighs about ten pounds. It'll keep the cable taut. Attach the load to the hook on the bottom of the ball. I threw in a few picking straps and chokers. You a roger-copy on that?"

"Roger-copy," Liz replied.

Standing on a step ladder, Jerry clipped the pulley to a shackle hanging from a steel beam and threaded the cable through the pulley. "Tie the winch to a car bumper or a big healthy tree. Battery is good for three hours. Plug it into your idling car's cigarette lighter to keep the charge. Once it's rigged, push the red button, the cable will coil, load will go up. Start praying after five feet." He repacked the rigging in the box. "Don't stand under the load. If something goes wrong, they'll bury you in a pizza box. And tie a tag line to the load so it won't sway out of control."

"Roger-copy," Liz said.

Jerry put the box of rigging into Liz's car trunk. In the shade of the Dungeness parking lot, she showed Ruby the wire and gear. "Down at the basin, I saw a sailor hop into a harness connected to a cable. Another guy turned a winch, in a few seconds the sailor was at the top of a mast. Let's do a dry run, over in those trees. I'll rig it up, you push a button, raise me up, lower me down. Easy as baby's breath."

"Hold on sis," Ruby said. "What happens if you get stuck up the tree and the Fire Department gets called? If I blow probation, I'm back in the can, for a long stay."

"I'm on probation, too" Liz said. "I'm also hell-bent to get back our stuff. You only break probation if they catch you. Let's try it out over there."

They wheeled the rigging box a few hundred feet to a stand of trees. Liz climbed twenty feet up a tall fir, wrapped the pulley over a thick limb, threaded the cable over the sheave, shimmied down, and chained the winch to the car. She stood on the hook below the headache ball, clutching the greasy cable with gloved hands. Ruby pressed the winch button. Liz ascended like Peter Pan. Fifteen feet above the ground, she said, with shaky voice, "No problem. Safe, quick, and easy."

"Try the stunt in dark fog with the wind blowing and a nutcase loaded for bear ready to pepper you with buckshot," Ruby said after Liz landed softly on the ground.

"Dammit," Liz said. "I paid your way out here. If you don't want to help, get on a bus, go home. I'll make pretty, go downtown, have one of them sailor boys help me."

Ruby borrowed a bus schedule from the innkeeper. Liz loaded the rigging into her car. She told Ruby on the porch stairs, "You may think I'm a spoiled Brooklyn chick. I'm really a hard-ass, smashed a few heads, done hard time."

"Figured as much," Ruby said. "You talk with an in-your-face prison way. How'd you end up in jail?"

"Stupid boyfriend wanted to take me on a vacation. Idiot made me wait outside a bank as he cashed a check. He pulled a gun at a teller, got a bag of money, came to ninety-five large. We hid out for a day. I'm making reservations for Tahiti, a hundred cops busted down the door. Boyfriend tried to save his ass. He told the judge I planned the stickup because I had a drug habit. I don't do drugs. He got twenty in the can. I got one for driving the getaway."

"You still have feelings for him?"

"Yah, I'd like to shoot him, chop him up for lobster bait. He's a bad combo of stupid and arrogance."

"Seeing we're both on the good girl track," Ruby said, "let's forget the circus act. Us city babes will screw this up. As we say on the street, it's the last three feet, people talking to people, one on one. I did my best cons six inches from the mark's face, looking them in the eye. Wore tight threads, spicy scent. I purred in their ear, they quivered and shivered. This afternoon, we'll get pretty and knock on April's door when she's good n' stoned."

Liz screamed into her palm, and then, in a hoarse, calm voice, agreed to Ruby's suggestion.

9 PLUCK

Liz and Ruby stopped at Kanga Rigging on the way to April's house. Their womanly scents rendered the mynah bird speechless. Jerry's eyes almost fell from their sockets when they lifted the box of rigging to the counter. He felt faint when Ruby ran her bright red fingernails over her shimmering white blouse. Liz said the pick went as planned. A family of eagles had moved into the birdhouse and her friend's mother loved watching the birds feed their young. Jerry thanked the rigging gods for letting this transaction occur without mangling the customer.

Liz parked on April's driveway behind an orange 1966 Dodge Dart station wagon. The boxy vehicle with a push-button transmission shifter and slant-six motor was the same vehicle April had packed with flower children and drove to the first Woodstock festival. She could have bought a new Ferrari with the money spent on its reacquisition and restoration.

April, hidden by a purple drape, watched the unexpected visitors land on her porch. She greeted Ruby with a hug. Ruby introduced Liz as Cassy Collins, a guitar thief from Jersey City. April's yellow sundress skimmed the floor as she led her guests into the living room, across the cloudy rug, to pea green leather chairs. Tall windows overlooked a watery expanse and snow-capped Mt. Baker. April's long blond hair glistened when she sat in front of the windows.

"We're chasing axes in Seattle," Ruby said, "figured we'd take the boat over and say hello. We're checking out the usual places like blues clubs, hotel rooms, apartment closets. A shill wants a Martin D-2. Cassie's looking to lift a 60s Telecaster for a guy in Boston. So far, no luck. Old pickers sleep with their guitars. They get paid in cash, most pack heat. Stealing is hard work these days."

"Take a load off and suck in the new view," April said with an angelic smile. "Last time, you couldn't see the water. Steve cut down every tree in the way. Couple neighbors lost some big firs. Tree warden fussed. Steve growled at him and resolved the matter. Neighbors threatened a lawsuit. Steve flashed his pistol, haven't heard boo from them."

"Steve here?" Ruby asked.

"Got business out East."

"Tell him I said hello."

"Better not. He hates you for some reason."

"He's jealous. I get the good axes before him."

April lit several cinnamon scented candles and set them on the coffee table. "No patchouli?" asked Ruby. "Last time this place was patchouli heaven."

"I inhaled too much of it over the years," April said. "Stuff makes me queasy."

"You still smoke pot?"

"Oh, yeah, but not for fun," April said. "I've got a serious, old hippie chick disease called fibromyalgia. Every morning, I feel like I got thrown out of an airplane. Only cure is medical marijuana. I send Trillium, my herb facilitator, to San Fran every month. She brings back medicine with more kick than the weed sold on Port Townsend streets. In fact, my joints ache. You girls care to share a dose?"

"Let's do it," Ruby said. "It may cure my hot flashes."

April emptied a jar of golden cannabis on the coffee table. She pinched a few spongy buds, slid a cigarette paper from a leather case, and with one hand, twirled the paper and buds into a chubby joint. She licked the paper edge, ran the joint through her pursed lips, settled the joint with her front teeth, and lit it with a wooden match. When she inhaled a cubic yard of pungent smoke, the end of the joint glowed like a nebula. Liz, holding the joint with swagger, sputtered on a half-hearted drag. Ruby took a timid toke. "Can't inhale," she said, holding a cough. "We're on the prowl tonight. Got to stay on the up and up."

April drew on the joint like a noosed convict puffing their last

Lucky Strike. With her eyes closed, she held the medicinal smoke in her lungs for a full minute. Liz and Ruby, feeling the potency of the medicine, declined additional tokes. April puffed and wheezed until the joint became a dark speck. She sat back and stared at the wall, ending her trance by asking Ruby, "Still got the Martin lifted from a minister? Twenty grand for a five grand guitar didn't work for me."

"I sold it to a musician. He gave it back to the blind bastard. I'll steal it again if you'll pay ten."

"Naw, Let the old boy keep it. You'd steal a gold tooth from a corpse."

"Price of gold makes it a no-brainer."

April set her squinty eyes on Liz. "What brings you into the picture?" she asked.

"Ruby and I shared a cell at Bedford Hills," Liz replied. "Found out Ruby knows guitars. These days, I play guitar, hang with musicians, make a nice living stealing their instruments. They never suspect a musician."

"Who you playing with these days?" April asked.

"During the week, rhythm with a South Jersey band. Fill-in with Manhattan bands on weekends."

"If you clip anything vintage, give me a call. I pay cash for gear played by the famous. If you girls have a spare minute, you want to check out my music room? Just don't steal anything."

"I've seen it," Ruby said. "Cassy would get a kick out of the wall hangings."

April led them past a hallway wall covered with random orange and purple brush strokes to a gray metal door. She punched four numbers on a keyboard. They entered the studio and walked by a storage room to an orange wall holding several dozen instruments.

"Got two million bucks, or fifty prison years, on this wall," April said with a laugh. She stepped onto a small stage. "A dude from Stellar Studios in LA built the room. I spent a hundred grand on security with motion detectors." She pointed to hefty gun barrels mounted on the ceiling. "If anyone breaks-in through the skylight, they'll be mincemeat before they hit the ground."

Liz asked about the vintage amplifiers and speakers cluttering the stage. "Bought them from a guy who lifted them from a LA studio." April said. "I hate digital junk. It's only loud analog for me. I want my music sounding like it did when my generation ruled the world. The wall insulation is thick as a mattress. We fired blanks from those guns up there and didn't hear anything in the main house. I can grab a guitar, play till dawn. Neighbors think I have an exercise studio in here."

Liz noticed framed black and white photographs on the wall next to the storage room. "Jimi Hendrix's favorite sound engineer was a world-class photographer," April said. "I bought the photos from him. I'm a Hendrix freak." She pointed at a row of autographed black and white pictures. "When I was a groupie, I slid under the covers with these the guitar gods. When I got a few wrinkles, they didn't want any part of me, so I had my people steal their guitars. I live and breathe these babies, think about the old days of no work and loose morals."

"Whose purple Strat is on the rack?" Ruby asked. "Wasn't here last time."

"You're looking at Lance Perkins' Violet. A collector paid a million for it, loaned it to the Seattle museum where Steve volunteers. Steve bought some banged-up Strats on the Internet and made one guitar from the parts. Scuffed it like the original, switched it during the loan. Crowds grooved at the phony guitar. Owner doesn't know the difference. Let's take a listen." She took Violet from the rack, stepped on the stage, wired the guitar for sound, tuned the strings, and toed a kick-pedal. Lights dimmed. Shades covered the skylights. A video of a loud audience appeared on the floor-to-ceiling monitor behind Liz and Ruby. A light beam shined on April's picking hand. Another monitor behind the stage showed Lance's band tuning their instruments for a 1968 concert.

April clipped on a wireless microphone and pointed at a stainless steel box near the stage. "The computer holds video of '70 Isle of Wight, '67 Monterrey Pop, the first Woodstock, and a hundred other rock concerts. Newest one is '73 Watkins Glen. After that, disco ruined the scene. I'll play the first track, mute Lance's playing."

Roars from thirty thousand stoners made Liz and Ruby to block their ears. Lance's bassist and drummer laid down a sweet line. April fumbled a few chords and sang some kooky lyrics. "This place makes me feel like a hot chick without a care in the world," she said while noticing the bag of potato chips next to a speaker. She tore the bag open, stuffed a handful into her mouth, then another, and another. The speakers broadcast the ravenous demise of the rippled chips. She tossed the empty bag on the floor next to an empty, crinkled bag of Cheeze Doodles. "Bad thing about medical marijuana is chronic munchies," she said. "I gained twenty pounds since I upped my dosage. Let's get takeout delivered."

April reactivated the security system. A half hour later, she put six cartons of Chinese food on the dining room table. Liz and Ruby nibbled on fried rice. April emptied the fried shrimp carton and devoured most of the chicken fingers. Her eyes now crimson slits, she pushed aside the General Tso's chicken, cut short a sloggy sentence, rested her head on the table, and shut her eyes.

"Same thing happened last time." Ruby whispered to Liz. "Food tasted like it was cooked in motor oil. Halfway through a sentence, she crashed. A bomb won't wake her. Follow me."

Ruby punched the four correct numbers on the security door keyboard. "When I was jacking ATM's," she said. "I got good at looking over shoulders, stealing pins."

They walked past the stage to the storage room where a workbench held some cardboard boxes. Ruby read the shipping label of the top box, sent by a Chicago used guitar shop. The box below it had a Phoenix, Arizona return address. The bottom box, shipped from Leeward, Maine, made a clanky sound when lifted. Ruby put the box on the floor with the shipping label down. She cut the box with her switchblade and brushed aside a layer of balled newspaper, exposing Jasper's baby-blue finish.

"I've got it! I've got it! I've got it in my hands!" Liz said. Under the guitar she saw Spoon's coiled washboard and a spoon shaped package wrapped with newspaper and duct tape.

Ruby put her hand over Liz's mouth. "Hush up," she said. "Grab the box, follow me, put the box in your car."

Liz carried the box by sleeping April to their car. A mile away, parked on a church parking lot, Ruby told her nervous accomplice, "If she finds out we stole her toys, we're goners. Watch how a real guitar thief works." She took the items from the box and put them in the trunk and left the box of crinkled newspaper on the back seat. They traveled a few miles to a department store. Using different checkout lines, they each bought a cast iron skillet, three metal pie pans, and packing tape. They went across town to a heavily treed section of Fort Worden State Park and parked on a secluded street. Ruby wrapped the skillets and pans with the Maine newspapers and packed the utensils in the box. By flipping the box over before cutting it, the shipping label remained intact. Liz sealed the parcel with tape. When she shook the box, the package sounded and hefted like it did in April's studio.

They sped to April's driveway. Liz waited in the car while Ruby looked in the living room window. April was prone on a sofa, looking embalmed, but breathing with vigor. Ruby waved Liz into the house. In the studio, they placed the repacked parcel under the two other packages. Before they left the house, Ruby wrote a note, "Good to see you, hun. Thanks for the chow. Keep in touch. I'm scooping a nice Tele next week, one you'll love. Rube and Cass." She put the note under a pair of chopsticks. A breeze fluttered the parachute on the ceiling as they left the room.

To avoid conversing with the chatty Dungeness innkeeper, Liz carried Jasper, wrapped in a blanket, to their room. Ruby hid the washboard and silverware with a sweater. In the room, under a light, Liz looked for a new dent or ding on Jasper. The guitar looked like it did when Johnny first put it on her lap. She read aloud a note taped to the guitar body: "April, got this new Durrell 335 from a young bitch. Overnight 5K cash to my NYC address. Pluck."

When Ruby heard the name Pluck, she threw her hands upward and said, "Oh, no, not Pluck. Sells to gangsters. Master of disguise. Fearless. Twice as mean as Steve."

"Come on," Liz said. "He can't be all bad."

"Sure is," Ruby said. "Your life means nothing to him. He's been clipping guitars for years, bagged some good ones."

Ruby stopped Liz from cutting the newspaper covering the coiled washboard. "Rule number one with hot gear, mail the stuff out of town, quick, in separate packages. We're in deep trouble if the cops or baddies find us with the booty." She refused to ship the goods from Port Townsend, so they drove an hour to the coastal town of Sequim and shipped the instruments to Liz's New York City apartment.

Liz and Ruby checked out of the Dungeness the next morning. They drove directly to the Sea/Tac airport, bypassing the humorless ferry dogs capable of picking up cannabis scent on their clothes. They landed in New York City at dusk. Liz handed Ruby five, hundred dollar bills during their cab ride to Manhattan, money destined for Reverend Whitley's collection basket.

10 HARD MONEY

Minutes after landing at JFK, Liz called Spoons. He answered the call while riding in Bucky's bus on the Baltimore Beltway. "Holy mother Mary," he said after hearing the news. "You saved my ass. Figured my stuff was melted scrap by now. My new washboard sounds like a wet towel. The spoons sound plastic. They gave me gravy stirrers, not tin slappers. You get your guitar?"

"Sure did. Found the person who stole it, stole it back."

"I'm damn thankful. We're gigging in D.C. all week. Text me when you have the metal. I'll take the next train going your way."

"Will do," said Liz. "I can't wait to see you slap your frot on Broadway."

Jetlag and fatigue kept Liz in pajamas the next day. Sarah visited her that afternoon. "Glad you made it back alive," she said. "I've been worried about you being with Ruby. How'd it go?"

"Got what I wanted." Liz said. "Ruby pulled it off."

"Flat out amazing," Sarah said. "Left town with a hooker and came back with your guitar. This sounds like one hell of a story. Or a good song."

"Keep the notebook in your purse. If you print this tale, you'll find me and Ruby floating in the Hudson, face down."

"Ruby behave? She do any tricks for spare change? Shuffle through your wallet? She must have stolen something."

"The only thing she shuffled was about a hundred Bible pages.

She was all-in after I convinced her God would go along with stealing my guitar back. She sweet-talked her way into the bad girl's house, everything went smooth. Anything happening in your world?"

"Lenny is pushing me every day. He's got his team ready to make a hundred thousand copies. His Internet sites are ready to charge twenty dollars for a download. He guaranteed a million dollar gross the first year. In short, now we'll get two hundred grand if you hand over the music."

Liz, ignoring Sarah's plea, carried a cup of coffee into the living room and watched television. Sarah, standing in front of the screen, unloaded a swear-laden tirade about her sister's selfishness, lack of a steady boyfriend, and money stolen from their mother's pocketbook in 1997. Liz responded with a pointed batch of insults. She ended the vitriol by calmly saying, "I'm trying hard not to beat your head into pulp. Stop jamming me about selling the music. For now, I'm keeping the *Chessman's* out of Lenny's hands. I don't like the guy. He spent time in prison for swindling royalties from half-dead musicians. If I sell to him, I'll get blackballed from the blues scene. I'm holding-off for now. If I need money, I'll build a website, sell downloads, but only after Chaz croaks. I'm keeping record companies out of the deal. To get you back on your feet, I've got a plan B to make some quick cash."

"Will it top two hundred grand plus residuals?" Sarah asked.

"No, but it'll be easy money. The stoner bitch we stole my guitar from has a Hendrix fixation. Babe is loaded with money with a brain cooked on weed. She'd pay big for a copy of the *Chessman's*."

"Hey, wait a minute. Are you whacked out? I've got a line to a big payout and you're blowing me off? I'm days from foreclosure, owe thirty grand on credit cards. You want to go back to the scene of your scam to pull another con job?"

"You've got no say in what I do with the *Chessman's*," Liz said, inches from her sister. "You had nothing to do with stealing it. I've got years of probation left. If Chaz turns me in, I'm back in the slammer."

"Who cares if Chaz gets pissed? If we sell out, we'll swim in money. I'll tell the tale of the *Chessman's* in my book, sell millions of copies. Prove Hendrix and Miles recorded together. I'll be on talk shows and book tours around the world. You'll play stadiums. We'll send Chaz a few bucks to shut him up. You won't need him and his twangy guitar anymore."

"Your plan ain't happening," Liz said. "April, the woman we stole from, will melt when she hears the *Chessman's*. She hates digital music, so we can't sell her a CD copy. I know a place that'll copy the CD's to vinyl. I'll fly out west, lay it on her turntable, drop the needle, stuff big bucks in my purse. No one will ever know what I did. She's paranoid, won't let anyone hear it. Chaz won't know. I'll pocket the cash. Get another look at her guitar collection."

"How much will she pay?"

"I'll ask for fifty thousand. Pocket change for her."

"How you paying for the trip?"

"Savings bonds. Aunt Jane gave me an envelope full for college."

"I'll go with you."

"No way, this is big girl stuff. I'm calling my assistant."

Sarah, angered by the snub, paced the apartment. Liz took her phone into her bedroom and called Ruby. "You took a shine to those hundreds," she said. "You want more? I have something April would love to own. I need your help selling it to her. You'll get another five hundred and expenses if you fly back to Seattle with me, help me do the deal. It'll take three days, maybe four.

"Honey, I went along with stealing your guitar," Ruby said, "Selling booty ain't happening. I've made a commitment to the Lord: no more stealing and hooking. I want a clean slate and a nice pad when he calls me to heaven."

"I figured you could use the money. No problem. Say hi to the boys."

Liz told Sarah, "Ruby is a no go. You're in. I'll book two seats on a Friday flight to Seattle. Gives us three days to pack."

Sarah scanned her smart phone calendar. "Yah, that'll work. I'll blow-off some research, hide from my agent. When we get there, you deal with the stoner princess. I'll look pretty, smile, stay quiet."

"Stoned out April isn't a problem," Liz said. "Steve, her boyfriend, sounds like trouble. He wasn't around last trip. I hope he's still not around. Let's pull it off and make a buck."

"I'm in," Sarah said. "I'll go get my clothes from the dry cleaner."

The next day, a Times Square record shop technician copied the *Chessman* CD's to four vinyl LP's and slid each one into a paper sleeve and white album cover. Liz stored the LP's at her apartment then took the subway to Chaz's apartment. After a dozen knocks, sleepy Chaz welcomed her. "I was dreaming about playing in front of a million people," he said. "Just as I struck the first note, you knocked. How was your trip?"

"We got most of our stuff," Liz said. "Ruby did the trick. She knows Port Townsend like a native. Talked me out of a high wire act. We picked the instruments from some rich babe. They should be in my apartment in a few days."

"What a relief," Chaz said. "Solves our guitar shortage. I'll tell Johnny we're all set. Ruby is something. I've never seen a woman change overnight from a backstabber and arm stabber into a do-gooder. She steals from the rich and gives back to a couple poor-ass musicians."

"She's a hundred percent with the Lord. Sure helped us in the luck department."

"The guitar OK?"

"Jasper seems fine. Thank God, whoever stole the stuff knew what they were doing. Me and my guitar are good to go. Kenny and Pearly rested and ready?"

"All systems normal. They called every afternoon from the Backbeat, feeling no pain. Said they loved me like a father and felt bad because they charged up my tab."

Chaz put a list of upcoming gigs on Liz's lap. Over the next few months, they'd play in Trenton, Long Island, Boston, and New York City. Her enthusiasm waned when the song list showed the same twenty blues standards at each gig. The newest song on the list, a blues ballad written in 1967, had a sluggish beat and lewd lyrics guaranteed to clear the dance floor. The other songs, with their lazy, string-bent notes, would make patrons dawdle in the restroom, chat at the bar, or dash to the exit. She tossed the list on a table. Playing second guitar in a four piece band felt like a waste of time. She knew the real action was in New Orleans, where zydeco bands like Bucky's played packed night clubs.

"I'll see you at our next gig, week from this Friday," Chaz said. "Small club off Time Square."

"Sounds good. My sister and I are visiting our aunt for a few days. I'll call you next week, when I get back."

When Liz got home, she accepted delivery of two boxes from the state of Washington. She opened the smaller box first and unwrapped the washboard and spoon. She told Spoons by phone, "Your frot looks pretty on my belly. No dents or kinks. Shining like a headlight, ready for a good whupping. Only got one spoon."

Spoons, distraught over the missing silverware, said he'd take the next train from DC. Liz put the larger parcel on a table, cut the wrapping, opened the flaps, and spent a few weepy seconds staring at her treasured guitar resting on a bed of packing. Eager to check out the guitar's condition, she failed to notice a few manly fingerprints on the guitar's body. The neck and headstock seemed OK, but the guitar had a half-inch wide dimple below the fingerboard. Fortunately, the guitar wood wasn't cracked, only the finish, so the ding wouldn't affect the tone. She plugged Jasper into an amplifier, aimed a speaker at an open window, turned the volume to its highest level, and sent a dozen bluesy chords over the buzzing Manhattan street. The guitar sounded like its first play in the Arkansas church.

Spoons dashed into Liz's apartment around dinner time wearing a dark blue jump suit with a prominent spoon embroidered on the lapel. He hugged Liz for a full minute. Freed from his embrace, she placed the washboard over his shoulders and put the spoon in his hand. Spoons responded with one of the toothiest smiles ever seen in New York City. He spooned his shiny breast plate and sang a few bars of "Jambalaya", adding the lyrics, "Sweet Liz, the blues queen who saved my ass." A dead sound made him check the frottoir from stem to stern. He found some spongy newsprint stuck in a ripple, easily removed with a toothpick. His joy turned to anger when he saw fifty years of tarnish missing from the spoon. He claimed tarnish gave the spoon a soft tone and polished silver made the frot sound hollow.

"Get over it." Liz said. "The tarnish will return in a few days. The crook probably wanted the spoon to look good when he fenced it, so he buffed it up. When you get back to DC, buy another spoon from one of those stores where brides buy silverware. You're lucky some of your stuff is back. Whoever stole your frot sold it to a whack job with a thing for stolen instruments. I found out the hard way Durrells are worth their weight in gold."

"Why'd she buy my board? She need a new grill for her Rolls?"

"She'll buy anything musical made between the late 50s and the early 70s. She hangs the stuff on her wall, plays them once in a while. Our instruments aren't wall hangings, they need playing, by us."

"Will I get shot if I play my frot?"

"You may. Tell everyone you're playing a new one. Someday the bad people will find out we replaced our boxed-up instruments with skillets and pie plates. I'd hate to be the person who shipped the goods from Maine. The woman who had the stuff isn't nice."

Spoons stroked his washboard and talked about his recently completed Louisiana tour. "I played ten jukes in ten days. Swamp people hollered for encores, the cops plowed them to the street."

"I'm headed down your way someday," Liz said. "Keep me in mind if you need a lead. For now, I'm hanging with Chaz. After that, I'm willing to travel, eat Cajun."

Liz accepted Spoons offer of dinner. He strapped his washboard to his belly and put the spoon in his lapel pocket. When they entered the dining room of a Midtown restaurant, waiters and diners ignored Spoons' regalia. Spoons maintained his smile through the main course, desert, coffee, and numerous drinks. He paid the check around midnight, ten minutes after the last southbound train left Penn Station. He wanted to take a bus, but Liz talked him into staying the night on her couch. In the early morning, feigning discomfort, he crawled into Liz's bed. The next morning he gave Liz a prolonged kiss and boarded a train.

A couple days after Spoons departure, Sarah and Liz landed in Seattle. They bypassed the ferry and drove two hours to Port Townsend where Liz rented a room in a peach-colored motel on the harbor edge. She paid for two nights with cash and signed the guest log as Cassandra Collins and Erin McKenna. After dropping their luggage in their room, they walked to a downtown pub. Over burritos and beer, Liz told Sarah, "Time to ditch your Ivy League look. Lay on some eye shadow, uplift your sag, frizz your hair. Let's slide you into tight clothes, make you look like a grifter, not a stockbroker."

"You're not whoring me up," Sarah said. "I spent hours in finishing school learning to walk like a lady. I'm not doing the perp strut, like you."

"This town is the end of the world," Liz said. "You've got to fit in with the scene. Do it for the money. We'll do some errands, rest up, make our pitch to April tomorrow afternoon. Steak and martinis on me after we pull this off."

They followed lunch with a visit to a boutique where Sarah tried on a pair of black jeans. Liz, noticing a loose fit around the waist, made her shoehorn into one size smaller. A saleslady topped Sarah off with a black tee shirt with pink musical notes embroidered on the front, several gaudy bracelets, and a tinny broche shaped like a G-clef. Sarah left the fitting room looking like a cast member of a punk rock musical. Liz hid Sarah's corporate haircut with a red-banded pork pie hat. Sarah nixed black, webby, stiletto heels in favor of black sneakers. Liz paid cash for the new outfit. A block from the boutique, Sarah said she needed a long walk to break-in her new footwear. Liz, needing a break from her sister, went back to the motel.

Over breakfast, the sisters planned their visit to April's house. "We'll let her wake up, smoke a few joints," Liz said. "She's a mean cuss if you show up early. We'll get there about five this afternoon. As long as Steve is gone, we'll be fine. When we get to her house, I'll start the conversation. When you smoke her pot, don't inhale, it's strong enough to drop a mule."

"I'm not smoking drugs," Sarah said. "Stuff is addictive."

"Just take a little puff," Liz said. "Pretend you're stoned. Say far out and smile."

With a half day wait, Liz and Sarah, dressed like frugal tourists, traveled to a beach near Fort Worden with a windy view of the Strait of Juan de Fuca and the Canadian coast. They walked through a lapse in the grassy dunes to a sand spit where fishermen dancing lures in the surf tempted ling cod. Early afternoon, they returned to the motel and changed into their blues chick outfits.

"You look like Suzie the Floozie," Liz told her sister. "Eye shadow makes you look like a cat, hat tops it off nicely. Tight jeans show every curve, even your beer gut."

"It's not a gut," said Sara."If I knew you were going to put me into little girl clothes, I'd have dropped a few pounds."

"Don't worry about it," Liz said as she pointed to her belly. "Blues babes have beer guts. Overall, you look cute."

Liz parked in April's driveway a few minutes after five, behind the hallowed station wagon. She strutted to the stoop and rang April's doorbell. Sarah cowered in a shadow with the brow of her hat hiding her eyes. A wide-shouldered man with a ruddy face wearing a red flannel shirt opened the door and barked, "Whatta you want?"

Liz, holding a plastic shopping bag, stepped forward. "Hey dude," she said. "Let me see April. I'm an old friend."

"She's napping," he said. "What's this about? You trick-or-treating a few months early?"

"It's about some business," Liz said. The bag slipped a few inches, but her grasp held.

"What kind of business? I'm the Lord of this Manor. I handle all the business around here."

"I'm princess Cassandra Collins, a friend of Ruby Ralston. I was here last week with Ruby. This is my friend, queen Erin McKenna."

"You girls into a goth thing?" he asked.

April's sleepy face and pillow bent hair appeared next to his shoulder. "Cassie, what brings you back to fog city?" she asked.

"Got some music you should hear," Liz said.

"Please come in," April said with a sunny smile. "Meet Steve, my business manager." Steve ignored Liz's extended hand. April led them to the dining room table where a silver tray held a brick of marijuana partially wrapped with cellophane. "My herbalist just drove this up from Los Angeles," she said. "She claims this medicine cures every ailment known by man and I believe her. Smoked some for breakfast; turned my life into a silly movie. Let's fire some up."

Steve sat on a long redwood bench between Liz and Sarah. He placed a gleaming handgun flat on the table with the business end aimed at Liz's breastbone. "Varmint problem around here," he said. He sliced the brick open with a box cutter, sprinkled a pinch of spongy pot onto a cigarette paper and rolled a pudgy joint with one hand. Sarah felt a sneeze gestate after breathing the pungent herb. Steve eyed Sarah's uplifted bust like a panther stalking a gazelle.

April lit the joint with a diamond encrusted Zippo She filled her lungs with blue smoke and passed the joint to Liz who pretended to suck in the same volume. Steve's clothespin-like fingers snared the joint. He cupped his hands and simultaneously sucked smoke through his nose and mouth. He held the smoke for a half-minute then exhaled a smoke ring that dispersed on Liz's hair. Sarah drew confidently on the joint, but inhaled when she was supposed to exhale. Too afraid to cough, she squeaked like a caught mouse as her lungs fought the smoke.

"Hey babe, leave a little for me," April said with a giggle. She eased the joint away and killed the ember with a monstrous toke, cackling like a witch as she put the roach into the belly of a porcelain Buddha. With the conversation stopped dead, Sarah's manner changed from deer-in-the-headlights fear to nonchalance. Steve, unaffected by the dosage, chewed cashews, scanned phone messages, and looked mean. Liz disrupted the communal stupor by taking the *Chessman* LP's out of the bag and saying, "Here's a secret session with two famous musicians and their friends. Let's play it. You guess who's on it."

"You're a good girl bringing me vinyl," April said. She led everyone into the studio. Steve put the first album on a turntable. Seconds later, loud guitar chords filled the room.

"Sounds like Hendrix," April said. "Never heard this session."

When a brash trumpet sounded familiar, April gave Steve the cut sign and asked Liz, "Is this Hendrix and Miles Davis playing together? This never happened. You trying to screw me with some fancy track splicing?"

"It's real," Liz said. "Don't worry about how I got it. You're hearing Miles and Hendrix jam with a few friends. It's the only copy and it's for sale."

Steve rolled up the sleeves on his sweaty shirt. "I smell a scam," he said. "You mixed a few stray tracks, made it sound like they played together."

"Sorry for making you hot and bothered," Liz said. "You're listening to real music, just as it happened"

"Let's hear it through," April said. "Then we'll figure out whose bluffing who."

Steve lowered the stylus on the first track. April shut her eyes and grooved on the hefty guitar chords, brash horns, and gutty percussion. Steve played all four LP's, isolating Hendrix's guitar on the last track. When the music ended, April said, "Far out sounds. I want it. Where was it recorded?"

"In Harlem, place called Chessman Studio," Liz said. "I knew the tech who recorded it. When he died, I found the records in his closet."

Steve examined one of the LPs. "No way. This is new vinyl,

shiny and flexible. Old LP's are heavier, have a dull finish. You got the master tapes or acetates?"

"This is all I got," Liz said. "The guy died with no relatives. He's not talking."

"How much for the LPs?" April asked.

"Fifty thousand cash," Liz said.

A second after Liz said the word *cash*, Steve turned into a bellowing monster. The outburst made him short of breath and shaking. He told April, "No way, honey, she's crazy. I care for you, and I want you to know these are copies, not source. Miss Cassie will copy the masters; sell them to everyone and their mother."

"Shut up for once in your life," April said. "They're Dynaflex, from the '70s. If someone had the masters they'd have cashed in a long time ago. When did the tech die?"

"He passed a year ago, without a will," Liz said. "Estate got caught up in probate. A few months ago, Erin and I jimmied his lock, looked for guits, found the records. Grabbed a few old Martins and a Gibson bass."

April relocated the negotiations to her spongy lawn. Sarah and Liz stayed on the upper terrace close to a stone sculpture of a feminine form thrusting a sword into a man's back. April and Steve walked down a stone stairway to a religious shrine where they swore and argued for ten minutes. When they returned to the upper lawn, April said, "Not doing fifty, I'll pay fifteen cash. Take it or leave it."

"You make it twenty, it's a deal," Liz replied.

April shook Liz's hand. Steve handed Liz a loose stack of hundreds. She stuffed the cash into her pocketbook without counting it. "We have an early morning flight," she said. "Must leave now. Pleasure dealing with you."

Steve offered the sisters lodging for the night. "Thank you for the kindness," Liz replied. "We're staying at Layla Point, at a condo owned by a friend."

"It's lovely over there, as long as the wind is blowing east," April said. "Thanks for bringing the tunes. I think I'll smoke another bone, listen to my new music. Keep me in mind if you run into any more goodies."

Liz and Sarah skittered across the lawn, past the Dodge, to their rental car. They sped to the motel and hid their car next to a stretched-out camper. In their room, Sarah put ten thousand dollars into her pocketbook. Liz hid her share under a stack of towels in the bathroom closet. They showered off their makeup, changed into casual garb, and walked to a natty restaurant where they celebrated their good fortune with delicate cuts of beef and martinis. Several times, the sisters laughed about April's bossy personality that surfaced when Steve talked tough.

Toward the end of her second martini, Sarah gave weepy thanks to her sister for having the fortitude to fly west and easily score twenty grand. Half the proceeds would delay her foreclosure and hold-off tenacious collection agents demanding payment. With no financial stress, she'd have the resources and relaxed attitude to finish her book.

The sisters returned to the motel and entered their room, lit only by stray lumens from a streetlight. Liz slid her hand along the wall and poked the light switch. Sarah removed her sweater and reached into the closet for a hanger. Steve jumped out and pointed a gun with a silencer at her pulsing carotid artery. "Shut up." he said. "I've killed before, I'll kill again."

Liz landed a punch on Steve's back. Sarah clawed his head. He swung his arm and struck Sarah's forehead with the gun butt. Liz heard the muffled crack of broken skull. Blood streamed down Sarah's face. She collapsed to the rug, whimpered for a few seconds, and lost consciousness. Liz jumped on Steve's back and landed a few stiff punches and cat scratches. Steve grabbed Liz by the hair and threw her to the floor. He pointed the gun at her head and said, "Gimme the twenty grand."

"Let me help her, you nasty bastard," Liz said. "You rip off people after April pays them? My sister is bleeding to death, you want money?" She crawled over to Sarah, who had regained consciousness.

"The room is spinning," Sarah said with blood dripping into her mouth. Ignoring Steve's guttural threats, Liz soaked a towel with cold water and held it to her sister's head.

"Forget about her, give me the cash," Steve said.

"We mailed ten grand back home," Liz said. "I spent a hundred on dinner. You can find what's left in the silver pocketbook on the floor."

Steve rifled Sarah's pocketbook. He removed the loose hundreds and stuffed them into his pocket. He took over three hundred dollars from Liz's wallet. "Your story had one hole in it, they don't let your type stay at Layla Point." He dropped a hundred dollar bill on the floor. "Get out of Port Townsend, don't ever come back. If you say a word to anyone, I'll hunt you down, fill your head with lead." He walked down the stairs and drove away.

Liz removed the towel from Sarah's face. Blood gushed from an inch-long gash over her right eyebrow. Her swollen forehead was blue and black. Sarah raised her head a few inches off the floor and asked what happened. Liz called 911. Within minutes, an ambulance squealed into the motel parking lot. Two EMT's and a police officer ran into the room. The bloody towel fell to the rug when they loaded Sarah onto a gurney. Sarah moaned and sobbed as the ambulance sped to the hospital. Liz sat on the ambulance floor, holding her sister's hand.

Sprinting emergency room nurses wheeled Sarah into the critical care unit. After a doctor took a lengthy look, he told Liz, "We'll stitch her up. It's a concussion with vertigo. I asked her what happened. She said she was drinking a martini and the lights went out. How many martinis did she drink?"

"It wasn't the booze. She's a sleep walker," Liz said. "I was asleep, heard a crash, found her banged up on the floor. Happens often."

"She's had quite a trauma," the doctor said. "You may say a few words to her."

Liz followed the doctor into a critical care ward where a nurse was sponging blood from Sarah's forehead. "What really happened to your sister?" the doctor asked Liz. "I interned in a big city hospital, saw hundreds of blunt force traumas. Someone smash her head with a baseball bat or a hammer?"

"No way," Liz said. "In the middle of the night, all hell broke loose. She's been a sleepwalker since her teens. I found her on the floor, near the edge of a coffee table."

The doctor, looking closely at the wound, said, "Your story doesn't fit. I'm reporting the injury to the police. I'm required by law. They'll get the real story."

Sarah moaned during her ride to surgery. Nurses updated Liz during the three hour procedure. At sunrise, the surgeon told Liz, "It took a hundred stitches to close the wound. It's near her eyebrow, a plastic surgeon can hide the scar. She has a concussion and a cerebral contusion. We shaved a few inches of hair. She'll have a black eye for a few weeks."

"When can she fly home to New York?"

"I'd like to keep her for a month, but her health insurance lapsed last week. If you can't work something out with billing, she must leave tomorrow."

Several hours later, a nurse led Liz behind a white linen curtain. Sarah opened her uncovered eye and said, "I'm a hurting girl."

Liz, seeing her sister's head mostly covered with gauze, said, "You sure got a whupping."

"Who hit me?" Sarah asked. "Last thing I remember, I'm in a restaurant. Then everything went blank."

Liz told her Steve struck her with a gun butt and stole ten thousand dollars from her purse. Sarah raised her head a few inches from the pillow. "Steve who?" she asked. "What ten thousand? What are you talking about? Is this a dream?"

"I'll explain later. For now, tell everyone you fell while sleepwalking."

A nurse checked the tubes and monitoring wires connected to Sarah. Minutes after the nurse left the room, a Port Townsend policewoman stood next to Sarah's bed. "Detective Ricker here. Who assaulted you?" Liz said a few words. The detective told her to keep quiet.

"Ma'am," Sarah replied. "I walked into a table or something."

The fifty year old detective with a curt demeanor paced the room. "Seems you girls are city slickers," she said. "Came to town for no good reason. One dressed like a prostitute, one dressed like a blues queen. Used phony names. You're Sarah O'Malley, a writer. Cassandra is really your sister Liz, a musician. You should have made up another name. Nobody names their kid Cassandra. I'm here because a doctor thinks you got assaulted. Tell me what happened or I'll arrest you both for obstructing a police report."

The detective's stern voice made Sarah's head throb so she pushed the help button. The responding nurse made the detective and Liz leave the room. In the hallway, the detective ended a quick phone call and told Liz, "Your sister doesn't remember anything and you're talking trash. I'll investigate this further. Right now, I've got a big horror show to tend to. A house burned to the ground last night. Two deceased." She ran to an unmarked cruiser and sped away.

Liz saw the nurses treating a coding patient at the far end of the ward. She snuck into Sarah's room and whispered in her ear, "We're going home tomorrow morning. Leaving this crazy town before the cops figure out what happened." Sarah responded with a vacant smile.

Liz returned to the motel intending to clean up the mess and pay for the damaged furniture. Two Washington State Police cruisers with every light flashing passed her on the way. She followed the cruisers to a street blocked by police tape. A State Trooper waved her away, so she parked behind a row of media cars. Holding one of Sarah's reporter pads, she smiled at a cop and walked by ten tidy Victorian houses to a row of fire trucks parked in front of April's iron fence with the peace sign finials. Beyond the fence, under dense nozzle spray, all that remained of April's house was a blackened stone chimney and smoky embers. The Dodge Dart was a smoldering blob of metal, upholstery, and rubber.

A fireman made Liz leave the scene. She returned to the motel and found the innkeeper leaning on the counter reading a newspaper. "How's the other lady doing?" he asked.

"She'll be OK," Liz said, "damn sleep walking. Something cooking up on the hill?"

"Double killing last night," he said. "Burned the hippie estate to the ground. People real nervous. Cops think a drug deal went bad."

Liz offered to clean-up her room and pay for any damage. The innkeeper gave her a mop, a bucket of cleaning solution, and a new scatter rug to replace the bloodied one. The furniture looked fine after a wipe down. The innkeeper offered her a chambermaid job after he saw the cleaned room.

Liz used her credit card to reinstate Sarah's health insurance, making the policy active in two days. The next morning, she checked out of the motel and drove to the hospital where she found Sarah on the bed, counting ceiling tiles. Thick gauze covered her hair, one eye, and one ear.

"Got some goofy pills," Sarah said. "My mind is shot, can't remember anything."

"Don't worry about it" Liz said.

A nurse helped Sarah change into street clothes. In an office, a doctor told Liz, "Sorry for sending her home so soon, but the state of Washington plays tough with freeloaders. I understand you ladies live in New York City. Your welfare system will give her fine medical care." He gave Sarah enough pain medication for the flight home. The doctor said, upon landing at JFK, she should go by ambulance to a hospital emergency room. Sarah signed her discharge papers with an X. She nearly fell over when she stood to thank the doctor. A nurse wheeled her to Liz's car. Sarah wiggled onto the rear seat and rested her head on a few pillows.

They arrived at Sea-Tac airport several hours later. An airport attendant and wheelchair met them at the rental car return and sped them through security and ticketing to the plane's door. Two flight attendants helped Sarah to her seat. The exhausted sisters said few words during the flight to New York City.

11 TINKER TALKS

Before exiting the plane, Liz covered most of Sarah's head with a pink towel wrapped Bedouin style and sunglasses. She looked like Norma Desmond after a rough night. A flight attendant helped her to a wheelchair outside the airliner hatch. The pilot, a combat veteran, felt queasy when he saw her battered face. Liz called a few ambulance companies, but they wanted two thousand dollars in cash or credit card for the ride to Manhattan.

Liz tossed their luggage into a taxi trunk. Sarah sat on the back seat. She rested her head on the side window and warned of imminent vomit. The driver, a twittering Irishman, refused to transport a nauseous passenger. Sarah got the taxi moving by promising to hold the thought. The driver sped to Liz's apartment in record time, set the luggage on the sidewalk, and thanked her for not following through with her prediction. As he drove away, she dropped to her knees and fulfilled her prediction on the sidewalk. It took twenty minutes for her to slog from the stoop to the apartment. She went directly to the couch, plopped her head on a pillow and slept within seconds with the turban still wrapped around her head.

Liz practiced unpowered chords in her bedroom to calm her nerves, but quit when flashbacks of Sarah's assault made her hands tremble. Endangering her sister's life on a quick-buck scheme now seemed foolish. Sarah made a living with her spunky personality and lively writing. If she suffered permanent brain damage, she'd loose her skills, never finish her book, and become Liz's responsibility. Also, they'd be in serious trouble if the Port Townsend police traced their rental car parked in April's driveway hours before the house burned. They'd serve lifelong prison time if convicted of double murder.

She powered her computer and typed April Peters into a search engine. The first result showed *The Seattle Times* home page with a color image of April's blazing home below the headline: "PT Hippie Heiress, Boyfriend, Murdered." The accompanying article said police had a few suspects.

Feeling it was time to destroy the source of much aggravation, she removed the *Chessman's* from a bedside drawer. On one hand, she thought, if she sold the discs to Lenny, *Rolling Stone* would put her face on a cover. She'd ride in the Hamptons in a chauffeured Bentley to her oceanfront villa bought with royalties. She'd buy a studio, write music, and stay away from Harlem. Chaz would get living money sent in an envelope with no return address. Sarah would live a simple life in a ritzy rest home paid with royalties. On the other hand, if she cut the discs into tiny pieces, she'd save herself from the plastic culture she deplored: individuals who preferred electronica over blues, slinky dresses over jeans, heels over sandals, money over craft. All she wanted from life was to play blues guitar in bars filled with edgy people clawing a life from the thankless city. The world would keep spinning without the *Chessman's* release. Classic rock worshippers could still listen to the hundreds of published Hendrix and Davis tracks while dreaming about a collaboration that never happened.

She took a pair of shears from a drawer, spread the blades over the edge of one of the CDs and squeezed firmly, making a slight diagonal cut. Her conscience told her to continue cutting and do the same to the other disc. She cut another hair width, then stopped and thought about her half-dead sister in financial, physical, and mental freefall who'd need plenty of money to pay for her care. The shears fell to the blanket. The *Chessman's* discs went back in the drawer.

She stood and looked at the tall mirror above her bureau. Her sparkling eyes had a dull, grayish tint. Lost weight and paled skin had cragged her face. Feeling ready for a full-blown cry, she looked down at the bureau and saw the business card of Stephen P. Stevens, the effervescent music executive she had met on the dank night someone stole her guitar. On his yacht on Leeward Harbor, he had offered to connect her with a sound engineer who worked at Chessman Studio in the late 1960s and swore he saw Jimi and Miles play together. She dialed his number. Stevens answered with a hundred decibel hello and dominated their ten minute conversation with music industry bluster and braggadocio. He gave Liz the phone number of Tinker Martin, the sound tech, and ended the call with, "If there's a story to tell about the night, Tinker will know it."

The next afternoon, Liz brought Sarah to an appointment with Dr. Anna Athena, a head trauma specialist at Mount Sinai Hospital on Manhattan's Upper West Side. The doctor's lengthy examination confirmed Sarah's concussion and brain contusion would require months of bed rest with intensive monitoring. The doctor said to expect significant memory loss for the next few months.

A couple hours after the examination, Sarah, with blank expression, watched the Three Stooges on Liz's television. She giggled like a toddler when Moe smashed Larry's head with a pipe. Liz interrupted the foolishness by telling Sarah to abandon her condominium and stay at Liz's apartment. A cousin who owned a moving company would store her furnishings. Sarah's eyes went back to the Three Stooges when Liz said the unfinished book needed completion. The revenues would help pay for Sarah's high insurance deductibles and a split of the rent. Liz shut off the television and called Sarah's literary agent, referred to as "Snarly Marley" by the sisters, and put the call on speaker mode. After Marley's snappy greeting, Liz described Sarah's injury and lengthy recovery that would require bed rest and no writing. She asked for a sixth month delay of the book. Marley's swear-laden contralto filled the apartment. Seven times she threatened a lawsuit. Six times she demanded a return of the advance payment. Twice, she called Sarah a phony who couldn't deliver the goods.

Sarah leaned toward the speaker. In pained voice, she promised to fight nausea and write a few words each day. Marley said the publisher wouldn't accept a long extension, so she'd try for a month. If Sarah couldn't finish the manuscript within the window, Marley would hire a ghostwriter to complete it. Marley summarized her compassionless tirade with another lawsuit threat. Liz hung up the phone after hearing a scatological insult directed at her sister.

Marley's diatribe gave Sarah a pounding headache. Liz wrapped an ice pack on her sister's forehead. "Somehow we'll get the book done," she said. "Right now, you can't write your name, let alone a chapter. Don't get someone else involved. They'll steal your work and put their name on it. Tomorrow afternoon, I'm meeting a dude named Tinker Martin, used to be a Chessman engineer, claims to know all about a Hendrix and Davis session. I'll take notes. If I have to write the final chapter, so be it. Split the royalties with me, we'll be fine."

"Yup," Sarah said. "Have a nice time. I'll be here with Moe and the boys."

Liz barely-passed freshman English, but in her senior year she won a writing award after a friend told her to "write the way you talk and don't worry about grammar if it sounds right." She asked the friend, now a feature writer for a Long Island newspaper, how to interview a subject. "Put heels on the ground," the friend said. "Get a reporter's notebook, the narrow, tall ones you see at breaking stories with the cardboard cover stained with coffee and ice cream. Use a cheap plastic pen. Watch out for leakers. Drink a few coffees, so you'll be amped and talky. Easy on the makeup, dress in baggy clothes. If you're dolled up, the conversation will drift from facts to frisky. Get in your subject's face. Smoke 'em out early, see if they're for real. If you smell booze, don't write anything down. I learned these lessons the hard way."

"I flunked penmanship," Liz said. "People can't read my handwriting when I send them post cards."

"Take a recorder," said the friend. "Then go home, replay the interview, type out the useful info, skip the bragging, name-dropping, pickup lines, and sales pitches."

Tinker told Liz to meet him in a few days outside Gate 2 at Yankee Stadium. He said to look for a "big white dude, late sixties, long sideburns, red hat." The day of the interview, she dressed in chino pants, faded black blouse, and scuffed work boots. She tied her hair in a ponytail and skipped makeup. Outside the stadium, she blended with a spectator swarm rushing to the four o'clock game. Near a gate, she saw a red cowboy hat amidst thousands of bobbing Yankee caps. Working her way toward the hat, she elbowed away a calloused hand that had touched her belly, pushed aside a ticket scalper, and chided a Boston Red Sox fan who had stepped on her toe. Near the Gate 2 sign, Tinker, wearing the reddest hat in North

America, chatted with a woman in a Derek Jeter game jersey. Liz tapped his nape and shouted, "Stevens sent me."

Tinker shook her hand like a stevedore tugging a rope. "Follow me," he said. They walked the sidewalk, savoring the spicy aroma of sizzling sausage. A tee shirt barker turned away when he saw Tinker's face. The crowd thinned when they approached a boulevard teeming with speeding taxis and provision trucks. Tinker stood on the closest lane and held his arms upward like a football official signaling a touchdown. The vehicles stopped and let them cross to a park. When a panhandler pleaded for fifty dollars, Tinker gave him the scarlet hat.

Four blocks from the stadium, Tinker leaned on a mailbox and lit a cigarette. "Ten minutes to go," he said. Liz recalled her mother's rule to never walk a city street with a strange man. Twelve blocks from the stadium they entered an infrequently painted apartment building. Tinker turned the doorknob of his basement apartment. "No keys. Nobody messes with Tinker. Bad guys know I'm badder."

Liz walked by stacked tape decks to a 1950s kitchen table surfaced with Spam color linoleum. Tinker took two cans of soda from the refrigerator, sat at the table, and smiled at Liz. She counted one good tooth and a dozen needing attention. Although parched from a long walk on a hot day, she declined the other soda after seeing the filthy top. Tinker downed his soda and belched into his fist.

"You're a pretty one," he said. "Just the way I like. Not painted up. Nice rear quarter."

Liz blushed. She moved her chair a few inches closer to the door. "Thanks for the review. My husband tells me the same thing every night."

"Where's your wedding ring?" he asked.

"Don't wear it in this part of the city."

"Good idea."

Liz took a pen and notebook from her pocketbook. "I've got fifteen minutes to chat," she said, "got serious business to tend to in Brooklyn. Stevens told me you spent years talking about a supposed recording session with Jimi Hendrix and Miles Davis. If you made the story up, no problem. I'll leave, life will go on. Only reason I'm sitting in this stuffy apartment with a man I don't know staring at my crotch is my sister. She's in bad health, trying to finish her book, needs the story of the Davis and Hendrix session, if it did happen. If she finishes the book and makes a few bucks, I promise she'll throw you some. Time to tell your story; someday you'll be in a pine box, holding a tale with no way to tell it."

"Stop disrespecting me. That's a no-no in the Bronx. I'll talk for ten grand or a half hour on my sheets."

"Forget about it. I'm carrying bad disease. Something I got in prison, causes horrible itching, makes your skin peel. You get it, you'll scratch your privates day and night."

"I get the point. No way on that action."

Tinker slurped foam from the second can. Liz opened her notebook to the first page. "You talk or I walk," she said.

"Ask me anything" he said. "I may answer, or may not."

Liz powered her hand-size recorder and asked a question. "Naw, Naw," Tinker said. "Ditch the recorder. This isn't a CIA interrogation. You're in the 'hood. Cops record people in the 'hood. You a cop?"

Liz put the recorder in her pocketbook. "Hey bro," she said. "I'm no cop. I play guitar for a living. Stevens says you know Chaz Russell, my boss. My sister heard Chaz knows all about the Miles and Hendrix session. Chaz got pissed-off when she asked him about it."

"You play with Chaz Russell? My old buddy from Chessman's. King of the String Benders. Met him in '66, must carry a pound of gold in his mouth. The boy would do anything for anybody, especially a woman."

"No question, he's nice people. So what happened at Chessman's that night?"

Tinker's eyes looked redder than his donated hat. He powered a table fan and aimed it at his face. "In '69," he said, "I told people Hendrix and Davis played music together. They called me crazy, say I drink too much, which was true. I ended up in a V.A. hospital. Doctors dried me out, blamed my boozing on Agent Orange, the death fog the Army sprayed all over me and most of Vietnam. These days, I keep my mouth shut. Still drink a little. You taking me serious?"

Liz turned the fan to share the breeze. "If Stevens says you're the real deal, you're the real deal," she said. "You OK with me asking a few questions?" Tinker took a jug of whisky from a kitchen cabinet, poured a belt into a stained paper cup, and bathed his throat with the spirits. Liz declined a swig.

"Oh, all right," he said. "I'm too old to worry about backstabbers. Time to get my story on paper. Do I get a free book if I talk?"

"Sis will send you a case of books if you tell me what happened. How'd you end up working for old man Chessman? You fall into the job?"

"Yah," he said. "When I got home from Vietnam, government paid my college tuition, gave me a full disability with a couple hundred a month to live on. The money didn't go far in the city, so I put on my Army coat, looked for work. Knocked on a hundred doors and had many slammed in my face. People with work hated veterans, hated the war, hated longhairs.

"One day, I banged on the door of Chessman Studio. Old man Chessman saw my Army jacket, shook my hand, thanked me for my service. Turns out, he was a former paratrooper; 82nd airborne, same division I was in. We sat in his office, talked for hours. He made me call him Chessie. We emptied a pitcher of stuff called special blend, light on the punch and heavy on the vodka. Halfway through the second batch, he offered me a job.

"I'd worked electronics in the Army, so he thought I qualified as an assistant sound tech. Asked for two bucks an hour, Chessie said four. Started work the next afternoon with a bad hangover; felt like I drank a barrel of Agent Orange. Worked ten years for him. Had a nice routine; came in every afternoon, three on the dot. He'd yell at me, down a snapper of special blend then take a nap in his office. The Army discharged him with a higher rank, so I was his gofer.

"Most nights, Chessie left at dinner time. I cleaned the studio, set up for next day's recording. If a famous group wanted to record at night, Chessie would stay, run the tape, send me home early. If a kid band from Long Island recorded on their daddy's nickel, Chessie went home, I'd run the show. Most nights I just cleaned up, listened to what the old man recorded during the day."

"Sounds like a perfect job," Liz said.

"It was. Bad part was Chessie yelling about everything from a scuff on the floor to the way I put toilet paper on the holder. For fun, I'd intentionally do something stupid, like forget to rewind a reel. That way he wouldn't have to make anything up. Yelling made him tired, nap sooner.

"I showed up one afternoon, saw Chessie slicked up in a purple velvet sport coat, pressed bell-bottom slacks, spit-polished shoes. Looked like an uptown doorman. I turned my ear for my daily yelling, got a smile instead. Chessie had me sweep the floors and load a fresh reel on the recorder. Around dinnertime he handed me an envelope. Dead sure it was layoff time. Opened it, found fifty in cash. Chessie said he felt bad I was working too hard, wasn't relaxing enough, told me to take the rest of the night off, cab to the Cotton Palace, meet a nice girl, have drinks on him."

"So Chessie wasn't all bad?" Liz asked.

"Not all bad, a pinch of good, the rest bad. I knew something was brewing. Chessie never dressed up, always wore chinos and a tan work shirt with Chessman Studio on the front. Looked like a chicken farmer. He was pushing seventy at the time, hated working nights.

"I left the studio about 7. Chessie watched me get into a cab. I took a one dollar ride and walked back to Chessman's, hid in the bushes near the parking lot; me and five million mosquitoes. About ten, a white limo parked twenty feet from my eyes. Jimi and his girlfriend got out with Miles Davis and his wife. No question it was Hendrix; he had on orange flared pants, swirly shirt with French cuffs. Miles wore a lime green jumpsuit, giant sunglasses, and elevator shoes. Looked like a praying mantis."

"What'd you do after they went into the studio?" Liz asked.

"Second limo unloaded another bunch of musicians. A few carried guitars. One carried drum sticks. I'm telling you something about that night I've never told anyone: I put my good ear up against a dressing room widow, listened to the best music ever played in Chessman's. Those boys played all night, didn't wrap up until dawn. Heard some great stuff and a loud fight."

"They record the session?"

"Yes ma'am," Tinker said. "Following afternoon, I found Chessie sleeping in his office, still wearing the purple jacket. On his desk, I saw the same reel I had put on the Ampeg the day before. We painted dates and session numbers on all our tapes."

"Then what happened?"

"While the old man slept, I got a blank tape, painted the same date and number on it, swapped the blank for the reel on his desk. I had tape machines at my apartment, planned to borrow the music for a day, play it, bring it back. I wasn't trying to make trouble. I wanted to hear the session again.

"Chessie slept to five. I did my usual chores and unpacked a crate of new recording tape. The boss walked into the studio holding the blank reel. Thank god I dried the paint with a heat gun. He yelled about bubblegum stuck on the sidewalk, made me scrape it off with a putty knife and scrub the sidewalk with a hand brush. Like a good soldier I did my duty with a smile. While I was hosing down the sidewalk, he grabbed my arm. Dragged me into the studio, called me an idiot. Chessie had a high pitched voice when he got pissed. He was so mad he squeaked like a train on a sharp turn. Had to mix a pitcher of special blend to get him talking in a pitch I could understand. Turns out he played the tape from the night before, heard only hiss."

"He blame you?"

"Sure did. Said I didn't clean the tubes. We opened the recorder, every tube twinkled. To prove a point, I put a brand new reel on the Ampeg, hit the record button, let the old man yell for a few minutes. I played back the recording, heard Chessie screaming, loud and clear. The mike even picked up a car horn."

"He figure out what happened?" Liz asked.

"I worked for the coot for many more years. He never again mentioned the bungled tape. He must have thought he forgot to press the record button all the way down, happened before on the machine. Miles stopped by a week later, wanted a listen, stormed out when Chessie told him the bad news. Hendrix's manager wanted the tape destroyed. Chessie never got paid for the session, denied it ever happened."

"You listen to the tape?"

"Damn right I did. Six times, real loud. Neighbors complained, cops went crazy. Unbelievable music. Hendrix's guitar screamed. Miles blew hot notes. Bass and drummer pounded the line. If I'd kept the damn tape, I'd be living off Central Park, dating girls like you.

"Back then, seeing I was a loudmouth who drank too much, I blabbered about the session to a few bar flies. I stopped talking about it when a *Crawdaddy* writer showed up at the Backbeat asking for me. Thank God I wasn't there. The next day, the Backbeat owner, Chessie's buddy, pushed me into the kitchen, said he kick my ass if I gossiped about the Chessman family in his place. These days, I slow drink and act like an altar boy in there.

"Chessie died in '90. I'd be dead meat if the music industry heard

I pooched his music. I hid the tape in my closet for twenty years. A month after Chessie's funeral, I saw Chaz at the Backbeat. He nearly fell off the stool when I told him I had the tape from the Miles and Hendrix session. Told him I found it helping Corky clean the studio after Chessie died. Chaz went to my place, listened to the tape. He was blown away."

"Chaz play lead or rhythm on the tape?"

"A little lead, but mostly rhythm, until Miles yelled at him. Chaz plays a drawn out stringbend like them old Chicago bluesman. Miles didn't like the sound, told Chaz to leave. I laughed like hell when I heard the door slam. I know how Miles was. He'd yell at anyone, didn't mean harm. Little man, big attitude. Chaz said he and Miles didn't talk for ten years after that night."

"Where's the tape now?"

"Far as I know, Chaz has it," Tinker said, pouring a whisky refill.

Liz moved her chair a few inches toward the door so one of his gestures wouldn't land on her thigh. With slurs creeping into his speech, she cut the interview short, and thanked him for the hospitality. Tinker gave her an unopened envelope from his probation officer. "Here's my address," he said. "Mail them books here, call if you get lonely." She walked briskly to the street and got a cab.

12 ACCUSATIONS

Liz, still spooked by the Tinker interview, found Sarah sitting on the floor eating popcorn and watching television. "Creepy dude," Liz said. "He went crazy when I pulled out the recorder. I jotted some notes in the cab." She handed the notebook to her sister.

"Good," Sarah said, tossing the notebook aside. "A man dropped-off an envelope. It's on the counter." Liz opened the envelope with a quick tear. The letter had the dark blue letterhead of the New York Police Department above a few paragraphs of cop-speak. An underlined sentence demanded that Sarah and Elizabeth O'Malley meet the next day with two Port Townsend Washington Police officers at NYPD headquarters.

Liz met with Detective Ricker and Lt. Kenneth Johnson in a padded room reeking of ammonia cleaner. The detective, sporting a fresh perm, wore a black pant suit fit for a gangster's funeral. Lt. Johnson, a fortyish man with a shaved head, looked honor guard ready with his military bearing and crisp police uniform.

Liz, fidgeting with a foam cup, explained Sarah's absence. Detective Ricker responded with a blank look and a recital of the Miranda warning against self-incrimination. Liz said she'd forego an attorney and answer their questions.

"Turns out you girls were at April Peters' house hours before the fire and homicides," the detective said. "Why were you there?"

"April asked us to visit," Liz said. "My friend and I had met her at the blues festival, had dinner at her house, she invited us back anytime. Sis and I went to Port Townsend on a sightseeing trip, we stopped by to say hi."

Detective Ricker pounded her fist on the table. "Honey, cut through the bull," she said. "You've got a history of lying to me. Cough up the truth. I know and you know April collected stolen guitars, smoked dope by the truckload. Did you sell her guitars during your visit?"

"No ma'am, we went to Port Townsend on a whim. My sister saw a Hollywood movie filmed at Fort Worden. She liked the scenery, we hopped a redeye, rented a car."

Lt. Johnson showed Liz a photograph of Sarah's swollen forehead and eyebrow covered with crusted blood. "Nobody believes she fell while sleep walking," he said. "This looks like an assault. Did you hurt your sister with a hammer?"

"You're crazy," Liz said. "She and I never fight. Last argument was in high school, when she wore my sweater without asking. Get this in your head: We drank a few beers, she tripped on the way to the bathroom. Middle of the night, I heard a crash, found her on the floor, blood all over the place."

"It wasn't beers, it was martinis. The grand jury will get the real story. Tell us about your visit to April's house."

"Got there about five, met Steve, her boyfriend, nice guy. We shared a marijuana cigarette with April, I didn't inhale. We laughed over a few jokes, passed around a bag of cheese puffs. April fell asleep, Sarah and I left, went out for drinks, got in about 10."

"First time I've heard Steve Kennedy called a nice guy. He's done hard time for manslaughter, suspected in a few rapes and assaults. Overall, a bad guy we tried to indict several times. He's a thug who even assaulted his mother."

"We only spent a few hours at April's. I didn't have time to hear his life story. I wanted to leave; show sis a big white sailboat in the basin."

Lieutenant Johnson leaned toward to Liz. "Why do you look away from us when you talk?" he asked. "I've interviewed many guilty suspects. They all act like you. You can tell the truth now, or under oath, in front of a jury. Give us a minute-by-minute description of what went on at April's house, without the lying."

Liz's mouth felt dry as Sahara sand. After drinking a few cups of water. she rambled a half hour of minutia about the Dodge Dart, the fence posts, the lawn, the statue, the rug, the potato chips, Steve's bad breath, and the cruise ships seen passing the strait. She denied seeing or discussing April's guitar collection. Lt. Johnson, feeling the interview was a waste of time, ended the session. He told her the Port Townsend Police website would soon post a sketch of a person of interest in the crime.

Liz told Sarah the session went well. She didn't mention they were suspects in a double murder. Sarah, with her eyes fixed on a televised commercial, uttered a blasé response. Liz, unwilling to engage in one-sided discourse with an inanimate object, tilted her laptop screen away from her sister's view. On the Port Townsend Police website, she saw a sketch of a white man with neatly trimmed black hair, wearing sunglasses. Liz suspected Ruby knew who stole the guitars and covered the crime with murder and fire. During their cross-country flight, Ruby talked about some Japanese collectors who craved custom-built American guitars. Some bought their guitars legitimately at auctions and private sales and others dealt with guitar runners who worked for the Yakuza, the Japanese mafia. During their ride to Port Townsend, Ruby valued April's guitar collection at a couple million dollars if sold to a shady collector. The Yakuza could have hired Ruby to scope the theft for a split of the proceeds, or Ruby, working with the slick man, shadowed Liz and Sarah in Port Townsend and when Steve left April's house, they butchered April and stole the guitars. They shot Steve dead when he returned from the robbery, set the property afire and splashed gasoline over the Dodge Dart, the car Ruby despised.

Liz printed a copy of the police sketch. In a Harlem fast food restaurant, she told Ruby about April and Steve's death. Ruby held her hands in prayer and recited a Biblical passage. She said the murders didn't surprise her because Steve's enemies and April's money attracted many stalkers and bloodsuckers. Liz showed her a printout of the suspect. "It's not Pluck," she said, "he's a heavy man. It must be someone working for him. Guy looks like a vacuum cleaner salesman, could be a minister. A clean-cut man would stick out in a blues crowd. Big money guitars attract ruthless, vicious crooks. If the guy shipped April's guitars to Japan, he made a quick hundred grand. Cops will never find them in a Tokyo mansion."

"He'd have gotten Jasper if we didn't get there first." Liz said.

Ruby, feeling uncomfortable talking about larceny and guitar lust, put three dollars on the table. Before walking away she said, "Come to think of it, last month in Leeward, I saw a guy who looked like the sketch talking to the big dude in the tan overalls leaning on the stage."

Liz spent the next day cleaning her apartment. Sarah, captivated by a run of Clint Eastwood Westerns, offered no assistance. After the late news, Liz slid under a blanket and shut off the light. Anxiety, sirens, and sidewalk banter kept her awake for hours. She tallied imaginary sheep, but lost count after eighty. For hours she thought about her sister's condition, the interrogation about a double murder, and having ten grand stolen. Cash flow was now a problem. Her recent rent payment left her with less than five hundred legitimate dollars.

She awoke with a fine attitude after a few hours of sleep bolstered with a few shots of tequila. Early afternoon, she drove a van over the George Washington Bridge to a gig on the New Jersey shore with her bandmates in their usual seats bickering about the usual petty issues. Chaz tried to calm things down with fatherly advice: "Let's knock the crowd out with an ass-kicking set. Doc says I'm fit for a two-hour solo. Liz got Jasper back. On my nickel, Kenny and Pearly have analyzed and reanalyzed every music note played by mankind."

"Boss," Pearly said. "We go to the Backbeat for a drink, try to leave after one, get stuck to the seat, stay for ten more."

"I've heard the line before," Chaz said. "I'm sure you two covered the payroll for a few distilleries over the last month."

"Ahhhh," Kenny said. "We did have a situation to borrow some future earnings by using your charge."

"Vinnie, the accountant, said you cuffed me with a two hundred dollar tab. Lots of high-shelf vodka. Don't you idiots know all vodka tastes the same?"

"Brother Chaz," Pearly said. "No hangover from the good stuff. We knew you was feeling good, band was playing good, we'd be earning good. Dun a couple hundred from our checks, make us all good."

"Yah right," Chaz said. "You better keep a tight beat or I'm docking you fifty bucks for every bungled note. I've got kids willing to play for pennies and learn the ropes from the String Bender. I bet

Liz would learn bass real quick. Drum machines rent cheap."

Liz parked behind Smokey's Saloon, a wooden building built in 1920, with a long, wide porch butting the Atlantic City boardwalk. In the early 1990s, a casino developer offered owner Ricky Simpson millions for the property. The afternoon before signing the letter of commitment, Ricky, his staff, and hundreds of regular customers crowded Smokey's beach stone bar for a funerary salute to the renowned blues club. The gathering ended at sunrise when wobbly Ricky, cheered by a raucous crowd, burned the commitment letter.

Ricky, seeing Chaz stretch outside the van, yelled a greeting from his second floor apartment window. He slapped drugstore aftershave on his face, brushed back his thick brown hair, slathered baby oil on his puffy hands, and set his dentures. From his rack of black clothes, he chose a silk turtleneck and beltless, polyester slacks.

Standing on the sidewalk, he gave Chaz a garlicky hug and an oily high five. He eyed Liz for a feely greeting. She saw it coming and took a step back, settling for a wet kiss on the cheek and a touch on her hip. Kenny and Pearly smiled like lottery winners after they removed their Dodger baseball caps and showed new haircuts with shaved sides, scrub brush tops, and thick sideburns extending to their jawbone. Ricky said they still didn't look like brothers.

Ricky made the band comfortable in the dressing room. The promised ten minute wait for dinner turned into an hour. Chaz, knowing Smokey's had the worst food in New Jersey, considered repeating a successful scenario from previous visits: ordering delivery from a Mexican restaurant. As he looked up the phone number, a cook who hadn't smiled in ten years carted in a stainless steel tray laden with tired leftovers from the poorly attended brunch. Kenny and Pearly downed cheeseburger sliders drowned in bacon fat. Liz chose a sealed bag of potato chips over the soggy bean salad. Chaz fought and won a battle with a leathery hot dog on a crunchy roll. When they finished eating, Chaz referred to the cook as "public enemy number one." He drank a can of seltzer and hoped his meal would stay down.

Chaz passed out copies of the set list. "Forget what I told you last week. I'm shaking things up. We make money playing for white boomers weaned on blues riffs. They're getting tired of the same old stuff. Tonight, for one song, we're not only playing from the old blues catalog, we're playing a fusion song, see what happens. If they like it, we'll play more at the next gig. We may play all fusion if it makes customers drink more." Kenny and Pearly smiled like pardoned prisoners.

"Hold on," Liz said. "I joined you guys to play electric blues, not some funky offshoot. I thought you were blues to the bone and now you're switching to funk. A white chick in a fusion band? They'll laugh me off the stage. I never thought you guys would go back to fusion. Where'd this fusion thing come from?"

"Started with Tony Williams," Chaz said, "a drummer I met at Chessman's. Boy got sick of playing suit-and-tie jazz, formed Lifetime, the best fusion group ever. Hooked up with Larry Young on organ, and the father of fusion guitar, John McLaughlin. I tell you, they made the jazz guys play fusion, blues guys too. When Miles heard Lifetime, he got hooked, went from playing quartet to blasting full-blown fusion at the Fillmore, for hippies. When I saw the fusion guys driving Ferrari's, I formed Chaz Russell's Electric Fog. We played kind of a blues fusion, still got the white jumpsuits and boots in my apartment ready for a show." He turned to Pearly and said, "We're going back to those silky outfits, get yours cleaned for our next gig."

"I ain't wearing those pimp threads," Pearly said. "You promised no chiffon ever again. Kenny and I are retiring if you're going back to them clothes."

"Only kidding," Chaz said. "Stick with your bowling shirts. Tonight, we'll play a fusion song, see what happens. If the crowd throws bottles at us, we'll go back to electric blues. If they dig fusion, next time, we'll play more."

"Why'd fusion die out so quickly?" Liz asked.

"Music went to hell when the hippies cut their hair and got jobs selling insurance," Chaz replied. "Then disco took over and fusion tanked, so we drifted back to electric blues with a healthy dose of improvisation. The music scene is circles and my circle is coming back to fusion. When you called me an old buzzard, it made me think about a playing a new vibe."

The band spent fifteen minutes on stage tuning their instruments and toying with notes and beats. Liz studied a chord chart for "Gallivant", a fusion song Chaz wrote for the Chaz Russell Electric Fog in 1974. Chaz played the opening notes on Thelma. Kenny and

Pearly hadn't played the song in thirty years, but they picked up the beat after a few bars. Liz added a few innocuous chords. After five minutes of head nods, toe taps, string wails, and drum rolls, Chaz pronounced the song fit for Smokey's crowd. Liz crumpled the chart and stuffed it in her pocket.

A few minutes after nine, with three-hundred patrons filling Smokey's to capacity, Liz, Kenny, and Pearly warmed the room with an opening number. After a punchy drum roll, Chaz walked to the stage like a statesman and played four bars of squeaks, cries, sirens, duck calls, and thunder. The crowd yelled for more, so Chaz pulled Thelma close to his chest and made the guitar talk. He started with wah-wah-woo-wah that came through the speakers as "how are you tonight?" The crowd loved it when he stretched his fingers over the lower strings and played "love you all" in string talk. He ended the schlocky demonstration with a funky "God Bless America," then he rolled up his sleeve and showed the crowd the pink scar on his arm. "They tried to steal my Thelma. I fought 'em off. Doc says my bad hand is now my good hand. Let me show you what I mean." Playing soft notes, he told the crowd, "Back in the late 60s, when hippies ruled the world, jazz and blues musicians got bored playing old music over and over so they created fusion, a jazz and blues blend; only lasted a few years. When I was healing, I got sick of soap operas, so I played my old fusion records. Got me thinking you'd like to hear some. So tonight, my spunky band will play "Gallivant" from my Electric Fog songbook."

Kenny tapped his cymbal twice. Chaz followed with guitar chords sounding like car horns, the sound made by simultaneously pinching and sliding three strings made Thelma honk. Kenny and Pearly smiled like toddlers on Christmas morning. The funky vibe brought them back to a time when life involved little sleep, plenty of partying, and steady work. Liz stood in the shadow of a speaker. She looked downward when Chaz told the crowd, "I haven't seen such an excited crew since the Baxter in '69 when some of you were only a mother's want. You want another dose of fusion, or more twelve bar blues?" Ricky, seeing bar flies jostling for barmaid attention and waitresses carrying laden trays, demanded more fusion.

"Sure will, boss," Chaz said. "Let's honor a boy who came from Seattle to New York City, got tired of the scene so he played around with this." Chaz stepped back a few steps and told Liz to "just air guitar it." The stage lights darkened. A spotlight shined on his face. "Most people think Hendrix never played fusion," he said. "Well, late 60s, he got up with Larry Young and Buddy Miles. Those boys recorded "Young/Hendrix," a song we'll play for you. My bass man Pearly White will help out on the Hammond B3 organ. Ricky, spin the Lesley."

Chaz played seven notes over thirty seconds. Pearly piped a funky line. Kenny played his drums so soft one stick left his hand and rolled toward Liz. He waved her off and pulled a spare. These Electric Fog veterans had played this song hundreds of times and it showed. Chaz shortened the song to ten minutes. After the final note, he said, "My friends, you heard Hendrix's take on fusion." He coughed on his drink of water when a thug leaning on the stage shouted, "Play more fusion."

Chaz's affable stage manner turned to a glare. "I'll play what I want to play," he said. "Get the hell away from the stage, or I'll have Ricky toss you out of here." The thug grabbed the microphone stand. An off-duty cop wrestled him to the floor. A few customers abandoned full drinks and left the club. Ricky, knowing the thug was on the Atlantic City mayor's staff, told Chaz to apologize, or unplug his equipment and go home. Chaz strolled to the center microphone. "Hey young fella, I didn't mean to get cross. To make amends, I'm buying you and your lovely a drink and singing her a song."

A waitress brought two plastic shot glasses of cheap whisky to the hooligan and his girlfriend, a by-the-hour seductress known to rob stupid men. Chaz sang her the crooner classic "Lust in Your Eyes."

Chaz told Liz to get Jasper and join their next song "Red House." She asked if she should plug her guitar in during the song. "Don't get flip," he said. "You got no clue about fusion. Play something you know, stop bitching."

Chaz led things off with a run of fuzzy chords. Pearly and Kenny played well enough to keep their jobs. A minute into the song, Chaz deferred to Liz and over the next two minutes she played furious, angry guitar. When most in the crowd thought her guitar would destruct, she slowed things down with a ten second snippet of "Woodstock Improvisation." When she completed her solo, Chaz, making the "Red House" vamp his, ended the song with a thirty second blast. They played electric blues until Ricky dimmed the lights at 2 a.m. The crowd rushed the stage and yelled for more fusion. Chaz posed for a picture with the drunken thug and his lovely.

Liz left Atlantic City with her passengers uncharacteristically awake. "Heard a whole new Chaz tonight," she said. "I'd like to learn to play fusion."

"You'll never pick it up," Chaz said. "It's too complicated. You'd have to spend years in a fancy jazz college to figure it out."

"Or a year in your band," Liz said.

Kenny and Pearly offered to unload the van at Chaz's place, so they dropped Liz at her apartment. She found Sarah awash in incandescent light, watching an infomercial for an apple peeling device. Despite doctor's orders to stay in the shade, every light in the apartment shined.

"Strange night indeed," Liz said, pouring a nightcap. "Last month, the CRB played half dead on stage. Tonight they played their asses off, even played some fusion, right out the 70s. Chaz thinks fusion will become popular again. Kenny and Pearly are onboard. Crowd got into it. I had no clue what was happening. I only played a few notes."

"Good," Sarah said as he switched the channel to a movie.

Liz put on blinders, crawled into bed, and slept until early afternoon when Detective Ricker called. "Got some video of a suspect," the detective said, "Go to our website, take a look. I'll wait."

Liz viewed the blurry video of the back side of a white man leaving a restaurant. "Looks like a wimp, walks like a pompous ass," she said.

"You're right," said the sergeant. "He's about five foot six. The FBI has pegged him in a few other thefts. Has a nose for expensive guitars. We allege he executed the couple then stole April's guitar collection. A few days after the fire, he shipped a container east, used a phony name."

"I'm glad we didn't meet."

"Be careful, he's still at large. We don't know his name. Think hard, did you see him in your travels? Call me back if you have any thoughts. Have your sister take a look at the video."

"Not sure she can offer much. I get about six words a day from her. Lots of migraine headaches. Brain is running on one volt."

"Hope she heals quickly. We'll need her testimony. Contact me if you want to change your story."

After the call, Liz expanded the video so it covered the entire screen and placed the computer on Sarah's lap. Sarah glanced at the screen, pushed it away, and focused on a movie shootout involving a sheriff and a horse thief. The laptop landed safely on the carpet. Liz shut off the television, put the laptop back on her sister's lap, and said, "Don't give me a one word answer. If they arrest the guy, we're off the hook. You see this guy in PT?"

Sarah gave the screen a half-hearted look. "Never seen him," she said.

The day after the Smokey's gig, the Backbeat lunch crowd buzzed about Chaz's fusion experiment. By late afternoon, the news drifted from Harlem, down Broadway, to Mim's, the epicenter of musician gossip. The online magazine *Live the Music* featured a post from a twenty year-old musician:

> Whenever my hippie parents played fusion, I ran outside and covered my ears. I should have listened because last night I heard the Chaz Russell Band play one hot fusion song. Hey hip-hop dudes, check out this group if you want to hear a new take on this short-lived jazz crossbreed that died too soon.

Chaz told his band, "The blues scene needed a kick. We delivered the goods. Music magazines, booking agents, and club owners want a piece of our band. I'm going all in on fusion, playing our 70s set list. It works on Broadway; every year they recycle a musical, make millions. Some of those plays have come back from the dead two or three times, the next generation loves them.

"I've got more music exploring to do before I see my baby sister up in heaven. You see the crowd the other night? They was in a trance when I played them solos. From now on, we're a fusion band. Screw those bastards who call string bending 'twanging' or 'fiddle fingering.' I'll shove bent notes down their ears, make a few million. Today, we start a new music life. You all in?"

"We're in under one condition," Kenny said. "If you're talking millions, we want our deal redone to an even split, a third for Pearly, same for me."

Chaz rubbed his chin. "How many times over the past years

have we had this discussion? When we play trio, I pay you each twenty-five percent of the gig. I get forty percent because my name is painted on the big drum. When Liz came on board, you all got twenty and I got thirty. I took a pay cut because of my wound. Ten percent goes for van rentals, meals, rooms, your tabs, reserve for bail money. So, to answer your question, shut up and play."

Kenny and Pearly debated the fairness of the offer. They could quit now and spend their days mooching drinks at the Backbeat, or take Chaz's offer. Several minutes later, Pearly told Chaz, "We'll shut up and play." Chaz, grinning like a cheesy salesman, shook their hands.

"One problem," Liz said. "You guys played fusion years before I was born. I heard my first live fusion a few days ago. I'm not playing air guitar in the shadow of a speaker. I'm done with you guys. I'll find a new electric blues band or call my buddy Spoons."

"You'll pick it up," Chaz said. "I need you to play a little rhythm. I'll show you what you need to know. This fusion thing may be over after one gig. We could get booed out the door and be back playing blues."

"The other night," Liz said, leaking a few tears, "I felt left out, standing like a mannequin. You guys smiled like kids at a carnival. Bands change all the time; it's my time to go."

Kenny rubbed Liz shoulder. "Stay with us," he said. "Just play a few notes here and there, look good, collect a paycheck. Watch us do fusion."

"Guys, it's over," Liz said. "The band sounds better without me. Let's stay friends, play together sometime."

"Boys, hate to say it, but it's time for her to go." Chaz said, "I think this fine musician should find a new band. Let's give her a salute."

Liz hugged Chaz like he was a husband going to war. She comforted bawling Kenny and Pearly with long hugs. Chaz set a pitch pipe on his lips, blew a sustained C, and sang "I'll be Missin' You", a spiritual played when respected band members depart. Kenny and Pearly wailed during the last stanza. When the song ended, Chaz put a few Chaz Russell Band guitar picks in Liz's pocket. Liz put Jasper on a chair. "It's your guitar," she said.

"No way," said Chaz. "It's Johnny's. You take care of it for him."

She left with Jasper in hand. On the dusty bench outside the apartment, under a canopy of leaves hinting of fall, she strummed a bluesy riff for the old men sitting on the grass, drinking wine.

13 LOST LUTHIER

Liz left Jasper at her apartment. She brushed dust from the backside of her jeans and walked two blocks to a bar where she sat next to Brie Piper, a musician who had played with Liz in a blues band that destructed after the lead singer suffered an onstage breakdown over a mismanaged love triangle. She now played bass for a classic rock cover band. Her bandmates loved her husky laugh and timely bass lines. Bar patrons loved her taut figure and shaggy blond hair. Her four former husbands disliked her frequent affairs and tendency to overspend. When husband two found her under the covers with a horn player, he beat her so bad with a saxophone she spent two months in a hospital. On her fiftieth birthday, in the middle of a set, husband three gave her a bar napkin note with a handwritten divorce demand saying he wanted to marry a younger woman with a knack for numbers and home cooking. Brie crumpled the note and laughed into the microphone without chugging the beat. During the next song, a sarcastic ballad that demeaned men, she winked at a leering dude slouched on a front row table. A week later, in a drive-in Las Vegas chapel, he became husband four. Brie recently celebrated her sixtieth birthday with a spanking-new divorce and was scouting for new, seasoned bandmates and younger bedmates.

Liz told Brie about her parting from the Chaz Russell Band. "I dated Pearly about twenty years ago," Brie said. "Was like a two-for-one sale. I had two comps for a sold out concert, got into a cab, saw Kenny in the back seat next to Pearly. Kenny claimed his bouncer buddy would sneak him in. We get there, bouncer told him to screw. I offered to pay his cab fare home. He ended up walking a bread tray from an alley through the kitchen to our cozy table for two. Kenny's afro blocked my view all night. Didn't hear much music because Kenny and Pearly talked nonstop. Thank God, I haven't seen them since that night."

Liz asked for any job leads or contacts worth a call. "You'll never find a job playing blues guitar," Brie said. "There are so few blues bands left out there." Liz suggested they form a blues band with Liz playing lead and Brie on bass. A quick handshake closed the deal. Needing a drummer, Brie phoned a prodigious percussionist named Big Suzy. Midway through the next round of drinks, Big Suzy sat between Liz and Brie.

Big Suzy wasn't big. She got the nickname from her weighty drumming and bark that righted many tardy bass lines. A former champion arm wrestler, she kept in condition by weightlifting, kickboxing, and brawling. To celebrate her recent thirtieth birthday, she had abandoned peroxide blond for orange frizz and bought a vintage motorcycle with a sidecar. She considered men cheap toys, cast aside after play. She swore off marriage, preferring to rent men by the hour. She'd go toe-to-toe with any man, woman, or machine who doubted her toughness.

Liz asked Suzy about her last gig. "Just spent two years playing revivals with Jimmy Creed," she replied. "Love the guy. We played New Orleans, Tampa, far north as Leeward. Jimmy's having health issues; he's got the gout, so we're on hiatus. I'm looking for work. Anything but weddings, proms, or bar mitzvahs."

"Honey, we're playing electric blues," Liz said, "the way the Chicago boys play. May add some jazzy licks."

"Here's the deal," Brie said. "Liz just got done filling-in with Chaz Russell. You know what I bring to the table. Us white gals can keep up with them old blues boys. You in?"

Suzy downed a neat whisky and chugged a beer. "Sounds good," she said, soberly. "Jazzy blues, that's what I'm looking for. My degree is in jazz drumming; by the time I graduated, jazz was dead. Eighty grand in tuition, I drove a cab. Dad loved the scene. My life was a disaster. One night I drove a prettied-up gospel singer to a huge Harlem church; saint something-or-other. She went in. I parked out front with the windows open listening to sweet gospel. I told the dispatcher I was changing a flat. I followed the music to the back row of the church. One pasty face sitting in a church full of locals. I listened to a few minutes of preaching and an hour of God's music. The momma who had sat in my cab shouted out song after song to the choir's harmony. A dude about seventy played kick-ass guitar. A woman on bass pounded the beat. The woman drummer played like the best.

"I got the gospel bug that night. Next day, I answered Jimmy's ad for a drummer with blues and gospel bones. Jimmy said I wouldn't get rich joining his band, but I'd get on God's good side. Having spent years on God's bad side, it was time to even things out. I signed on, spent the last two years busing around the South, filling churches with blessed music."

"You're hired." Liz said.

"Let's show the world us gals can play blues," Brie said. "I know a place we can practice, over in Brooklyn, a no frills studio with nice sounding amps. Sweet old guy owns it. I'll rent some time. Let's meet there in a few days." Liz and Suzy went along with Brie's suggestion. Over the next hour, they nursed celebratory drinks and talked about songs to play at their first practice.

The next morning, Liz felt optimistic about her new band and aggravated over her sister's refusal to visit Dr. Athena's office unless given a sugary bribe. Liz got her there by promising to buy cotton candy on the way home. In an email, she had warned the doctor about her sister's decline; explaining how, one morning, Sarah had burned a hamburger and set off a smoke alarm resulting in an evacuation of the building. She tried to work on her book, but took a minute to type a word. Her one word answers became passive utterances. She spent most of her day watching movies and infomercials.

Dr. Athena, concerned over brain bleeding seen on Sarah's latest MRI, scheduled a more detailed scan and told her to stay in bed until further notice. On the ride home, finding cotton candy in Manhattan proved impossible. The cabbie, a Yemini, knew nothing about the swirled concoction. Liz called off the pursuit after several unsuccessful stops and paid the fifty dollar fare. Sarah, angry over the unfilled promise, sulked all afternoon on Liz's couch. Liz, needing to replace Jasper's strings, opened the guitar case on the kitchen table.

The socket wrench used for her slide playing was missing, so she called Chaz.

"Gracious be," Chaz said. "Awful thing last night; Johnny got killed."

"Oh no." Liz shouted. "Not little Johnny. No way. Couldn't be."

"His momma found him this morning, shot dead," Chaz cried. "On the shop floor, near the stove. She called me from the police station. Wants me to come down, help bury her boy."

"Who'd murder the nicest guy in the world?"

"Sounds like robbery, momma said they stole guitars. Not sure if they got all the good ones. I'm flying to Arkansas tonight. I need company. Can you go? I'll pay for everything."

"Let's see. I'm supposed to meet with my new band. My sister isn't doing well. I'll call you back in ten minutes."

Five frenzied phone calls cleared Liz schedule. Three of Sarah's visiting nurses would cover Liz's absence. Brie said they'd talk after the funeral. Liz endured a speedy rush hour cab ride to JFK. Around 7 p.m., she found Chaz sitting outside Terminal 2, dabbing his eyes with a plaid handkerchief. "This is the worst thing ever," he said. "Johnny was my best friend. We grew up together. Best guitar builder in the world. So good, got him killed."

"It's sad," Liz said, holding Chaz's hands. "I took a shine to him. Let's give him a king's burial."

They arrived in Little Rock after midnight and stayed in a hotel near the airport. The next day, an Arkansas state trooper guarding Johnny's driveway let them enter the property. A dozen police cruisers and a medical examiner's van blocked the path to Johnny's shop. A bus with CRIME SCENE UNIT lettered on the side idled outside his mother's house. A trooper leaned on the rusty Harley, drinking a coffee. Johnny's cousin Minnie, dressed in black, led Chaz and Liz into the parlor where Johnny's mother Mae sat on a sofa next to Moline and Ralph, listening to Minister Lancaster mumble prayers. Mae, seeing Chaz's drawn face, wailed, "Thank you Jesus for sending Johnny's best friend." Chaz gave her a long hug and promised they'd send Johnny off in style. Minister Lancaster offered his church for the funeral. Moline said she'd host the post burial dinner and help plan the wake. Liz volunteered to contact Johnny's musician friends through the Internet. Chaz said he'd line up the music for the funeral and reception. The funeral home director, hearing that Johnny's friends would need time to travel to Arkansas, suggested two days of reflection, then an afternoon wake, with the funeral the next morning. Mae nodded her approval then welcomed friends offering condolences and hugs.

The sobbing and hugging stopped cold when a studious man in a white laboratory coat yelled into the parlor, "Medical Examiner, looking for someone in charge." Mae nearly fainted when she saw splattered blood on his coat. A retching woman ran to the bathroom. Chaz led the examiner to a picnic table behind the house.

"We checked out Mr. Durrell's body in the van," the examiner said. "Victim shot four times; nine millimeter dum-dums, quick death. Shipped the deceased to Kimmell Funeral Home in Lincolnville."

"Oh Lord," Chaz said as he signed the release. "Johnny never hurt a grasshopper."

Liz brought Mae's Christmas card list of several hundred friends to the Lincolnville library next to the general store. The store owner leased a storage room to the town for a dollar a year and had donated an Internet connected computer. Liz spent three frustrating hours searching the web for Johnny's friends. Most had no Internet exposure, some showed up on court proceedings, a few had vague obituaries, and several were musicians with no contact information. Her efforts identified twenty-four friends of Johnny in legal trouble, sixteen currently jailed, ten deceased, and over fifty missing in action. She gave the results to Johnny's uncle, a sappy alcoholic known for breezy phone calls. Over a few hours, the uncle emptied a glass of moonshine and got the sad news to everyone on the list.

Liz sent Leslie, the day nurse, an email describing the situation at Johnny's house. Her speedy response said, "Your sister is talking strange. Said she got hit by a bad man. Words get twisted when she talks. I called her doctor; she doubled her medication. See you later this week, if not sooner." Liz knew that memory loss was an expected result of the bludgeoning, but Sarah's inability to write and speak coherently was worrisome. When healthy, she claimed to write five thousand words per day. Now, she could only stare at the keyboard.

Chaz and Liz walked to Johnny's shop. A detective stopped

them at the doorway, but let them watch the action for a few minutes. Forensic technicians swept the shop with electronic wands. A detective on his knees panned the floor with a large magnifying glass looking for assailant hair or fibers. A fingerprint expert dusted the splintered wood left from the wall mounted guitar rack. Chaz felt queasy when he saw coagulated blood on the floor near the woodstove, so they walked away. Under a shade tree, a tall state trooper named Williams invited them into his command trailer.

Williams sat at a plywood desk, removed his trooper hat, and scratched his fresh whiffle. "I've seen murders that make sense," he said, scanning a legal pad, "this isn't one of them. Poor guy, making a buck, whacked on his farm. Near as we can tell, perps stole twenty-seven guitars. The mother saw a white van leave the crime scene and thought it was a delivery truck. She didn't see the driver. Johnny didn't come in for dinner. She found him on the shop floor, bled out."

"I warned my boy to be careful," Chaz said. "His guitars got real expensive on the open market. He knew nothing about money; charged me five hundred for my Thelma in 1973. A few months ago, he built Liz a guit, wanted to charge me the same price. We fought like heck on the phone, gave him eight-hundred, figures to a buck an hour."

"An officer who knows guitars told me some of them Durrells are worth north of a hundred thousand," Williams said. "If you own a Durrell, store it in a bank vault."

"Oh mercy," Chaz said. "I'm not hiding Thelma. I'll just get a bigger gun."

"I'll never hide mine," Liz added.

"We interviewed a local guy who helped Johnny with chores," Williams said. "He found a copy of Johnny's customer list. We made a list of the stolen guitars and contacted the head of the Durrell Collectors Society. He had pictures of every stolen guitar and told us they were worth over two million if sold overseas."

"You hear about the West Coast guitar theft and murders last week?" Liz asked.

"We're on it," Williams said. "Sounds similar, with murder and missing guitars. Couple FBI agents from Seattle are flying in this afternoon."

Chaz and Liz went back to the house. "My son spent his life in his shop," Mae said. "I'm going to make it into a museum." She asked Minister Lancaster, "Please have them play some blues during the funeral. Let's have a row of playing Durrells send Johnny to Heaven's Gate. Johnny hated dirt, so no burial, we'll cremate my boy. Spread his ashes near the creek behind his shop."

When dinner time approached, many mourners left for their homes or motel rooms. Liz drove to the general store for beer. Chaz stayed with Johnny's uncle and Mae, taking phone calls from Johnny's friends. Kenny and Pearly told Chaz they were leaving New York City on a bus and would be in Lincolnville the following noon. Pearly had pawned a bass to pay for the trip.

Liz and Chaz stayed at Mae's house that night. They viewed scrapbook pictures of Johnny playing baseball, building a guitar with his father, and receiving an award from a guitar magazine. Before retiring, Mae said, "Remember, I want a room full of pickers sending Johnny home."

A bus from Little Rock dropped Kenny and Pearly at the Lincolnville town common, a weedy lot at the intersection of two state roads. Liz found them sitting on their suitcase sharing a bottle of beer. She dropped them off at Molly's. Moline had invited them to stay for free in an outbuilding provided they stayed away from the bar, helped set up the stage, and paid for any meals. Liz then drove Chaz to the funeral home. After a peek at Johnny's body, he requested a closed casket.

The day of the wake, every telephone pole in downtown Lincolnville displayed a limp American flag and a black, plywood guitar silhouette made by the high school shop class. Haze hid the view of the foothills from the town common. An ice cream truck made its rounds with its music silenced. Laborers with sweaty flesh rushed to fix a broken water pipe before the funeral procession.

A black Chevy sedan delivered Chaz and Mae to the wake. Over the next four hours nearly every Lincolnville resident prayed at the casket and spent time with Mae, a former grade-school teacher in the town. In an adjoining room, a young woman played spirituals on a Durrell. Johnny had paid for her guitar lessons at a Little Rock music school and had given her the guitar after her acceptance to a Boston music college.

FALLEN FRET

The wake ended after Captain Keith, a Memphis bluesman, prayed at the casket with Audrey, his purple Durrell, over his shoulder. Before the lights went out, Chaz and Mae said a few weepy words over the corpse. They returned to her house and talked about Johnny for hours.

The funeral began at ten a.m. Two hundred seated mourners, thankful of a tepid breeze, listened to an organist play "Soon and Very Soon," an uplifting spiritual. With Liz, Chaz, Mae, and close relatives seated on the first pew, twelve musicians in coal black three-piece suits walked two abreast down the middle aisle, set their instruments on the pulpit stand, and stood in a row behind the lectern. Liz counted six Durrells, two trumpets, two saxophones, and two drum kits. Stewie Rogers, a renowned piano player from Memphis, sat on the right side at a grand piano lent by a local college.

The organist increased the tempo. Fifty red-robed gospel singers walked single file down the center aisle singing "Soon and Very Soon." Each singer bowed at a life-size picture of smiling Johnny sitting on his plastic bucket with sawdust in his hair. They split into two lines and walked the outer aisles to the balcony stairs. When the last singer stood at rest on the balcony, the organist began a dirge. Six wet-eyed pallbearers wheeled the brass cart holding the casket down the center aisle. Minister Lancaster, holding the Durrell family bible, followed the procession. The mourners stirred when Johnny's two teenaged nieces entered the church, each carrying a gilded Durrell. Liz recognized the instruments as the Golden Sisters, two guitars built for late bluesman John Lee Johnson. A hedge fund manager had purchased the guitars from his estate for a million dollars. The girls placed the guitars on the rack near the other guitars and then sat on the front row next to Mae.

Minister Lancaster told the mourners, "The Lord has taken our Johnny. Let's celebrate this little man who turned wood and wire into pleasing sounds. Just last week, I stopped by his shop and sat by the wood stove. He had just built his two-hundredth guitar and planned on building many more. Let us sing."

The choir, packed against the balcony rail, sang "Amazing Grace." After the second stanza, Minister Lancaster said, "Johnny's best friend, please come up." Several dozen mourners dispersed throughout the church shuffled to the aisles. The minister, seeing frilly dresses and starched white shirts headed his way, apologized for the confusion and sent them back to their pews. He called Johnny's real best friend to the lectern. In a sullen voice, Chaz told the assembled, "Johnny loved hearing his guitars played. Next to me are eight Durrells along with kits, piano, and horns. You all know who's playing them, so no intro needed."

The guitarists tuned strings, horn players fingered silent scales, and drummers loosened their wrists. One of Johnny's nieces handed Chaz a Golden Sister and strapped the other Golden Sister over her shoulder. Chaz, wanting to send Johnny off with sizzle, chose the upbeat spiritual "John the Revelator," a fitting tune for a steamy church holding fifty mellifluous voices, dozens of famous musicians, and pews filled with angry adrenalin. He paused after the opening stanza and pointed to the balcony. The choir sang a hundred decibel "tell me, who's that writing?" and answered the question with "John the Revelator."

Chaz replayed the opening stanza. The choir responded with a louder, "Tell me, who's that writing? John the Revelator."

All eight guitarists played the third stanza. The longleaf pine timbers supporting the balcony creaked as the swaying choir sang "Tell me, who's that writing? John the Revelator." The choir followed with a glorious "He wrote the Book of the Seven Seals."

For six steamy minutes, wiry fingers on steel strings drove the loudest choir ever heard in Arkansas. Mourners' facial expressions turned from sadness to joy. Sunlight made the plaster statues glow. Several couples danced in the aisles.

The spent performers gulped iced lemonade after the song. Minister Lancaster said from the lectern: "Johnny wasn't big on church services, but he sure loved church music like that. Seeing it's about a hundred-fifty in here, let's end the service with the Lord's Prayer. You all are invited to air-conditioned Molly's Restaurant for a tribute jam and meal of celebration." He recited the prayer at auctioneer pace. Pallbearers in sweaty white shirts and sagged ties scooted the casket down the aisle into a hearse. The fifty car procession travelled a mile to Molly's. School buses carried the musicians and choir. A bread truck carried their instruments.

Moline, wearing a white chef's jacket with a black arm band, greeted the mourners. A state trooper unloaded the Golden Sisters and Johnny's two nieces at the service entrance. Kenny and Pearly helped Jimmy Shine carry his keyboard into the restaurant. California drummer Mary Kelly's friends carried her kit.

When the main restaurant seats filled, Moline led mourners to an adjoining room that accommodated another hundred people. The previous night, Ralph and a volunteer crew built a long stage at one end of the restaurant and helped volunteer sound techs set-up amplifiers and monitors while Kenny and Pearly watched from bar stools. A guitar guru had tuned and set twenty Durrell guitars and three Durrell basses on a rack on the stage.

Minister Lancaster told the mourners, "Thank you all for coming to Johnny's farewell. Johnny would want to hear them Durrells sing, so we parked his body and soul out front and left the door wide open so he can take-in his send-off. Let's say a prayer, then Johnny's friends will say a few words. After the formalities, we'll fire up these guitars and celebrate Johnny's life."

The Minister mumbled a quick ode. Moline told a story about Johnny sleeping in the kitchen one night when he couldn't find his car. Turned out, Johnny didn't own a car. Johnny's cousin Bubba Brown described Johnny's chase from a creek by a catfish bigger than him. Chaz recalled Johnny sending money to a Brazilian wood broker's family after the man died felling a tree. Moline introduced the owner of Ark Ale brewery, Suds Johnson, who had donated enough ale for everyone. A dozen waitresses passed out chilled bottles of the cherished brew. The minister offered a toast. Four hundred bottles emptied.

Over the next hour, electric blues spilled from the stage as mourners converted a truckload of barbecue into a bushel of bones. After dessert, the trooper said from the stage: "A good man died and with your help, we'll figure out who did it. Please think long and hard. You see anyone acting suspicious the days before Johnny's demise? If you want to talk, I'll be in my cruiser, out front."

The trooper went to his cruiser and reviewed mug shots of known guitar thieves. Moline, holding a plate of pulled pork and corn bread, tapped on his window. "Been wanting to talk to you people," she said. "Something strange happened the day of the murder."

The trooper rested the plate on the dash. He took a notepad and pen from his shirt pocket and asked her to speak slowly. "Molly's is out of the way," she said. "Most of our customers are from the county. Half hour before closing, man from away ordered a cheeseburger. I sell ten cheeseburgers a month, mostly to seniors who can't chew."

"Describe his clothes," he said with pencil on paper, "any scars, how he walked, how much he tipped. Tell me everything."

Moline closed her eyes and in five sentences she recalled her encounter with the suspicious individual. The trooper radioed his second-in-command, "Do an APB for a white male, late-forties, medium height, black hair, fresh haircut, thin build, driving a new Ford box van, color white, no lettering, suspect probably armed and nasty."

Around five o'clock, Minister Lancaster told the audience, "I want everyone who owns one of these Durrells to come back up and play one last song for Johnny. Let's have the choir stand in front of the stage. Johnny's nieces will play the Golden Sisters."

Chaz, carrying a borrowed acoustic, got on stage with studio musicians and blues legends. Roadies carried wheelchair-bound Mickey Groundwater to his bass. Chaz told the mourners, "Last time I saw Johnny, he strummed "I'm Going Home" on a new Durrell. Let's do it again. And a one and a two…"

Twenty pounds of mahogany, three pounds of maple, and a hundred feet of steel string played by vengeful musicians chilled the backbone of everyone in the room. The nieces wowed everyone with a worried string solo. A deliveryman, a mile away, heard the choir sing.

The celebration ended with a gloomy prayer. Chaz, Mae, and ten of Johnny's closest friends formed a condolence line in Molly's lobby. After an hour of weepy hugs and boozy kisses, the funeral director took Johnny's body to a crematorium in a nearby town. Exhausted Mae leaned her head on Chaz's shoulder during the ride back to her house.

The next afternoon, Chaz, Mae, Liz, the twins, and a few relatives, stood on the knoll behind Johnny's workshop. Mae cast Johnny's ashes toward heaven. A soft wind carried the grit and powder to a stand of reeds.

On Mae's front steps, Liz told Chaz, "I just got bad news. Sarah is failing. Hate to leave you alone. I must return to New York. I'm taking a bus from Lincolnville to Little Rock in an hour."

14 DECLINE

After a bumpy flight through a pack of thunderstorms, Liz helped the third shift nurse steady Sarah's walk from the bathroom to the couch. In the kitchen, the nurse told Liz, "She's a goner. Her memory is failing. It's way more than forgetfulness. She called the refrigerator a cold box the other day. I've told her six times my name is Jan. She's called me Pam, Jim, Jenny."

Despite the early hour, Liz called Dr Athena's office. Twenty minutes after the call, Sarah, strapped to a gurney, stared at a grimy ambulance ceiling. Liz sat on the dimpled metal floor, rubbing her sister's hand. Seconds after the ambulance backed to the emergency room entrance, EMT's wheeled Sarah into a critical care room where Dr. Athena took a quick look. "This is serious," she said. "We must take a scan. Sarah, sign here."

"Am I dead?" Sarah asked.

"No, but you're in a life-threatening condition. I'm your doctor. You need a scan, now. Sign the release."

"No way," Sarah said. She asked Liz why they were in a hospital. Liz took the clipboard from the doctor and made Sarah's fingers hold the pen. "You're going downhill," she said. "Sign here so they can scan your head, see if anything is in there." With the pen point on paper, Sarah paused. Liz made her sister's hand write an x. An orderly released the gurney's brake and whisked Sarah to the imaging department. Dr. Athena said it would take a few hours to read the results.

Liz bought a journal from the hospital gift shop and went to a waiting room with walls painted sugar cookie white. Gray couches with mushy springs and coffee-stained cushions held jumpy spouses and siblings ignoring nurse requests to wait at home for a surgeon's call. She removed the dark cellophane from the journal. The cover featured a white bird sitting on a guitar, a promotional image from the first Woodstock festival. The last time she saw the image was at April's house. She considered tossing the notebook into the trash, but kept it as a reminder of Jasper's rescue.

She thumbed through a stack of housewife magazines, drank a coffee machine tea, and ate a desiccated pastry. Unable to relate to articles about nurturing zinnias or canning peaches, she tossed the magazines aside and watched gloomy faces waft in and out of the waiting room. Three young women with their eyes fixed on a soap opera waited for news about their father's heart surgery. An elderly man with a bandaged head cried out for his wife, a fellow car crash victim. A woman fled from the room shouting to God after a nurse whispered in her ear. To evade the drama, Liz moved to a small conference room. In the quiet setting, she worried that Sarah may be disabled for life, or would die, because of a scam. She felt shame because they had become close friends after years exchanging snide remarks and insults. Their tepid relationship softened after Chaz told them, "You have one breathing sister, so be thankful."

Over the next few hours, she wrote in her journal. The first few pages described the bank robbery, the celebration of her ill-gotten wealth, and the shock when police handcuffed her. She described a prison beating she endured after brushing a gang member. Two pages described her frustrating work search after her release, when few would hire a felon. Her eyes flickered when writing about her visits with Johnny Durrell. As she began writing her tenth page, Dr. Athena breezed into the room and said, "First off, she'll survive, but plan on months of bed rest."

"How long before she gets back to work?" Liz asked.

"Full cognitive recovery could take a year. Brain injuries take time to heal. I want to send her to Longview Hospital on Long Island, the perfect place for her recovery. Your sister is a lucky lady. A little more trauma, she'd be vegetative. If she approves, an ambulance will leave soon. I'll write a summary for her new doctors, but I can't include your story about how the injury occurred. I know this isn't a sleepwalking injury. The next round of doctors will want to know what happened. Tell me the real story, for your sister's health."

Liz's lack of sleep resulted in a spell of sobbing, coughing and faintness. She cried into a towel for a few minutes and recovered after a hug from the doctor. "Truth is, in a little town across the bay from Seattle, a man attacked us," she said. "We fought him off. He bashed Sarah's head with a pistol butt. I heard her skull crack. Dude stole some of our money. Sarah bled all over the rug. I thought I saw brain bits on her head; turns out it was strands of rug. Thank God I slowed the bleeding until the ambulance arrived." Dr. Athena thanked Liz for telling the truth. They rushed to the intensive care ward where Liz hovered close to Sarah and wrote an x on the transfer form. Minutes later, an ambulance dashed Sarah to Longview Hospital.

Back at her apartment, Liz packed Sarah's clothing and belongings in three corrugated boxes. She stuffed vomit and urine stained blankets and sheets into plastic bags and tossed them into a dumpster. Their cousin cleaned Sarah's apartment and stored the contents. Around dinner time, Liz received a phone call from Dr. Leonard, Sarah's new doctor. "Looking at the scan, I'd say your sister took a good blow to the head. Dr. Athena gave you the correct diagnosis. We must stop the bleeding. It's only a few drops, so it should heal without surgery."

"How soon will she return to reality?" Liz asked.

"Hard to say. With rest and therapy, most of her memory should return. It takes time, the brain must heal. If she plays by the rules, she should recover. There's a chance she'll be disabled emotionally, or could have difficulty speaking. She's having more tests tomorrow morning. You can visit her in a few days."

With Sarah under care, Liz went to the Brooklyn music studio for the first practice of her new band. A taxi dropped her outside a long, concrete block building with unmarked doors every fifty feet. In the first unit, Liz encountered several young men stripping parts from an Italian sports car. They didn't speak English, so Liz played air guitar. One of the men showed seven fingers.

Standing outside unit seven, Liz watched Suzy rumble in on a vintage BMW motorcycle with the sidecar brimming with snares, cymbals, and beer. She parked her bike, took off her fluorescent orange helmet, and shook her carrot-colored hair. She gave Liz a tight handshake and confident smile. The stitching in her purple leather riding pants strained when she bent over the sidecar to remove her gear.

They walked through a cluttered office to a high-ceilinged studio with a glass-walled mixing station on one end. Six pitted chrome stands held squarish microphones with 1952 patents. Brie chatted with an elderly white man wearing white frame sunglasses and a white linen suit. "Ladies, meet Mugsy Walters," she said. "I've known him since he owned Rage, the punk rock capital of the world, down in SoHo. After Liz shook his hand, she rubbed her palm in her pocket.

"Blah, Blah, Blah," Mugsy said. "You're talking three bankruptcies ago. Nice to meet you girls. Let's talk money. Hundred an hour in cash before you plug in. Four hour minimum. Unplug ten minutes before your time is up. Chuck your empties and snipes in the barrel or you won't be back."

"Wonderful," Brie said. "Three in the afternoon to seven on Saturday open?"

Mugsy said the time was taken. Brie put four, hundred dollar bills in his hand. On a calendar, he crossed out the name of a slow-paying boy band and wrote Brie Piper band on the Saturday afternoon slot. The band-to-be left the studio and walked a few hundred feet to a stand of weed trees on the edge of the parking lot. Suzy carried a chilled six-pack of beer in a cooler. Using tree trunks as chair backs and cardboard as pads, they drank beer and talked about their new venture.

"The studio is a dump. Mugsy is a creep." Liz said.

"I know it ain't Chessman's," Brie said. "He won't bother us as long as his wallet is heavy with cash. He's like a kind uncle until he's short on money."

"I'll brain the bastard if he tries any shit with me," Suzy said.

"I'm sure you will," Liz said. "Seeing we have a chick band, anyone know a chick singer?"

"Kim Sanders from Queens might fit." Suzy said. "Gal sings everything from screaming rock to babysitter ballads. I'll call her tonight."

They drafted a song list for their first practice. When dark clouds crept over the Manhattan skyline, they finished their beers. Liz and

Brie returned to Manhattan by cab. Suzy covered her sidecar with a canvas tarp, pinched a fresh beer with her thigh, and plowed her motorcycle through raindrops to a Queens biker bar.

Liz entered Sarah's hospital room expecting to see a zombie attached to wires and intravenous tubes. Sarah had only a small bandage on her head and no attachments. "I'm doing fine," she said, rubbing a teddy bear sent by Dr. Athena. "This is like a hotel. Good food, funny nurses, hot doctors."

"You look and sound damn good," Liz said.

"Met with doctor something or other this morning. Guy sounded British. I'm staying for a while. No idea how long. Bed rest, no noise. TV with the sound off. No phone. Probably basket weaving lessons. They gave me happy pills. Everything seems funny, you're funny, the wall is funny, my life is funny."

"I told your mortgage company you're disabled and willing to hand over the keys. Cuz stored your furniture."

"Do what you gotta do."

"Next problem: Marley called your cell six times."

"Why you checking my phone?" Sarah asked."

"You told me to check your messages every day."

"I did? Any other messages?"

"Lenny, four calls, asking about the *Chessman's*."

"Oh, forget about him."

"OK, back to the book," Liz said. "You gotta finish it somehow."

"I can't write anything. Talk to Marley for me. Don't tell her what hospital I'm in. Have her hold the book for a year."

"The call will be fun. By the way, Lenny wants to squeeze your ass. He said the other deals went well. What other deals? You working around me?"

"Stop drilling me with questions. I just woke up, can't deal with you. Go away, leave me alone."

Sarah threw the stuffed bear at her sister and pushed the buzzer attached to her bed. A nurse ran into the room and told Liz to follow her to the nurse's station. Sarah shouted, "Let me go home…I want to go home…"

The nurse told Liz, "You must leave. Head trauma patients are moody. She's having a bad spell. She's hurt, can't do much about it.

Stay away for a few days. Give the meds time to work. Call us if you want an update on her condition."

Liz dashed to her apartment. She opened a cookie jar on her kitchen table and removed eighty-seven, hundred-dollar bills; all that remained from the Port Townsend debacle. She put thirty-six hundred dollars in an envelope to pay Sarah's foreclosure fees. Five thousand dollars went into an envelope for her sister's insurance deductable. With more financial issues to address, she crawled under the table and detached a black fanny pack wired to the underside of the tabletop. She unzipped the pack. Four stacks of hundred dollar bills fell to the table top.

When Mick robbed the bank, he tossed the first bag of stolen money into an office where the dye pack exploded. He then held a gun to the head of the quivering teller, got a bag of clean money, and ran from the bank with over ninety thousand dollars in a deposit bag. Inattentive Liz, thinking Mick was only cashing a check, drove away slowly. Mick screamed, "Get outta here! I robbed the bank!" as he stuffed the stolen cash in the black fanny pack.

Within minutes, Brooklyn's Flatbush Avenue filled with wailing police cruisers looking for Liz's dark green Toyota sedan. She evaded capture by being stuck in traffic along with hundreds of other dark green Toyota sedans cruising Brooklyn that afternoon. Unfortunately, an hour after the robbery, she parked her car near an abandoned house under police surveillance.

The next morning, a police officer parked behind Liz's car noticed the wanted license plate and called in reinforcements. When they barged into Mick's apartment, Liz tossed the fanny pack out the bathroom window. The pack slammed against a three story tall oak tree and settled in a cavity used as a squirrel residence. The police tore the apartment apart looking for the cash, but didn't find a penny. The cash stayed in the tree, dry and secure, during their arraignment. Mick couldn't make bail. Liz's relatives pooled their home equity to pay her bondsman. Hours after her release, Liz went to Mick's apartment to get her clothes. She climbed the tree under moonlight and retrieved the fanny pack. Before starting her prison sentence, she sewed the robbery proceeds into a pillow unknowing Sarah kept in her living room.

Liz pleaded guilty, testified against Mick, and got a year. Mick got seventeen plus another year, when, in the courtroom, he threatened to kill Liz and all her relatives. Mick assumed the police stole the robbery money. The cops had no idea where the money went. Mick's lawyers appealed his conviction, placing the blame on Liz and her alleged drug addiction. Liz's lawyers countered with clean drug tests taken when she was employed by a hospital. The judge denied the appeal. Liz knew Mick's snarky demeanor would keep him in prison for the full sentence. She felt entitled to the money because she was snookered into the crime and had served her sentence.

With several thousand dollars due for rent and utilities, she sliced the paper band of one stack and counted three thousand dollars, crinkling each note to make it look circulated. She stuffed the cash into her back pocket and noted the withdrawal in her notebook. Seventy-two thousand dollars remained in the stash. With her expenses covered for the next month and Sarah under competent care, Liz could focus on her new band and finish Sarah's book. The process would begin the next day during lunch with Marley.

Liz, wearing a black dress and twiggy heels, entered a Midtown restaurant known for its chromy motif and steely waiters. The hostess, a cherubic princess in a size two dress, seated Liz in a sunny room near a group of loud lawyers. Marley arrived a few minutes late. She extended her long fingers and murmured a greeting through a forced smile. When they shook hands, Marley's fat diamond ring brushed Liz's barren fingers. Marley positioned her phone so she could simultaneously converse and read emails. "Your sister is lovely person, a skilled writer, and a budding literary star," she said. "I pray every morning she recovers quickly." She patted her tight black perm while checking out faces in the room. "I also pray she finishes her fucking book."

"Doctors say several months, maybe more," Liz said.

"Listen girl, I've got big money on the line. I can't wait several months." Marley said with her eyes fixed on a table of slick men. "I've got a few options. Excuse me for a second. One of my authors just sat over there."

Marley stood and passed her hand over a crease in her buttercup-hued pantsuit. Liz caught a whiff of perfume fit for a king's bride. Many in the room watched her cattish gait cross the velvety carpet. They knew that during her Mt. Everest ascent she had pushed aside a suffering climber begging for help. She flattered the author with compliments and returned to the table. "He's happy as a clam," she said. "Just got him a half-million advance on his next novel. Now the lush has to sober up and write the damn book."

"There's money in writing?" Liz asked.

"Yeah, if the author has a following. Sarah's on a different level. She's a fine writer with no following. Her first book must have blockbuster info that'll knock the literary scene on its ass. Lead to talk show interviews. Sell books and more books. Make me money, her money."

"Seeing she's on the mend, can't write her name, how do we finish her book?"

"I've got a few ghostwriters up to the task. A chapter is only five thousand words. Any half-wit can thumb through Sarah's notes and pound out a chapter in a few days."

"Do you know Sarah has some shocking information?"

"Listen babe, in my thirty years as an agent, all I hear is the word *shocking*. Give me Sarah's laptop and files. I'll finish the book. She'll get a royalty check every month."

A waiter put a stainless steel plate holding Marley's watercress sandwich on a woven wire placemat. She read emails during her meal. Liz ate a silver dollar sized filet mignon in two bites. Marley waived away a cheery waiter pushing a tea cart loaded with pastries, gave the bill a disgusted look and slid a black credit card into the presenter.

"Let me finish the book," Liz said. "I've got a handle on my sister's work. I've also got a writing jag from my mother's family. My uncle was a novelist. My mother studied journalism at Columbia. I'll get a draft done in a month."

"Oh come on girl," Marley said. "Stop wasting my time with this foolishness. You don't know jack-shit about writing. My authors must have style. Never use the passive voice. Do you even know about the passive voice?"

"Is it pillow talk?"

"No, no way. I don't have time for high school grammar lessons."

"We'll make it work. It'll be a joint effort with me typing and Sarah talking."

"All right," Marley said. "I'll give you a few days to resolve this. If I see one form of the verb *to be*, your work is going in the trash. Just remember, when I gave your sister a thirty-thousand dollar advance, I got the power to hire a ghost to finish the book."

Marley gave Liz a handshake and trotted to her town car. Liz stayed at the table, slow-sipping a twenty-dollar cocktail while plotting how to fulfill her promise to finish the book. She planned a quiet night at home to rest for her next day visit with Sarah.

Sarah, sporting a short institutional haircut, told Liz, "You like the look? Us whack jobs get a boy's regular. What's happening out in the world?"

"Met with Marley. Went smooth as sandpaper," Liz said.

"You tell her my brain is mush?"

"She knows all about it. She wants a ghost writer to finish the book. Get it on the market. Send you royalty checks after you pay off the advance. I didn't know you got an advance."

"I did?" Sarah said, with a confused look.

"Someday, tell me how you spent the money. I offered Marley a sensible option: You and I write the book. I'll stoke your memory. We'll talk things out. I'll type what you say. It's only five-thousand words."

"Whatever," Sarah said.

Liz sent Marley an email saying the sisters would finish the book as a team. Several minutes later, Liz read aloud Marley's snappy response and the first sentence of an attached, lawyer-drawn confirmation of the arrangement. Sarah interrupted the reading by shouting, "Stop talking junk! My brain is useless! You want to write it, go write it!" Her attention turned to a muted talk show. Liz put the stuffed bear next to the pillow and went to Mugsy's studio.

Suzy strolled into Mugsy's with Kim, a trash talking singer with a debutante's strut, whose father, a snooty Manhattan lawyer, disowned her after she showed a fondness for flirty singing and a dislike of arias. He had paid her Julliard tuition, but refused to listen to her concert performances because her vocals hurt his trained ears. She regretted choosing a career in punk rock after a ruffian grabbed her leg during a performance and dragged her into the crowd. Her broken femur took three months to heal. His broken jaw healed in a jail cell. She won a two hundred thousand dollar civil suit against the club. Her fifty thousand dollar donation to the Metropolitan Opera restored her father's love.

After Kim nailed a two song, a cappella audition held in Mugsy's office, Brie and Liz hired her. The band had a twenty minute wait before their studio time, so they bandied names for their new group. Suzy insisted on Hormonal Distraction, Liz wanted Bitchin' Blues, Kim liked Blues Babes. They settled on Brie's offering, Simply Blue.

Mugsy ordered a dawdling group off the studio stage. Brie told Mugsy they would jam, not record, so he stayed in his office. Simply Blue settled behind microphones and tuned their instruments. Liz called out "Motherless Child," a slow spiritual with a bluesy touch. Simply Blue responded with cacophonic chaos. Brie's pushy bass disrupted Liz's slow playing. Suzy's furious drumming suffocated Kim's tender vocals. Simply Blue tried a dozen songs over three and a half hours. Nothing worked. The session ended with a collective belief the band had no chance to succeed. Mugsy shook his head as he swept the stage of dust and agitated women. The band gathered near Suzy's motorcycle and drank beers. Suzy suggested renaming the band Simply Awful. Brie told her bandmates to stop showing their strengths. If they thought about the band as a whole, they could make it work. The group agreed to another session after a five-day cool down.

Liz spent the next morning reading digital folders in Sarah's laptop. She couldn't access a password-protected folder titled Len. The Hendrix folder held hundreds of entries downloaded from an academic portal. Other folders contained scans of Hendrix written letters, contracts, and newspaper clippings. The Miles Davis folder contained over a hundred files. A separate folder held Sarah's draft of three-hundred and fifty double-spaced pages divided into twenty chapters.

Liz had a copy shop print and spiral bind the manuscript. Fueled by caffeine, she spent the evening in her apartment reading the bound draft. The first few chapters described the birth, decline and renaissance of blues music. Twenty pages explained how rock and roll artists from England and the United States borrowed heavily from the blues songbook. A chapter described Hendrix as a softy surrounded by aggressive agents. Another chapter characterized Davis as a mean spirit with a snappy tongue. Latter pages hinted at an impending collaboration. Liz figured the last chapter would have to deny they jammed, or claim they did by telling the story of Tinker and the *Chessman's*.

Chaz heard Simply Blue was falling apart. He invited the band to a Sunday afternoon session at his apartment so they could meet some seasoned musicians who had survived band drama and stylistic differences. The day of the session, Suzy parked her motorcycle in front of Chaz's apartment. Kim took a minute to wiggle from the sidecar and shake blood to her legs. Liz and Brie arrived soon afterward. From the foyer, Suzy watched a bearded waif eye the motorcycle and run away after seeing the Protected by PMS sticker on the gas tank.

In Chaz's living room, Liz introduced the other members of Simply Blue to Kenny, Pearly and Ruby. Brie countered Pearly's syrupy greeting with a caustic reminder of their three-way date costing her a hundred-dollar bar tab and two taxi fares. Chaz softened the tension by introducing the Waywards, the aged musicians who spent their days sitting under the trees in front of the apartment building. The attendees parted for Reverend Whitley, guided by his daughter Lucy, a gospel singer. Liz quashed the Reverend's request to feel Simply Blue's physicality.

"First-timers," Chaz said, "we jump-start Sunday get-togethers with "Wade in the Water." I'll open the windows so the neighbors can hear it." Lucy said she'd sing a cappella, so Chaz kept his hands off his guitar. When her voice filled the apartment with perfectly pitched, melodic devotion, a family in church clothes listened from the street.

"Now we made the Lord happy," Chaz said, "let's talk about a new band with a broken engine; four woman needing advice on how to work together. Young ladies, tell us about your musical leanings."

Liz claimed an obsession of Chicago-style electric blues. Brie admired the late jazz bassist Jaco Pastorius. Suzy, pounding a string of beats on the Manhattan Yellow Pages, said she worshipped drummer Buddy Rich. Kim's said her immersion in punk music fueled her need to sing with snarl.

"Too many styles going on," said one of the Waywards. "Never works. Once we settled on a style, we've played together for forty years with no problems."

"I get your point," Brie said. "We've got to blend our styles into a stew and serve it."

"Everyone plays music different," Reverend Whitley said. "Pick out what you like and run with it. Take a guy like Hendrix. Boy threw out the rock and roll book, played blues, jazz, country, whatever felt good. Chaz, you remember the night we laughed like hell when he blew out Mim's sound system?"

"Sure do," Chaz said. "She spent ten grand fixing the woofers."

"The best way to blend a band is gospel," Lucy said. "Next time you're warming-up in the studio, don't play instruments, sing a barebones "Walk on the Water." Keep working it. Let jazz blend with punk, blues mix with rock. Start out sweet then add a growl or two. Make your voices one, then transfer the blend to your instruments. You get out of sync, into a bitch-fight, sing gospel. Girls, give it a try."

Simply Blue stood in front of the open window. Lucy sang the first stanza and encouraged them to sing along. It took a few bars for things to sync. Suzy softened her blues-mama voice. Brie, singing with vigor, pounded a bass line on her hip. Liz harmonized the tune while fingering air chords. Kim hid her brash contralto by singing softly. Reverend Whitley, impressed with the harmony, howled after the song.

Every Sunday session, Chaz followed gospel with a Hendrix song. Pearly suggested "Hear My Train a Comin', a song Hendrix played on a twelve-string acoustic guitar.

"The boy kept a guitar company busy," Reverend Whitley said when the song ended. "He must have burned a hundred Strats in his day. Shame only a couple survived. Glad the white one from Woodstock is still around."

Over the next hour, the musicians stood in the center of the living room holding hands, singing gospel numbers. During the final stanza of "He's Got the Whole World in His Hands," Chaz stretched his arms and yawned. Lucy took Reverend Whitley back to his church. Kenny, Pearly, and Ruby headed for the Backbeat. Simply Blue promised to carry the sisterly spirit to their next practice.

In the hallway outside Chaz's apartment, Liz listened to Detective Ricker's phone message request for another interview. The call shocked Liz who thought the investigation was focused on a man, not the two sisters. She'd have two days to tweak her alibi.

15 JOHNNY'S REVENGE

In a Lower Manhattan police station, Detective Ricker led Liz past a shackled suspect to a windowless interview room. "Let me be clear," the detective said. "You and your sister are back in the middle of the double-murder investigation. Seems you two were involved in suspicious activities near the scene. You being a convicted bank robber adds to the story."

"Sightseeing and socializing isn't suspicious behavior," Liz said. "I told you, we visited PT, dropped by April's house, had a nice visit, left on good terms."

"Why'd you rent rigging a few weeks before the murders? Something about hanging a birdhouse?"

"For picture taking. I wanted to get a shot of the harbor from a tree. I sat in a sling until the light was right. Rig worked out fine."

"You can buy cheap posters downtown with that view. On another matter, why'd your sister buy outrageous clothes the day before the killings?"

"Sarah felt out of place looking like a Long Island princess. For fun, she bought some chick clothes, tight jeans and the like. Got hit-on by a dozen guys; got more action since college."

"Yah, right. Next issue: The doctor said you changed your story about your sister's injury."

"Sarah writes for a living," Liz said, dabbing sweat from her brow. "Got to have a good reputation in the word business. I thought she'd get a bad rap. The truth is, a strange man barged into our room, robbed us, bashed Sarah, ran away."

"Well, this changes things. What'd he look like?"

"Kinda tall, mustache, short black hair, ruddy white face, missing a few teeth."

"Give me an hour. I'll show you images of local thugs."

From another office, the detective called her office. Liz, uncomfortable on the steel, cushion-less chair, rested her head on her crossed arms. The aggressive questioning made her consider hiring an attorney. Detective Ricker returned with a dozen printed images. Liz viewed the suspect photos. "None of these guys did it," she said. The detective concluded the interview by saying a convening grand jury could indict the sisters.

Liz experienced a panic attack on the ride from the police interrogation to her lawyer's office. A short stay on a park bench normalized her heartbeat. The lawyer offered to review her case for ten thousand in cash or equity. She didn't sign the retainer, but said she'd be in contact in a few days. On the ride home, she had another panic attack while worrying about her next day meeting with a team of doctors who'd describe Sarah's current neurological and psychological condition.

The Longwood doctors gave Liz an optimistic report. An x-ray of Sarah's head showed her brain bleeding had stopped. A doctor said Sarah had performed well on memory tests. She had recalled her Social Security number, cell phone number, and third-grade teacher's name. With her memory restored, the doctors had given her a strong sedative that would keep her semiconscious for a few weeks and allow her injury to heal. They prohibited family visits during the sedation. If the treatment worked, Sarah could return to a normal life after a few months rest.

After the meeting, Liz peeked into Sarah's dimly lit room. Under a bank of blinking monitors, a feeding tube and an intravenous line fueled her deep sleep. Liz, comforted by the doctor's optimism, went to the hospital cafeteria and celebrated with a slice of light bulb warmed pizza. While chewing the crust, she listened to Lenny's voicemail request for an update on Sarah's condition and a meeting about the mystery recordings. Liz agreed to meet him at his office in a few days.

Liz, knowing blues casual wouldn't fit a Rockefeller Place

meeting, wore a scarlet business suit found on Sarah's clothes rack and a bracelet found in Sarah's jewelry box under a false bottom. During her walk from Times Square, many eyes focused on her tattooed arms, tight suit, wobbly heels, and the flash on her wrist. A policeman gave her a wink. Several young hoods, seeing an easy grab, turned away when she entered the tall building holding Lenny's office. A receptionist walked her to a chair facing Lenny's desk. Lenny breezed into his office and gave Liz a clingy handshake. His steady, ceramic smile shined as he removed his cream-colored sport jacket, sat at his desk, and powered his computer. "Sorry about sis. Why you wearing her bracelet?" he said.

"It's a probably a cheapie," Liz said. She uncoupled the bracelet and handed it to him.

"You sure?" asked Lenny. "I see bling like that at the Grammys."

"It's not worth anything. Sarah has five bucks in her checking account. She'd have sold it long ago if it had any value."

"The necklace cost fifty-five grand plus tax," Lenny said. "It's solid gold. I'd hide it in your pocketbook on the way home."

"You seem to know all about it."

"I gave your sister the bracelet on her last birthday along with a two-caret engagement ring. She kept the bracelet and declined the ring. Claimed she couldn't contribute a nickel toward the wedding. I offered to pay for a wedding at the Parkland. I still have the ring, hope she reconsiders."

"I knew you were friends," Liz said, looking stunned. "I didn't know you were really close."

"Things cooled after she said no." Lenny said, keeping his smile as he shuffled through a foot high pile of contracts and lawsuits. "We keep a working friendship. She sends musicians my way. If I sign them to my label, she gets a cut. Everything went smoothly until you guys refused to sell me the *Chessman's*."

"Never knew sis had so much side action."

Lenny rested his elbows on the desk top and took a boiler plate agreement from a manila folder. "I know you're Chaz Russell's buddy, scared to piss him off," he said. "The old timer won't be around much longer. Guarantee if you had a half-million in your pocket, you'd forget his name. I've made millions from old blues musicians like him who signed contracts they couldn't read. I sell music to keep the lights on. My lights are close to dimming, so let's get the *Chessman's* deal done. Shock the jazz and blues scene and take rock along for the ride."

"Hold on," Liz said. "Sure as shit, Chaz will know I stole his music. He knows every leg breaker in Harlem. I don't want to play guitar from a wheelchair. You want to calm your nerves, give me a twenty grand deposit. If we sell, you get first refusal. If you decline the asking price, I'll keep the deposit and auction the music to the highest bidder."

Lenny, looking like he was viewing a beaten corpse, rested his hand on a phone receiver and thought about the offer for a few seconds. "Give me ten minutes. I'll have legal draft a contract."

"Don't get lawyers involved," Liz said. "This is a handshake deal. Hundreds only."

A phone call from someone famous interrupted the negotiations. Liz left the office and chatted with a female intern, a comely Smith College student. "Don't let him lock his office door," the intern whispered. "You'll get the couch treatment."

Lenny summoned Liz to his office after the call. With his smile restored, he counted twenty thousand dollars, pushed the pile her way, and walked toward the door. "Get your hands off the lock," Liz yelped. "I'm not getting the couch treatment." Lenny, blushing brighter than a welder's torch, went back to his desk. With his cash in her pocketbook, she promised to return some day with healthy Sarah, ready to sign a deal for the *Chessman's*, if the price was right.

Back at her apartment, Liz put the yard-long cardboard box holding Sarah's book research on the living room floor. Fifty thick folders contained notes and copies of magazine articles about the late 60s Manhattan music scene. The Durrell folder included a handwritten list of guitars Johnny had built from 1965 to 1972. Liz rubbed the list with her finger tips. The paper didn't have the sheen of copy paper. It was sturdy rag paper, yellowed by time and wrinkled by humidity. The penciled notations looked like Johnny's handwriting. The list began with a 1965 guitar named Maxie, "burnt up" in 1970. Kahuna, built in 1967, was "drownded in hurcane." Johnny listed twelve guitars built in 1970. Bugeye Merchel bought the first guitar built that year and paid in "shine." The fifth guitar listed was Johnny-Strat delivered to Jimi and noted as "fixed fret."

When Tinker described Hendrix carrying a flashy guitar into Chessman's the night of the Miles Davis jam, Liz assumed he was describing a Stratocaster. Hendrix preferred these battle-tested electric guitars capable of generating wails, squeaks, whinnies, or clean chords. Astounded by the news of the Hendrix guitar, she called Tinker. Despite his drunkenness, he said she could visit his apartment the next afternoon.

Liz dressed in baggy jeans and an oversized, black hooded sweatshirt. She skipped makeup, distressed her hair, and wore scuffed hiking boots. The outfit made for an uneventful walk from the subway station to Tinker's apartment. Tinker responded to Liz's door knock with a growly "who there?"

She put her mouth inches from the door jam and yelled, "Liz here. We talked last night."

Tinker opened the door a few inches. His breath smelled of sour hops. "I kind of remember talking to you," he said. "You coming over wasn't talked about."

"Sure was, just give me five minutes," Liz said. "Got a couple questions."

"All right, let me get out of my pajamas."

Tinker changed into baggy shorts and a tank top tee shirt. Liz, seeing his scruffy beard holding pizza remnants, suggested he stay off the street until he shaved. "Speaking of looks," he said, "why you dressed like a grape picker? Where's them tight jeans?"

"Had to throw them out. Your eyes burned holes in them."

Tinker cleared pizza-stained newspapers from the kitchen table. He put a fresh can of discount beer on the tin cover of a muffler repair kit. Liz took a bottle of water from her pocketbook and sat on the chair closest to the exit. "You told me Hendrix carried a guitar into Chessman's," she said. "What'd it look like?"

The question shocked Tinker. In the many years he had thought about the night, he had forgotten about the guitar. A chug of beer rekindled his memory. "The body had pastel swirls, neck had gold inlay. Found out later Johnny Durrell built it for Hendrix, called it the Johnny-Strat. Back then, Johnny hung around studios, fixing guits, filling in for strung-out session guys. He built Jimi a half breed, half jazz, half rock axe. Thing had blues bones with plenty of muscle. Had to be; around that time Jimi played rough. He smashed and burned

Strats during encores. Rumor was Jimi's manager had a kickback deal, made Jimi play Strats, keep barbecuing them. Jimi talked about plastering the Johnny-Strat with Strat decals to keep the suits happy. Pretty sure the only time he jammed with the guitar was the night at Chessman's. He played it so hard he popped a fret. Probably saved it from the lighter fluid. Johnny fixed the fret. Jimi died before getting it back. Johnny told everyone he burned it after Jimi's funeral. Of course, Johnny played light with the truth."

"It look like a Durrell or a Strat?" Liz asked.

"Looked like a Durrell," Tinker said. "Not much like a Strat. Figure Johnny added Strat to its name so Jimi would feel comfortable with it. Somehow, the thing sounded like a Strat. Still think Johnny's father had something to do with it. JD built lots of wacky guitars for his friends. One had a keyboard, sounded like an organ."

Tinker finished his beer and got another. "One more secret you can tell your sister," he said. "Johnny never built guitars. JD left him hundreds of bodies and fretboards, probably built the gizmo that gave the guitar two tones. If Johnny got an order, he'd assemble a guitar from the parts."

"No way," Liz said. "I've been in his shop, seen him covered in sawdust. Bench and floor loaded with shavings."

"His saws never ran. He got free bags of sawdust from a saw mill and dumped it all over the place."

"You're crazy," Liz said.

Tinker, looking ready for war, told Liz, "Stop disrespecting me. If you're one of those people who think I'm a liar, get the hell out of here. Johnny couldn't press a fret without screwing it up."

Liz calmed him down with a smile. Tinker leaned back on his chair, rubbing his belly. She respectfully asked for a picture of the Hendrix guitar. He shuffled to a bedroom closet. Ten minutes later, on the table, he dumped a cardboard box with "family and friends" written on it. In a pile of faded, curled photographs, he found a photo of Hendrix playing an electric guitar that look like it had survived a paint store explosion.

"There's the Johnny-Strat," he said. "Found the photo on old man Chessman's desk. Taken the night Hendrix jammed there. Shame poor Johnny toasted the guitar, it sounded real good. I've had a few slimy dudes and a badass woman ask me about it, told them don't bother because Johnny scattered its ashes in the Arkansas wind."

"Got any idea who whacked Johnny and stole his guitars?" Liz asked. "Same thing happened on the West Coast. Two dead, bunch of guitars gone."

"To answer your questions, pay a guitar thief to talk. Cash loosens lips. They know whose stealing them. I'd say the guitars ended up on a collector's wall, probably in Japan."

Tinker, losing his battle with a grade ten hangover, dumped his beer in the sink, and made chocolate milk from a carton his drink of choice. The carbohydrate rush softened his demeanor. Feeling sentimental, he showed Liz photos of his murdered brother. He turned misty when showing an image of a former girlfriend who had jumped or was pushed off the George Washington Bridge. When his veiny eyes looked ready to spurt blood, Liz thanked him for his time and put twenty dollars on the table. He yawned, canted his head toward his bedroom and winked. Liz, ignoring his advances, gave him a pat suitable for a Rottweiler and left for Chaz's apartment. Tinker ran to his bedroom for a long nap.

Liz complimented Chaz on his yellow-framed sunglasses with yellow-tinted lens, black bell-bottom slacks, and billowing silk shirt with the top three buttons unfastened. He denied moonlighting as a pimp and changed the subject by playing a recording of his previous night, all fusion session at Blue Monday, a SoHo nightclub. Positive audience response led to an agreement to play four more gigs that week.

Liz asked Chaz about the Johnny-Strat. "I tried to forget about the dang guitar," he said. "Johnny worked his ass off building it Jimi's way. Jimi loved it, but his manager wouldn't let him play it in public, only on session work. Jimi busted it by playing too hard. Johnny fixed it, but never gave it back. He told me if Jimi couldn't play it, he'd burn it."

"Johnny wouldn't hurt one of his guitars," she said. "They were his children."

"I agree," he said. "Johnny told the world he ran out of apple wood halfway through a rack of ribs, so he threw the guitar on the coals. Turns out, Johnny kept the thing hidden in his shop. A few times we got into the shine and he let me play it. Thing could play blues, jazz, rock, country, gypsy. Boy made me leave his shop so I couldn't see where he hid it."

"Johnny's killers take it?"

"I doubt it. His shop has a bunch of hidden closets. I'm flying down to Arkansas tomorrow to visit Johnny's mother, stay at her place, go over his estate. I'll ask her about it. You want to go? Drive me around. I'll pay for everything. Back in two days."

"I'll do it," Liz said.

Chaz and Liz arrived at Mae's house around dinner time. Mae gave Chaz a bucket holding hundreds of envelopes addressed to Johnny. She was so upset about his death she couldn't open an envelope with his name on it. Liz slit each envelope with a steak knife and Chaz read the contents. One envelope held a seven thousand dollar royalty check for a song Johnny wrote in the '70s. A Los Angeles-based rap group had sampled the song on their best-selling album. Other letters contained hand-written tributes to Johnny. A few letters from law firms begged to process Johnny's estate. Liz totaled the checks received and current bank statements. Johnny's accounts held over two million dollars. "I'm leaving all my money for my kin," Mae said, "and if they find them stolen guitars, they're going to a museum." Chaz read the list of stolen guitars compiled by the Arkansas State Police. The Johnny-Strat wasn't listed so he asked Mae if she knew about it.

"Oh, the goddamned Hendrix thing," she said. "Pardon me Lord for swearing. Johnny burnt it, so he said. Whole thing started over Johnny being cheap. His father told him a hundred times to buy a new roll of fret wire for each guitar. Johnny ran out of fret on the guitar. Cut the fret groove wide to fit some spare wire. Damn fret fell out during a session. Johnny told him the devil messed with the wood, best to burn it. Jimi told Johnny to fix the fret and fly his ass up to New York with it. Of course, Johnny waited until he had to buy a new roll of wire. Jimi died before getting it back. Collectors asked my boy about it every once in a while. He told them all he threw it into a fire, tossed the ashes outside another guitar builder's shop. Put the guy out of business."

"I'm not so sure he burned it," Chaz said. "Few years back, we was in his shop, you was away. I went outside to get some air. Came back in, Johnny was holding the Johnny-Strat. We let her rip until the sun came up. Johnny played Hendrix better than Jimi. OK if we look for it?"

"Do anything you want around here," Mae said.

Liz and Chaz entered Johnny's shop. Fingerprint powder covered the fractured guitar rack. Investigators had shipped a dozen floor planks soaked with Johnny's blood to a FBI lab. Coffee cups and cigarette butts filled Johnny's bucket seat.

"Them murderers think they picked the place clean," Chaz said. "I think Johnny knew they were coming, so he hid some stuff." He gave Liz a hammer and told her to start at a corner of the shop and tap each floor fastening. Chaz, holding another hammer, did the same at the opposite corner. The tapping stopped after ten minutes when Liz's hammering loosened wood-colored putty covering a screw head. She eventually found twenty puttied-over screws fastening three planks. Chaz gave her a long-handled screwdriver. With her belly on the floor, she unscrewed the fastenings and pried the planks with her fingers. They wouldn't budge, so she slid the screwdriver under a plank edge and had Chaz step on the handle. The plank released. Liz removed the floorboard, reached into the spidery void and retrieved a rusted military ammunition box containing a spiral-bound notebook listing every one of Johnny's guitars. Thelma was the tenth guitar on the list. Jasper was the last. Under the notebook, she found a pinewood cutoff with a crude diagram of the shop. An X was drawn over a window facing the house.

Liz dragged a step ladder to the window. She stood on the highest step and tapped the ceiling boards with the hammer. The fourth tap released putty hiding a screw. Additional taps identified screws holding three boards. She unscrewed the fastenings, handed the boards to Chaz, reached in the cavity and removed a furled sleeping bag wrapped with chicken wire and baling twine. Chaz put the sleeping bag on the bench. He removed the wire, unraveled the bag, and nearly passed out when he saw the Johnny-Strat. When he put the guitar on a sunny splash on the bench, the rays made the finish glow like a thousand watt light bulb. Looking closely at the fretboard, he counted five frets down from the thumbscrews. The fifth fret was fatter and higher than the others.

Liz asked Mae to come to the shop. When Chaz showed her the guitar, she swore like a cut off trucker. Liz calmed her down with daughterly words and a held hand. "You found the devil's tool," Mae said. "Get the piece of shit outta here. Take some kero and burn it. All that work for nothing good. Johnny spent a month inlaying the neck. Brought it to church a dozen times to get the sound right. Things got bad voodoo, wasn't meant to be built."

Mae wouldn't let the Johnny-Strat in her house so Chaz sat on the porch with the guitar on his lap. Speaking through the door screen, he offered to pay Mae for the guitar. She gave him the guitar for free provided he took it out of Arkansas and never brought it back. Chaz hid the guitar in a black trash bag and put it in the car trunk.

The next morning, Chaz asked Mae if she had enough money to get through the next few months. She told him Johnny had given her over a million dollars of his royalties to pay her house expenses and she had deposited every cent in a local bank account. After her lawyer settled the estate, she'd use the proceeds to display what the great Johnny Durrell accomplished after his "no-good father died."

Around noon, after weepy waves, they left Mae's farm. Early afternoon, as the jet leveled high in the blue Kentucky sky, Chaz looked at the Johnny-Strat like a father admiring his infant. "If I die," he told Liz," give it to the museum, after Mae passes on. I want them kids to see what the world's best played, if only once." Chaz put the guitar back in the trash bag when the plane landed in New York. He carried it with both hands through the concourse and held it tightly during the taxi ride home where his rhythm section, low on funds, would get their overdue paychecks.

Kenny, Pearly, and Ruby stared at the Johnny-Strat on Chaz's kitchen table."Can I borrow an air sickness bag?" Kenny asked.

Pearly bent over and viewed the guitar from bridge to tuner. "Ugliest guit in the world. Bronx Zoo monkey paint it?" he asked.

Ruby rubbed the guitar's body and wiggled the tremolo bar. "Has to be a Durrell from the 60s mated with a gizmo. Got good wood. Old time pickups. Played hard. How much you want for it?"

"It ain't for sale," Chaz said, " it's for showing. Johnny built it for Hendrix. Jimi played it once, popped a fret. Johnny fixed it. Jimi died before playing it again. Johnny's mother gave it to me. She thinks the guitar has bad voodoo. Let's go fire it up."

Chaz carried the bagged Johnny-Strat into the Backbeat. The

ebullient Friday afternoon crowd quieted when they saw what looked like a bag of trash. They all knew Chaz wouldn't enter the Backbeat with rubbish. A few thought the bag held marijuana. The bartender offered to toss the bag into a dumpster. Chaz, sporting a cagey grin, declined the offer and ordered a round of drinks. The bartender waved Chaz, Ruby, Pearly, and Kenny to vacant stools. One of the patrons asked what was in the bag. "Machine gun," Chaz replied, "good for shutting up loudmouths." The bartender served Chaz a whisky. Kenny and Pearly got gimlets, easy on the lime juice. Ruby drank fountain cola. The standoff ended when the forewarned Backbeat owner waved Chaz to the stage.

Chaz sat on a chair, holding a microphone, with the bag at his feet. "I see old friends out there," he said. "Hey Snooks, you remember getting chased down a Memphis street by some husband?" Snooks pumped his fist and grinned. And Kiki over there, you remember me climbing the fire escape, visiting you with a bottle?"

"Sure do," she said. "You passed out ten minutes later. Had to hook a sailor for some live action."

"What I'm getting at," he said, with a wide grin, "most of you know me or played music with me. Seeing you're like family, I've got a treat." He slid off the plastic bag, exposing the guitar. Under stage lights, the swirly finish looked irradiated and the inlay sparkled like a thousand tiny mirrors. All fifty patrons rushed the stage for a closer look. "Here's the Johnny-Strat," he said. "A Durrell with two lives, jazz or blues. It's not for sale, so don't ask. And tell your buddies don't try to clip it. I've got heat in my pocket. Plan is to show the world what Johnny built and Jimi played once. Form a line with ladies first. I'll let you play a string or two. Hey sound man, juice me up. Kenny, bring me another belt."

The crowd parted for the ravishing singer Missy Alex who sang the intro of "The Wind Cries Mary" with the guitar strapped over her bare shoulder. Snooks kissed the guitar and speed-picked a few bars. Queenie Maximus, a twentyish music prodigy with restless fingers, played a hundred chords in a hundred seconds. After every willing patron held the guitar, Chaz played a five-minute, slow tempo take of Hendrix's "Voodoo Chile." Several times, he bent four strings at once. The guitar didn't mind.

Queenie asked how to make it play jazz. "I have no idea," Chaz said. "Johnny kicked me out of his shop when he made the switch.

Looking in his window, I saw him turn a socket wrench. You'd have to gut the guitar to see how it works. I'll get some guitar geek to figure it out, maybe have to x-ray it."

News of the newly-found Hendrix guitar quickly dominated Harlem gossip streams. A line formed outside the Backbeat a half-hour after Chaz unveiled the guitar. The house band became too drunk to play, so Chaz kept showing the guitar. The Backbeat owner called in extra bartenders. By ten o'clock, most of Harlem's elite guitarists had played the Johnny-Strat. Even the Honduran dishwasher played a few notes. Around eleven, the house band, sobered by several Irish coffees, took the stage. Chaz sat at the bar next to the editor of a guitar journal that would feature the Johnny-Strat in the next issue.

The headline "Hendrix Jazz Guitar Found" made the September 15, 2009 *Guitar Weekly* cover. A second page photo showed Chaz playing the Johnny-Strat in the magazine's Manhattan office. A lengthy, reverential article about Johnny and his guitars prefaced a four page photo spread with close-ups of the guitar's neck, body, and fingerboard. An image taken in a sound hole showed the penciled words *Johnny-Strat* next to Johnny's signature.

Over the next week, most of the New York City newspapers published front page articles about the instrument. Chaz played the Johnny-Strat and bantered about Johnny Durrell on a late-night talk show. Before entering a town car parked near the television studio exit, he showed the guitar to a group of photographers. As the cameras flashed, a man wearing a designer tee shirt, tailored shorts, and alligator skin loafers leaned in and got a close look.

16 FALLEN FRET

Simply Blue's five day hiatus ended at Mugsy's with a group hug and a pledge to make great music. The conviviality turned vicious when Brie suggested a song that reminded Suzy of a failed romance. Mugsy heard shouting and waved the band into his office. "Let me give you some advice, on my nickel," he said. "Forty years of music listening, I know junk when I hear it. You girls are from different planets. Leads got blues bones, bass plays jazzy, drummer should be with a hair band, singer should be fronting a punk act. I'll refund your money if you go home and don't come back. It's your call. Leave now or stay for your minutes. I'll go back in my office, put in ear plugs, do paperwork."

Brie led her bandmates back to the studio stage. With calm demeanor, they adjusted their microphones and stood ready for the first mellow note of a spiritual with lyrics of love and peace. Placidity turned to ferocity when Suzy called Brie "pushy." Brie responded with a right hook that smeared Suzy's makeup. Liz and Kim avoided a homicide by loosening Suzy's hold on Brie's neck. For ten minutes, the band bickered about phrasing, beats, hairstyles, shoes, stolen boyfriends, and song selection. The arguing and hysteria ended when Brie, mad as a hornet, limped to a chair and disbanded Simply Blue. Mugsy gave each band member seventy-five dollars and barred them for life. Suzy flashed a middle finger as she drove away on her motorcycle. Kim swore all the way to the bus stop. Liz and Brie, vowing to stay friends, shared a cab to Manhattan.

Unemployed and angry Liz began the new day by sorting Sarah's mail. Unopened get well cards, personal letters, lawyer correspondences, and utility bills went into a low-priority pile. A health insurer's demand for immediate payment of a two thousand dollar deductible got her attention, so she converted some of the allocated cash into a money order and paid the bill.

With Sarah's immediate needs addressed, Liz could focus on writing. Lenny's cash paid for a new high-speed printer and a ream of copy paper. To prepare for a furious writing session with little sleep, she loaded her refrigerator with frozen entrees and energy drinks. Jasper got a chamois massage, string loosening, and closet storage. She set her printer and laptop in her living room on a folding banquet table borrowed from a neighbor. With a writer's studio in place, she gave Sarah's paper files a second read, closing the window shades when late sun reflected off tall steel. Finding little of interest in the papers, she opened a digital folder containing twenty pages of chunky paragraphs, the bones of the last chapter. The time stamp showed Sarah last worked on the file the night before leaving on their ill-fated West Coast trip. Liz spent several hours fattening Sarah's sentences with adverbs and redundant modifiers then she cut and pasted the bloated sentences into a corpulent draft. She didn't mention Johnny's build of a custom guitar for Hendrix because Sarah's writing focused on musician deliverables, not on their instruments. When the word count reached five-thousand and two, she stopped writing. The completed chapter had no mention of the Hendrix-Davis session. She read the work aloud, deleted a few double commas and emailed the draft to Marley. She spent the night watching television, confident Marley would love her writing, publish the book, pay her a bonus, and make her the co-author.

Marley called Liz the next morning. "Total garbage," she said. "You're fired. You write this under the influence? I want meat, not gristle. Ever hear of a spellchecker? Why use *is* so much? Dozens of adverbs. I hate adverbs. You tune out English grammar after second grade? I'll rewrite the damn thing. I'll call with any questions."

Liz swore at the dial tone for twenty seconds. She vowed to release the *Chessman's* and use the proceeds to pay someone with a functioning brain to write a book about the recordings and her experiences owning a Durrell guitar; the eight and a half pounds of wood, wire, metal, and plastic that created so much joy and havoc.

The calendar on Liz's refrigerator door had a red smiley face on October 1, the day Sarah would awake from her induced sleep. Early afternoon, a nurse called with the news Sarah had awakened, bright-eyed and alert. Liz could visit her that evening.

When Liz entered her hospital room, Sarah shouted, "Hey sis, how's things? Nothing like a snooze to freshen the mind. What's with the book? Marley call you? Next time, bring my laptop. I must have five thousand emails to read. Lenny call? Chaz and the boys OK?"

Liz stood speechless for a few seconds. Although Sarah's mind seemed in order, she weighed under a hundred pounds. Her teeth had a yellow pall and her eyes had recessed into dark craters. Liz asked her the name of the street they were raised on, her Social Security number, and their mother's birth date. Sarah answered all the questions correctly. "Headache's still there," she said. "Starting to recall some of the Port Townsend trip."

Sarah talked nonstop for a half hour about her book. A doctor interrupted the overwrought analysis by examining Sarah's wound. "You're going home in a few days," he said. "Latest scan shows you're healed. Take it easy for four weeks. Don't play rugby or football. No loud noises. Stay calm."

Sarah clenched a fist and said, "You said what I wanted to hear."

Liz asked the doctor if Sarah's recovery was a miracle. "Could be," he said before leaving the room.

"Love you sis," Liz said, cuddling her sister. "You ready to rejoin the world? My apartment is ready for you."

"Thanks for all you've done, except for getting me beat-up," she said. She picked up a newspaper. "Got some catching up to do."

A week after the Johnny-Strat unveiling at the Backbeat, a music promoter met Chaz at Mim's. The promoter interrupted his liquid lunch by offering Chaz a seven gig, three-week Hendrix tribute tour that would begin in New York City, continue to Hendrix's hometown of Seattle and have subsequent stops in San Francisco, Los Angeles, Chicago, and New York City. The tour would end in London, a few miles from the apartment where Hendrix died in 1970. The promoter offered Chaz twelve thousand dollars per concert. Chaz could hire three backing musicians who would each earn a two thousand dollar fee each gig. The tour would begin in seven days to capitalize on the excitement generated by the newly-found guitar. The promoter promised to book and pay for all venues, hotels, meals, and transportation. The day before each concert, Chaz would bring the guitar to a local radio station for an interview and casual chord. At each concert, he'd play ninety minutes of Hendrix covers on the Johnny-Strat. The promoter gave him a list of the best backing musicians available. Chaz pushed the list aside. He knew some people who would deliver the goods so he signed the contract after a quick read. The promoter gave him a five thousand dollar cash deposit. With the contract in his blazer pocket, the promoter walked to his limousine. From Mim's office phone, Chaz told Kenny and Pearly to pack for a three week tour that would begin in a week. He agreed to take Ruby along as a spiritual advisor. Liz said she'd consider the offer after Sarah's release from the hospital. With his backing band in place, Chaz told the promoter they'd practice Hendrix covers in a few days.

The day before Sarah's discharge, Liz performed a frenzied reconfiguration of her apartment. A quilt hung from a taut clothesline sectioned the bedroom into two areas. Sarah's clothing went from corrugated boxes to hangers, hooks, and shelves. Notebooks and files went on a card table next to the bed. A single rose in a glass vase made the space right for creativity and recovery.

The day of Sarah's release, Liz and her cousin Brenda sped to Longview Hospital in Brenda's white SUV. Sarah, seeing her liberators, leapt from her bed wearing white scrubs and her first radiant smile since the assault. A nurse described post-discharge protocols: For the next few weeks, she could engage in a few hours of reading and light exercise. To gain weight, she should eat as much as possible. Her potent pain medication should temper any headaches. Dr. Athena would see her at five day intervals.

Sarah, wearing wraparound sunglasses with dark lenses, declined a wheelchair ride, but after a few teetered steps, she acquiesced. Liz and an orderly eased her onto the front passenger seat of Brenda's vehicle. She asked a thousand questions during the hour-long ride to Manhattan. With assistance, she ascended to Liz's apartment and signaled her approval of the bedroom configuration by falling asleep on the cushy mattress. Brenda, suffering from cousin overdose, left in a huff.

Marley disrupted Sarah's nap with the phone greeting, "You cured? Able to write me something?"

"I'm back on earth," Sarah said. "Just don't ask me anything about the last few months. Whatever the doctors did, worked. Time to finish the book, make some money. Can I have an update?"

"Your sister wrote garbage," Marley said. "I had a ghost write a chapter, but he didn't have any meat to put in the sandwich. The meat is in your head. When will you get it done?"

"Liz did her best," Sarah said. "Sounds like the grammar gods wouldn't let it happen. I'm ready to plow out the last chapter. Two weeks work. I'm warming my laptop right now."

"I'll tell the publisher to plan for a thirty day galley. Come visit when you feel better. Welcome back to earth. Keep me updated on your progress. Great to hear your voice."

Sarah retrieved the entire book draft from the thumb drive, read Liz's writing, and wrote a few paragraphs. Liz phoned Chaz and joined the Johnny-Strat tour, agreeing to play rhythm guitar and a few solos. Being a fast track gig, they'd practice at Chessman's the following afternoon. Chaz said to plan for an all-nighter.

The first morning out of the hospital, Liz served Sarah a breakfast of double-cooked English muffins thick with peanut butter. She described the upcoming tour that would keep her on the road for twenty-one days. Sarah was forbidden to listen to live music, so Liz promised to give her recordings of each concert.

"I'm fine," Sarah said. "Go, have fun, make a few bucks. I'm happy not looking at hospital walls. Plan is to review my work, get my mind into it. So far, I'm good, other than a headache here and there. But before you go, what happened with the *Chessman's*?"

"I made a deal with Lenny while you were whacked out," Liz said. "He gave me a twenty grand deposit. I paid your medical bills, bought some office supplies. Before I hand him the music, I want things to be right. It's all about timing. I figured we'd tie it into the book release."

Liz counted out ten thousand dollars from Lenny's deposit. She kept nine thousand for a split of the rent and reimbursements. Sarah got a thousand dollars without mention of the money left over from the Port Townsend trip.

"What about my emails and messages?" Sarah asked.

"A bunch of emails came in. I explained your situation. Said you'd contact them if you got out of the hospital. Sorry if I sounded pessimistic, things looked bad for a while."

"That's what I heard from the nurses. One told another my condition was hopeless."

"Those emails had some interesting stuff. I never knew you were researching Durrell guitars. I learned a few things about Johnny when I read them. By the way, how'd you get a list of Durrells?"

"It must have fallen out of Johnny's pocket. I found it in the car, cleaning out the trash. Before we had dinner with Johnny, I never knew he was tight with the 60s electric guitar scene. Turns out he *was* the 60s guitar scene."

"There's more to the story. While you were goofed-out, Chaz got his hands on a Durrell built for Hendrix."

"You telling me the Hendrix Durrell exists? I've waded through ten feet of Hendrix research without a mention."

"Johnny's mother gave it to Chaz. He's been showing it off around town. It's probably sitting on his lap right now. You want to take a look?"

"I'd love to."

Chaz almost fainted when Sarah entered his apartment. The ebullient writer was now a withered figure with a stubby haircut. A row of scarred stitch holes ran from the bridge of her nose, across an eyebrow. Her skin had the tone of overcast sky.

They went into the living room where the Johnny-Strat lay on a stand. "Remember when I said some guitars have good voodoo and some bad?" Chaz said. "Johnny said this one is bad. He bought the wood from a New Orleans lumberman. Turns out the guy was hoodoo. First time Jimi played it, the fifth fret fell out. They call five the quincunx, a bad hoodoo number. Some hoodoo tricks run in a five-spot or X-pattern."

"Hendrix know the guitar was spooked? Sarah asked, holding the guitar.

"Not sure. Jimi sent the guitar back to Johnny and told him to fix the fret and fly back with it to New York. Johnny called Jimi from his shop, claimed some bugs had eaten the wood, so he'd build him another guitar. Jimi laughed it off. He said the guitar sounded right and he wanted it fixed for a London trip. Johnny fiddled for a month looking for a two-dollar piece of fret wire. Jimi went to London without the guitar and died. Johnny blamed the guitar's voodoo for Hendrix's death, told everyone he burnt it. Good thing he kept it. After I play it on tour, it's going to a museum."

Sarah set the guitar on a chair. "No more bad luck for me," she said. "Let's get out of here." She waited near the elevator as Chaz and Liz reviewed the song list they'd practice that evening.

Liz entered Chessman Studio around 9 p.m. In a corner, Kenny, Pearly and Ruby gossiped about someone's wife. Chaz and Corky hovered over the Johnny-Strat. "How in hell did this guitar get by me?" Corky asked. "Chessie never mentioned it. And Johnny, rest in peace brother, why didn't you tell the world about this axe? At least sell the dang thing, get your teeth fixed, buy a round of drinks."

"For years, I figured he burned it after Jimi died," Chaz said. "I dang near fell over when Johnny pulled it out, about ten years ago, a night we drank too much in his shop, played the heck of it. When the sun came up, he told me the guitar had bad hoodoo, bugs had eaten it from the inside out. I couldn't see a bug hole. Thing sounded fine. I told him he was crazy. Course, later that day, I tripped on its cord, broke my foot. For about a month nothing went right, old girlfriend sued me, caught my agent stealing money, on and on."

Corky played a few chords. He claimed the guitar sounded better than any Strat he'd heard. Chaz read aloud the note found taped to the guitar. "Johnny says turn this to change the tone." He pointed to several threaded studs connected to the bridge. Corky loosened the studs a few turns with a wrench. Chaz showed him another stud located where the fretboard met the body. Corky wrenched the stud counterclockwise six turns. Two, six inch long panels shaped like the letter *f* receded into the body.

"I'd say it's now a semi-hollow," Corky said, shining a flashlight in the openings.

Chaz pointed to the fifth fret from the headstock. "Johnny built good guits, but you'd have to squeeze his head with a vice to have him spend money. When he came up a few inches short of fret wire, the cheap bugger wouldn't buy a new roll, used a stray piece. You look close, the fifth fret is a different color and thickness." Corky shook his head in disgust after a look through a magnifying glass.

Chaz turned three knobs near the pick guard. He attached a chromed clamp, called a capo, perpendicular to the strings, below the fifth fret. The device shortened the strings, creating a different pitch, perfect for jazz chords. Confident of the guitar's capabilities, he played a sweet take of Wes Montgomery's jazz classic "Four on Six" with the edge of his thumb, not with a pick. Impressed with the sound, he played a few block chords. The jazzy tone reminded Corky of Montgomery's L-5 Gibson.

Corky restored the guitar to solid body. Chaz delivered a by-the-book cover of Hendrix's "Purple Haze." Everyone in the room including the cleaning lady watched in awe because they had never heard a Durrell sound like a Strat. After the song, a muffled pop came from the sound system. Seconds later, a flame jetted from Corky's favorite amplifier. More tubes popped when he got closer. Corky and Kenny tossed the smoking amplifier into a dumpster. Corked told Chaz to remove the Johnny-Strat from the property. Chaz laughed him off, blaming the fire on old tubes that couldn't handle heavy notes. Corky kept the session alive by using a digital amp with wimpy output that made the Johnny-Strat sound waterlogged. Despite the bad acoustics, when the practice ended, the Chaz Russell-Hendrix Cover Band sounded ready for touring.

The next morning, Marley, in her office, yipped at a publisher through her speakerphone. Seeing Sarah's alabaster skin and opaque sunglasses headed her way, she ended the call. "Why'd they let you out?" she asked. "Are you dead?"

"Brain is fine," Sarah said. "Could use a tanning salon and a few pounds. Time to get back to work."

Marley tossed a folder of typed papers into a trash container. "The ghost's draft is going to the shredder along with your sister's rubbish. Go home, finish the damn book, or I'll junk the whole project." Marley took a phone call from an attorney and waved Sarah from her office.

Following a late-morning practice, the tour promoter introduced Stevens, the record company executive, as the tour producer. Chaz and his bandmates gave him an enthusiastic greeting. Stevens introduced Tinker as the chief of tour security and guitar tech. Chaz wrapped his arm over the shoulder of the grizzled veteran of the blues scene. Liz secured the top button on her blouse.

Stevens passed out the five-page itinerary. The tour would begin in two days at Manhattan's Baxter Theater, a cushy venue built in 1920. They'd fly to Seattle the next afternoon, rest for a day, and perform the next night. Over the subsequent two weeks, they'd play shows in San Francisco, Los Angeles, Dallas, Memphis, and Chicago. They'd return to New York City for another Baxter concert, have a three day rest and end the tour with three London concerts. Scalpers got a thousand dollars for a ticket to the sold-out tour.

The afternoon of the first concert, a vintage black Lincoln with six-inch whitewalls ferried Chaz and the Johnny-Strat to the Baxter. Dozens of photographers, held back by furry ropes, fought for choice angles. The chauffeur, a tuxedoed woman with no personality, cleared the cameras before opening the door for Chaz. He handed the Johnny-Strat to Tinker who held it against his belly inches from his exposed pistol. A hip young woman in a fluffy dress led Chaz to a microphone stand set on the sidewalk. Reporters from music magazines shouted questions about the mysterious guitar. He responded by thanking the Mayor of New York and the assembled media for fostering the blues music scene. His evasiveness angered the testy scribes looking for a scoop. Tinker cut off the questioning by pushing Chaz and the guitar into the venue.

Few noticed the slight woman wearing sunglasses leaning on a signpost twenty feet from the media scrum; the taut hood of her black sweatshirt covered her hair and most of her face. She watched Chaz serve clichés to the media, then entered the Baxter's main entrance and handed her ticket to an usher. A woman police officer, sensing odd behavior, asked her to step aside. She found a pair of military grade ear protectors in the woman's purse. The woman said she used them to protect her ears, tender from recent surgery. After a frisking, the officer let Sarah into the biggest Hendrix event since 1970. The concert wouldn't start for an hour, so she bought a drink and chatted with a husband and wife from Alabama who had met at a Hendrix concert in Atlanta.

Kenny, Pearly, and Ruby arrived in a white Cadillac limousine with a shark fin rear quarter. Ruby flashed her long legs as she slithered to the sidewalk. A hundred camera flashes landed on her sequined red dress and newly dyed auburn hair. The photographers chuckled when Kenny and Pearly, wearing lime sherbet tuxedos fit for a 70s prom, stood by the microphone. Kenny stuttered a few words. Pearly thanked his momma for making him and Kenny. A reporter asked Ruby if she was the legendary guitar thief. Hiding her face with her bible, she silently followed Kenny, Pearly, and the escort into the lobby.

Liz arrived in Suzy's motorcycle sidecar, escorted by police cruiser. She had remained friendly with all her Simply Blue bandmates despite their acrimonious breakup. In front of the Baxter, she hopped from the sidecar with Jasper and a plastic bag holding her performance clothing. A guitar magazine photographer talked her into a pose next to the motorcycle.

In the dressing room, Chaz told Kenny and Pearly they looked like ice cream vendors. He made them change into black tuxedos. In the next room, Liz put on a long black dress and silvery high heels.

An hour before the show, locked doors and husky men kept ticket holders from the velour seats in the theater. Chaz and Liz chatted with Stevens on the Baxter stage. Kenny adjusted a few loose screws on his drum kit. Pearly swore at Lucas for being out of tune. An undercover police officer watched Tinker polish the Johnny-Strat. After a quick sound check, the band had dinner in a chandeliered room.

Midway through the dessert course, Stevens shouted a ten minute warning to show time. Chaz, first to the stage, saw a thousand occupied seats when he peeked by a curtain. Corky stayed close to the sound system, ready for action if it acted up. The lights dimmed at eight o'clock and the towering curtains parted with a rush of air. Stevens stood at the center microphone, squinting at the spotlights. He uttered a few buttery sentences about Hendrix and Johnny, then introduced Chaz, Kenny, Pearly, and Liz. With spotlights shining on their Durells, Chaz told the crowd, "We're here to honor two dear friends who died too young. One by accident, one by murder. Could have been two by murder. Johnny's momma gave me this here Johnny-Strat. Tonight, we'll play Hendrix's best with a big surprise at the end."

Chaz retrieved the golden guitar pick from his tuxedo pants. He pinched it with his thumb and index finger, drew a full breath, and drove the pick into a string while pressing the finger tips of his other hand against a few frets. A fuzzy C chord led to "The Wind Cries

Mary." Video screens next to the stage showed a black-and-white film of Hendrix in concert.

A cannabis fog drifted from the balcony, making the audience of timeworn groupies, balding ex-longhairs, and drowsy Summer of Love participants long for the good old days of loose morals and little need for money. A retired banker passed Sarah a lit joint. She took a drag and shared it with a school teacher from Brooklyn.

Chaz, energized by cheers, unloaded a twelve-minute medley of "Crosstown Traffic", "Hey Joe", "Purple Haze" and "Like a Rolling Stone." Kenny did his best to imitate Mitch Mitchell's drumming. Pearly's tight bass sounded like Noel Redding's best work. Liz added the right backing chords.

The senior band members caught their breath after the medley. Liz took a demure walk to the center of the stage and asked all attendees of the first Woodstock to stand up. Hundreds of arthritic joints squeaked as half the audience stood. Liz thanked the standees for their service to the counterculture and told them to turn up their hearing aids to hear something Hendrix had played that day. The audience, expecting a wimpy blues number played by pretty girl, nearly suffered communal arrhythmia when Liz upped the volume and nailed the "Woodstock Improvisation" played at the festival, ending the solo by playing the guitar with her teeth.

Chaz told the exhilarated crowd, "You just heard some of Jimi's best. Hendrix freaks know Jimi was messing with other sounds just before he passed. Johnny gave the Johnny-Strat a second personality. Corky Chessman will now convert it to jazz." Corky set the instrument on a table next to the center microphone. A spotlight focused on his hands as he fumbled with wrenches and pliers. When he adjusted the mechanism hidden in the guitar's body, the audience heard the innards creak. A loud click indicated the transition was done.

"Jimi wanted to play jazz on this guitar," Chaz said, "but fate didn't let it happen. Pearly has in his hands one of the few Durrell basses built. We'll play a song we wrote called "Jimi Jazz."

Chaz slowed "Voodoo Chile" to one-mile-per-hour tempo. Pearly added a spare backing beat. Kenny barely touched his drum with his sticks. Liz closed her eyes and contributed a couple chords. A black and white movie of a 60s jazz club scene with men in seersucker suits and pencil ties dancing with bouffant-haired women in sheath dresses played on the screen behind the band. When the song ended, the crowd delivered tempered applause. Chaz, sensing they wanted more high-voltage Hendrix, made Liz play a shuffle while Corky converted the Johnny-Strat back to blues mode. Chaz praised Corky's mechanical skills and took a deep breath. The husky blues chords of "Voodoo Chile" filled the theater followed by another medley from the Hendrix catalog. For the first encore, they played Hendrix's version of "Wild Thing." Before the second encore, Chaz sent his band off stage and told the audience he'd end the night with a cover of Hendrix's "Star Spangled Banner." Several audience members bolted to the exit. Many in the front row covered their ears. Sarah put on her hearing protection.

Chaz, with a proud smile, set his pick on the strings. On the second sustained note, as some in the crowd mouthed the lyric *say*, the fifth fret fell from the Johnny-Strat. Chaz, looking like a witness to a bad car crash, stopped playing, picked up the fret, and told the audience, "Jimi is telling me don't play the song. I'm outta here. Have a good night, God bless you all." The tall curtains closed slowly as Chaz and his band held hands and bowed.

Tinker secured the Johnny-Strat, Jasper, and Lucas in an aluminum guitar box. He wheeled it to the Baxter lobby where Chaz and his bandmates greeted several dozen high rollers who had each paid ten thousand dollars to pose with the Johnny-Strat; money destined for the Durrell Guitar Museum. The hour-long photo and fawn session ended abruptly when a boisterous donor demanded to play the guitar and Tinker threatened to empty a clip in the man's head. Police dragged the screaming loudmouth past the ice sculpture, across the plush carpet, into a secure van. Chaz and his entourage retreated to a nearby lounge with the concert promoter and a music journalist. Mim and the Backbeat owner joined them during the second round of drinks. Ruby, feeling faint, had left after the concert ended. The journalist, on a 2 a.m. deadline, left before the third round. Chaz told those remaining at the table: "When the fret popped off, I should have run off the stage. I'm cancelling the tour. Jimi don't want his music played. This ain't about money. Johnny said voodoo got into the Johnny-Strat. I believe him."

"It's only a chunk of wire," Mim said. "You can buy fret wire anywhere. Tinker will make it good. Get out on the road, make some money. Don't worry about voodoo nonsense."

FALLEN FRET

"I suppose you're right," Chaz said. "I need money, but I won't play Jimi's 'Banner.' "

The morning after the concert, Tinker brought the Johnny-Strat to a respected Brooklyn luthier who had worked on many Durrell guitars during his forty year career and considered Johnny an overrated guitar builder. The luthier examined the vacant fret slot and found bare wood with no adhesive remnants. Tinker gave him the fallen fret. The luthier, swearing in German, tossed it into the rubbish. He offered to replace the fret with fine '60s era wire for twenty dollars. Tinker, with four thousand dollars in his pocket, accepted the offer and watched the repair.

The luthier, handling the guitar like road kill, attached it to an oak scantling clamped to a vise and taped both sides of the vacant fret slot with masking tape. After a few minutes rummaging through a room of guitar cultch, he returned with a roll of fret wire packaged in crispy cellophane. He cut a piece of wire slightly longer than needed, coated the fret slot with glue, and used a fret press to push the new fret into the slot. Tinker took the guitar home with six inches of the fretboard wrapped with surgical gauze.

The next morning, the luthier nipped the excess wire, and beveled and burnished the fret ends. Tinker brought the guitar to Chessman's and put it in the aluminum box with the other Durrells. He'd spend the night in the studio guarding the instruments. In the morning, he'd meet the tour members and fly to Seattle.

Corky dropped a few cushions, a shipping quilt, and a few pillows on the studio floor. He told Tinker to take what he wanted from the refrigerator. He locked the front door and went home. Tinker ate a cold anchovy pizza, drank several beers, and rested on the cushions, twenty feet from the guitars. He shut off the lights with his loaded handgun on the carpet near his preferred shooting hand. Volcanic heartburn made him toss and cough for a few hours.

A few hours after midnight, a door squeak interrupted Tinker's drowsy agita. He grabbed his gun, bolted from the cushions, and stood with his back against the wall. Two shadows pointed a flashlight on the box holding the guitars. A shadow opened the box, removed the Johnny-Strat, and strummed a few strings. The other flashlight shined on the pizza box, beer cans, and disarrayed cushions. Both beams of light skipped across the floor and landed on

Tinker's feet. Tinker fired shots at each flashlight. The flashlights fell to the floor. One lit a wall, the other shined on two moaning bodies leaking blood.

Panicked Tinker called the NYPD from Corky's office. Within minutes, a dozen squad cars parked outside Chessman Studio. Homicide detectives heard Tinker's self defense plea. They told him a prosecutor would make a decision on charges. Corky ran into the studio. Two blanket covered bodies lay on the floor. Next to the bodies, in a puddle of blood, was the bullet riddled Johnny-Strat. In the aluminum box, Jasper, Thelma, and Lucas had no damage. After seeing the shattered guitar, Corky cried, "Johnny didn't want it played. He took care of it from heaven."

The tour producer suffered a mild cardiac event after hearing the news. He told Stevens to spare no expense to fix the Johnny-Strat in time for the next show. Stevens took the news calmly; with thirty years in the music business, he'd experienced worse situations. He spent the afternoon calling in favors.

The next morning, ten of New York City's best luthiers met at Stevens' office to examine the damaged guitar. The luthier who had repaired the fret refused to attend. Corky led the luthiers to an office where the Johnny-Strat lay on desk. A few shook their head after Stevens asked them to make the guitar playable in 48 hours. Chaz nearly caused a walkout when he described Johnny as the best guitar builder in the world. Stevens, Chaz, and Corky, hearing the luthiers argue in German, left the studio for an early lunch.

One of the luthiers, a curmudgeon named Otto, held a hammer and chisel, ready to split the guitar in two. Common sense ruled when his colleagues let a younger luthier, also named Otto, examine the guitar's structure and internal mechanism with an endoscopic camera. The video feed, fed to laptop viewed by all, showed split wood and mangled steel. If the guitar were human, doctors would deem the injury terminal. For several hours, they debated how to repair the guitar. Bullets had pierced the body, shattered two ribs, and destroyed the gears and levers that gave the guitar two personalities. They concluded it would take a month to repair the instrument, but they couldn't fix the conversion mechanism. They'd need a donor Durrell to make the repair. Belly laughs erupted after Lucretia Stein suggested they use Thelma.

Stevens moaned after hearing the prognosis. He gave each luthier a check for five hundred dollars and sent them back to their shops. He called the producer, recovering on a hospital bed, with the autopsy results. The producer set off the bedside monitor when he cancelled the tour.

Chaz and Corky looked down at the Johnny-Strat and knew what to do. They brushed the guitar into a cardboard box and took it to Chessman's parking lot. Corky lit a pile of balled newspaper and pallet wood. When the flames reached waist height, Chaz tossed the Johnny-Strat into the pyre. The swirled finish ignited first. Tight-grained mahogany put up a noble fight, but eventually burst into flames. Frets shot from the fretboard like shooting stars. The conversion mechanism became a steamy blob. With tears and remorse, Chaz and Corky hummed "Amazing Grace." When the flames shrunk to shoe height and the crackle silenced, they doused the embers with a bucket of water and then shoveled the wet ash and singed metal into the dumpster.

The next morning, the coroner identified one body as Lenny, the record company owner. The second body remained unidentified until detectives traced Lenny's cell phone calls. The most frequently dialed number rang in Liz's apartment. Liz answered the call. A NYPD detective told her about the double killings. Liz, in a quivering voice, asked about the dead woman. The detective described a thin woman, late twenties, with a scar over her eye. Liz said it was her sister Sarah. The previous night, while Liz slept, Sarah had left the apartment dressed in dark clothing. A note explained her womanly need to spend the night with Lenny.

The detective drove Liz to the morgue where she identified Sarah's body on an autopsy table. Over the next few days, Liz cried, hyperventilated, kicked a hole in her apartment wall, screamed into a pillow, and sobbed when calling friends and relatives.

A week after the killings, the O'Malley family buried Sarah at Cypress Hills Cemetery in Brooklyn, next to her father. Bank robbery money paid for the funeral. Hundreds of Sarah's music industry colleagues and friends stood near her mother and Liz. Marley wept over lost revenue. Ruby put a rose on the casket. Chaz sang a prayer. Kenny and Pearly barely knew Sarah, but they were so upset, they watched the burial from a hill. After the other mourners left the cemetery, Liz stared at the casket, regretful she had replaced her trusted Les Paul with a Durrell.

A day after the funeral, NYPD detectives took Sarah's files and laptop from Liz's apartment. A rental receipt for a white van matching the one seen at Johnny's farm implicated Lenny in Johnny's murder. Lenny's credit card had a Port Townsend gas station purchase of two coffees and a tank of gas on the day of April and Steve's death. Surveillance video showed Lenny kissing Sarah next to the gas pump, a few blocks from the Uppity Deck. A pink golf shirt found in Lenny's apartment had traces of the gloss black paint on the surface of the Timely Pub fire escape.

With the Port Townsend and Johnny Durrell murders solved, the FBI assigned a dozen agents to finding the guitars stolen from Johnny's shop and April's house. Liz found a key and receipt for a Long Island storage locker in one of Sarah's shoes. In the locker, the agents found every guitar stolen from Johnny and April along with a Durrell stolen from a Connecticut museum. Mae donated Johnny's guitars to the University of Arkansas along with all the money needed to build the Durrell Museum on the campus.

A photo surfaced of Sarah and Lenny attending a Philadelphia concert the night of Chaz's stabbing. The FBI considers the Chaz Russell stabbing an unsolved, random act. Ruby still denies the assault. Mim's barmaid, a New Orleans native, still won't look Chaz in the eye.

A few weeks after Sarah's burial, Marley hired a recent journalism graduate, a woman in her late twenties, to finish Sarah's book. The published book, still meatless, sold a few thousand copies. A *New York Scribe* reviewer called the book "cobbled together with little insight into two revered musicians."

Liz, with little interest in playing or hearing electric blues, spent the day after the funeral in her apartment putting Sarah's clothing and shoes in boxes destined for the Salvation Army. She kept the gold bracelet and a black-and-white snapshot of the two sisters playing in a sand box.

The story of the Johnny-Strat made Chaz an in-demand performer. He signed a lucrative contract with the now-recovered producer to tour America with a Johnny Durrell tribute. The contract specified Thelma as the only guitar he would play. Chaz assumed

Kenny and Pearly would go on the tour. With room for one more Durrell, he called Liz. She suggested they talk in person, not at Mim's or the Backbeat, but at Harlem's Riverbank State Park on the Hudson River.

On a clear and breezy fall day, they sat on a wooden bench near the river edge with hands tucked in jacket pockets. Chaz told Liz his jazz fusion ride was over. Like the first time, audiences grew tired of the sound. He asked her to join the upcoming tour, promising her a substantial raise, co-billing, and a few songs to play as lead. Kenny and Pearly would join the tour only if Liz signed on. Chaz would let his band play a long introduction then he'd perform a half hour of guitar work. They'd end each concert with his new composition, a blues ballad called "Fallen Fret" about Sarah, her faithful sister Liz, and a guitar named Jasper. The song would feature Liz's guitar and singing.

He handed Liz a brown envelope containing a contract and a ten thousand dollar signing bonus. Liz gave back the unopened envelope. She said blue notes rekindled memories of Sarah. She couldn't play a note on Jasper without dropping tears on the guitar. The next day, she'd leave for New Orleans to join Spoon's new Zydeco band and play her Les Paul.

She put Jasper on Chaz's lap and asked him to give the guitar to a young woman playing blues on a dull guitar. Chaz, so upset he could only wave goodbye, carried the guitar across the lawn to a waiting cab. Liz walked to a railing hung over the rushing river and took the *Chessman's* from her pocketbook. She spun the first disc over the water. It fluttered like a wounded bird and pierced a whitecap, fifty feet from the rail. The second disc sailed for a few seconds over the current and dove into a trough. She walked away as the discs settled deep in the river sediment.

ABOUT THE AUTHOR

Ray Richard writes fiction and nonfiction from his Cape Cod home. In his spare time, he chases views on the Maine Coast or Ireland's Beara. He'holds a M.A in Professional Writing from the University of Massachusetts-Dartmouth

www.ingramcontent.com/pod-product-compliance
Lightning Source LLC
Chambersburg PA
CBHW051649040426
42446CB00009B/1048